RACE, RELIGION & RACISM

RACE, RELIGION & RACISM

Volume Two

Perverting the Gospel to Subjugate a People

Frederick K.C. Price

Faith One Publishing
Los Angeles, California

Unless otherwise indicated, all Scripture quotations are taken from the *New King James Version.* Copyright © 1979, 1980, 1982, Thomas Nelson, Inc., Publishers. Used by permission.

Race, Religion & Racism, Volume Two
Perverting the Gospel to Subjugate a People
ISBN 1-883798-48-5
Library of Congress Catalog Card Number: 99-75670
Copyright © 2001 by
Frederick K.C. Price
P.O. Box 90000
Los Angeles, CA 90009

Published by Faith One Publishing
7901 South Vermont Avenue
Los Angeles, California 90044

Publisher's Cataloging-in-Publication
(Provided by Quality Books, Inc.)

Price, Frederick K.C.
    Race, religion & racism, Vol. 2, Perverting the
  Gospel to subjugate a people / by Frederick K.C.
  Price. -- 1st ed.
        p. cm.
        Includes bibliographical references and index.
        LCCN: 99-75670
        ISBN: 1-883798-48-5

    1. Race relations--Religious aspects--
  Christianity. 2. Racism--Religious aspects--
  Christianity. 3. Race--Religious aspects--
  Christianity. 4. Race--Biblical teaching.
  I. Title.

    BT734.2.P75 2001   261.8'348
                        QBI00-500153

Table of Contents

Preface

In 1991 I was given an assignment from God to speak and write about race, religion and racism. In 1992 an incident happened in my life that catalyzed me into action.

A white minister with whom I had had a long and close fellowship made a racist statement to his congregation. Shortly after he made it, the statement was heard all over America on the tapes his ministry distributed. A group of black ministers gave me the tape, and as I played it I was shocked to hear someone whom I considered a friend say something racially biased against black people. I was further saddened when, despite my urging and the urging of other clergymen and Christians of all races, he refused to recant publicly.

Following this incident, I immersed myself in three years of research: reading books, magazines, newspaper articles, Websites — everything I could find that had to do with racism in America and, especially, its connection with religion. What I found amazed and disgusted me; as much as I already knew, I learned a great deal more, and I quickly saw how essential it was for me to teach others what I had discovered.

In October 1997 I began to speak on the subject of race, religion and racism on my *Ever Increasing Faith* television program. In December 1999 Faith One published the first book of what I planned to be a three-volume series based on those teachings.

In Volume 1 of *Race, Religion & Racism* I wrote in detail about the incident that led me to fulfill my assignment. I also gave an overview of race, religion and racism in America, traced the attitude toward black people from slavery to today, showed how it has affected African Americans, and suggested what our country can do to make restitution for the past.

In Volume 2, which may be read independently of Volume 1, I focus specifically on the insidious relationship involving race, religion and racism. As you will see, religion has played a primary role in developing and sustaining white America's racism toward African Americans. I examine this long and tragically effective connection in order to show how our country's past has created and fostered its racist present.

Race, Religion & Racism, Volume 2, is an exploration of facts and information. It is also a spiritual journey. After you read this book, it is my fervent hope that you will never again hear or read a racist statement supposedly made in the name of God without seeing it for the lie that it is. Once the lie of racism has been exposed, all that is needed to determine the relationship among all races is what God originally intended: love.

— Frederick K.C. Price, D.D.

1

The White Distortion:
Interweaving Racism With Religion

RACE, RELIGION & RACISM Religion has been the most flagrant perpetrator of racism in the world, and the Christian Church in America has been the leading perpetrator.

At first glance, to people who know God, this may seem paradoxical. How can religion, which we associate with the Word of God, be a perpetrator of something evil like racism? The answer is that religion is not necessarily the Word of God; religion is very often the word of man *about* the Word of God, and that has been the problem.

While *religion* can mean the service or worship of God, *Webster's Dictionary* also defines it as:

A personal set or institutionalized system of religious attitudes, beliefs and practices.[1]

Notice the word *personal*. People inject their personal ideas into religion, and with their personal ideas come their personal

---

[1] *Webster's Ninth New Collegiate Dictionary* (Springfield, Massachusetts: Merriam-Webster Inc., 1983), 995.

1

prejudices. These personal prejudices bring religion further and further away from the Word of God.

Notice the word *institutionalized*. In making religion into an institution, the ideas and biases of the people who created the institution become part of the system. Thus, the people in power within a religion can corrupt it with their own prejudices, which come from the overall society of which they are a part.

So when I say that religion has been the most flagrant perpetrator of racism in the world, and that the Christian Church in America has been the leading perpetrator, I'm not talking about the enlightened Word of God. I'm talking about how men have distorted the Word of God to foster their own racist attitudes, beliefs and practices.

The primary motivation for this has been the fear of interracial marriage between black and white people, a fear that has been fundamental to most of white society since the early part of the 17th Century. When black people were first brought to this country as slaves, the lie was propagated that Blacks were inherently inferior — really just animals — and therefore needed to be segregated from Whites, particularly from white women.

To illustrate how far some white people have gone to use religion in helping them to promulgate their belief that the black man is inferior, let's look at several passages from *The Tempter of Eve* by Charles Carroll:

> The white is the highest and the Negro the lowest, of the so-called five races of men; and they present the most striking contrast to each other in their physical and mental characters, their modes of life, habits, customs, manners, language, gestures, etc.[2]

---

[2] Charles Carroll, *The Tempter of Eve* (St. Louis, Missouri: Adamic Publishing Company, 1902), 255. Born in 1849, Carroll was known throughout the South as one of "the great Southern white gentlemen" who fought to uphold and preserve Southern culture. Elsewhere, he had the reputation for being one of a number of highly vociferous

So far Carroll is just stating racist beliefs with a pseudo-scientific style. But then he says:

> With this interesting family of animals, shading up from the lemur to the Negro, we are able with the assistance of the Scriptures...[3]

"With the assistance of the Scriptures" — this is how racists have distorted the Bible and how Christianity has gotten a bad name around the world with people of color. Every time racists present their lies, they try to cloak them in biblical principles. For anyone who knows the Bible, the racists' untruths will not fly, because racism is not in the Book, it's in them. But how many people really know the Book? How many are taken in by commentary that they assume is biblical just because the author says it is?

Despite having no biblical basis, Carroll says with an air of authority:

> ...we are able with the assistance of Scriptures and the sciences to determine that the Negro is one of the ape family; that he simply stands at the head of the ape family, as the lion stands at the head of the cat family. Hence, as the lower apes though unfit for general domestic purposes, are invaluable, in that they enable us to determine beyond question the Negro's true position in the universe — that he is merely an ape.[4]

---

polemical writers "obsessed with the need for race purity." His writings helped to "transform the stereotype of the Negro" from the kindly image of Uncle Tom to the menace of the black beast, and he advocated using the strongest conceivable means, including lynching, to keep "the beast" in place. See Daniel Joseph Singal, "Ulrich B. Phillips: The Old South as the New," *The Journal of American History*, Vol. 63, Issue 4, March 1977, 871-891. *The Tempter of Eve* was re-edited for publication in 1970.

[3] Carroll, 286.

[4] Carroll, 286-287.

Carroll further states:

> Besides, it should be borne in mind that, though the
> Negro is omnivorous, he manifests a strong preference
> for the flesh of man as an article of food. The character-
> istics clearly identify the Negro as the creature described
> in the Scripture as the "beast of the field."[5]

This is why things are the way they are today in America
between white and black people. Carroll believed that my family
and I and all of our black friends and neighbors — indeed every
black person on the planet — are animals, that we are the Bible's
"beast[s] of the field." He wrote his warped nonsense in a book, and
other people read it. He told his wife and children, and his children
told their children; his readers told their wives or husbands and children, and their children told their children. This is a microcosm of
how the pollution of racial bigotry came down to us today. We know
that everyone doesn't believe these and other racist lies, but you
don't need everyone to have division and racial oppression.

Carroll continues:

> Dr. Clark manifested a commendable independence of
> thought and action when he abandoned the absurd theory
> of the modern clergy that the tempter of Eve was a snake;
> he made a creditable advance upon the snake theory
> when he proved the tempter of Eve an ape; yet, it is at

---

[5] Carroll, 287. In regard to Carroll defining the black man as "the
beast of the field," two years prior to the publication of *The Tempter of
Eve*, Carroll had published *The Negro A Beast*, which was routinely
quoted by Southern Whites to justify their stand of racial superiority.
See Daniel Joseph Singal, 871-891. *The Negro A Beast* is said to have
been the catalyst for the decision of the renowned African-American
author W.E.B. Du Bois to pursue a career in literature. See Arnold
Rampersad, "W.E.B. Du Bois as a Man of Literature," *American
Literature*, Vol. 51, Issue 1, March 1979, 50-68.

once a matter of surprise and regret that after thus advancing so far in the right direction, he should have stopped at one of the so-called anthropoids — the orang — when a step further would have taken him to the Negro, the identical ape he was seeking.

The Negro meets all the requirements of the case, he is the only animal that does; he possesses the erect posture, articulate speech and more reasoning capacity than any other animal; and these characteristics place him at the head of the apes, and consequently "at the head of all inferior animals for wisdom and understanding. Besides, the Negro is an inveterate talker — 'babbler' — and is withal one of the noisiest animals in the world." [6]

In Carroll's view, it wasn't just any "babbl[ing]" Negro who tempted Eve, it was a specific Negro whom he identifies with certainty:

All the circumstances indicate that the beast of the field which tempted Eve was a Negress who served Eve in the capacity of a maid servant....[7]

Wouldn't you know it? Carroll is actually blaming the fall of mankind on Eve's black maid! In 1902 when Carroll wrote his book, they didn't laugh. It was 37 years after the end of the Civil War, 39 years after the Emancipation Proclamation, but here we can see just how strongly the perspective of the slave-owning society still influenced the consciousness of white people at the start of the 20th Century. "A Negress who served Eve in the capacity of a maid servant" — this foul stuff was written and printed and read and implemented. It was because of attitudes like this that

---

[6] Carroll, 391.
[7] Carroll, 402.

Whites Jim-Crowed us all those years.[8] That's why they required separate colored and white facilities. You don't want to use the same restroom as an ape, do you? You don't want to drink from the same fountain as an ape? How could people have thought this about us? Because of teaching like Carroll's.

Carroll adds insult to injury with this statement:

> Their acting upon the advice of the Negress by eating the forbidden fruit, was their second offense; when they accepted the Negress as their counselor, they necessarily descended to social equality with her. This reveals the startling fact that it was man's social equality with the Negro that brought sin into the world. This being true, it follows that man's social equality with the Negro will keep sin into the world and will bring upon man the just condemnation of God.[9]

---

[8] In response to the Emancipation Proclamation of 1863, in the latter part of the 19th Century and beginning of the 20th, all the Southern states adopted laws which, by various devices, impeded Negro suffrage and freedom. These laws, commonly referred to by the name of "Jim Crow," were seen as the answer to the South's race problem and involved the subordination, disfranchisement, and ultimately the legal segregation of black people by way of local and state laws. Jim Crow laws were the primary method used after the Emancipation Proclamation to maintain control of Blacks and sometimes proved more effective than slavery because their subtlety initially precluded outright protests. See Rayford W. Logan, "The Progress of the Negro After a Century of Emancipation," *Journal of Negro Education*, Vol. 32, No. 4, Autumn, 1963, 323. So prevalent and effective were these segregation laws that in 1944 the Swedish writer Gunnar Myrdal observed, "Segregation is now becoming so complete that the white Southerner practically never sees a Negro except as his servant and in other standardized and formalized caste situations." See C. Vann Woodward, *The Strange Career of Jim Crow* (New York: Oxford University Press, 1974), 118.

[9] Carroll, 405.

This material is not analyzed in school, but it should be. It contains the kind of root thinking that spawned all the actions against African Americans through the years. White people need to know this; they need to see the information their forefathers circulated. And black people need to see the lies that were circulated about us.

If you're a white reader of this book, I'm not writing it to put you in bondage to guilt. I'm writing it so that you will think about it and make sure that you're not operating from some of this false, racist information that may be hidden in some closet inside of you. Maybe it was passed on to you, perhaps subliminally, in childhood. If you're a black reader of this book, I'm not writing it so that you will feel like a victim of white oppression and use that as an excuse to be hostile to white people. I'm writing it so that you can understand how racist beliefs and attitudes have been formed and why you have experienced racism in your life, and so that you will not believe the false, racist information that would give you a negative self-image. If you are a person of color other than black, I'm writing this book so that you can think about what I say regarding white racism toward Blacks, which has been the most prevalent form of racism in America, and compare it to your own experiences. Only by understanding the past can we understand the present. And only by understanding why things are the way they are among the different so-called races can we end racism once and for all. As Jesus Christ says in John 8:32, **"And you shall know the truth, and the truth shall make you free."**

What a twisted idea Carroll has of the truth! With the same false air of scriptural authority, he goes even further in providing reasons why his readers should put as much distance as they can between themselves and African Americans.

> Man's social equality with the Negro tends to political
> and religious equality; and these three, or any one of
> them, inevitably leads to amalgamation — itself the

most infamous and destructive crime known to the law
of God.[10]

This is why I said earlier that the fear of interracial marriage is at the core of racist thinking within the Church in America. Otherwise, why would Carroll say that "amalgamation" between white and black people — not murder, not adultery, not breaking any of the Ten Commandments — is "the most infamous and destructive crime known to the law of God"?

This is the type of thinking that gave birth to today's racist garbage. Remember the house painter Adolf Hitler? At first, many people said, "He's crazy, he's just spouting off." They didn't take him seriously. By the time they decided to take him seriously, he had plunged the whole world into a war. He talked his hateful message before he ever put it into operation, but many who recognized it as garbage just laughed at it and dismissed it. So don't laugh when you hear similar garbage against black people. It might sound ridiculous to anyone with sense, but that garbage is what people have believed — it's what many still believe — and it's why many who have believed it have worked so hard to keep the races separated.

Let's look again at Carroll's statement that "amalgamation itself [is] the most infamous and destructive crime known to the law of God." Note that Carroll doesn't just present his feelings about interracial marriage as his own point of view. He doesn't say, "amalgamation is something that I personally think is wrong"; no, he weaves in his beliefs with the Scriptures, with God. He calls interracial marriage "the most infamous and destructive crime known to the law of God." That's why I say that religion has been the worst perpetrator of racism.

As you read these passages from Carroll's *The Tempter of Eve*, I wonder if you said to yourself something like, "That was 1902. Surely no one in the Church in America in the last 50 years would have written anything blatantly false about the races."

---

[10] Carroll, 405.

If you said that to yourself, you are wrong. In *Dake's Annotated Reference Bible* — one of the most widely read Pentecostal Bibles in the last half of the 20th Century[11] — there are what *appear* to be racist teachings. I say *appear to be* because I never met Mr. Dake; my comments are based only on what his Bible notes seem to indicate. But what something appears to be is extremely important. As the Bible tells us, **Abstain from all appearance of evil** (1 Thessalonians 5:22, KJV). And racial or color prejudice is evil. When we are prejudiced against any ethnic or racial group, we have sinned against God's creation. Because God made every racial or ethnic group the color that it is, in essence we are saying to God, "You are a stupid Creator, because you created these people and they are inferior, so you have created an inferior product line." If you consider the product to be inferior, you consider the manufacturer to be inferior — and you are in sin.

Before we begin our examination of Dake's Bible commentary, let's look at what Stephen L. McKenzie, associate professor of Hebrew Bible/Old Testament at Rhodes College in Memphis, Tennessee, has to say about *Dake's Annotated Reference Bible*. McKenzie writes:

> I shall never forget the session of a course I was teaching on the Book of Genesis several years ago that treated the story from Genesis 9 on the so-called curse of Ham. This passage, or rather interpretations of it, provided

---

[11] According to Stanley M. Burgess and Gary B. McGee, authors of *The Dictionary of Pentecostal and Charismatic Movements*, "Dake's impact upon conservative Pentecostalism cannot be overstated." Between 1961 and 1988, when Burgess and McGee published their book, 372,000 volumes of *Dake's Annotated Reference Bible* had "rolled off the presses," and an estimated 28,000 to 30,000 were still being sold annually. See Burgess and McGee, *The Dictionary of Pentecostal and Charismatic Movements* (Grand Rapids, Michigan: Regency Reference Library, Zondervan Publishing House, 1988), 235.

> the historical and theological basis among southern Christians prior to the Civil War for legitimating black slavery....

> I have since become aware that the abuse of this passage for racial oppression is not nearly so defunct as I supposed it to be.... I have heard a white supremacist preacher on television try to give this interpretation legitimacy by couching it in the guise of a reasoned explication of the text. I have even discovered a study Bible (*Dake's Annotated*), still being published in Georgia, that offers this racist explanation as the meaning of Genesis 9.[12]

While some might want to dismiss the comments I am about to make regarding *Dake's Annotated Reference Bible* as the ravings of an angry black man, no one can accuse Professor McKenzie, who is white, of being an angry black man. His assessment of the interpretation of Genesis 9 in *Dake's Bible* has nothing to do with his skin color; it has to do with his knowledge of the Old Testament. The fact that McKenzie and I agree is not based on my skin color, but on my knowledge of the Bible. I am righteously angry about racism because racism goes against the Holy Word of God.

Certain ailments require extreme measures to eradicate them, and it's not pleasant. When my wife was battling cancer, I was there, bedside and tableside, and I could see that the medication they gave her to help eradicate the cancer was more deadly than the disease,

---

[12] Stephen L. McKenzie, *All God's Children: A Biblical Critique of Racism* (Louisville, Kentucky: Westminster John Knox Press, 1997), 3-4. Although, as McKenzie notes, many in the white church before and since the Civil War have told us that Ham was "cursed" with black skin and have used this supposed curse to justify the oppression of black people, the Bible tells us that Ham was not cursed black, nor was he cursed at all. I've discussed the fallacy of "the curse of Ham" in Volume 1 of *Race, Religion & Racism*, pages 5, 122,149-150, and will analyze this racist doctrine in greater detail in chapters 9 and 14 in this volume.

and if it was not properly handled, it could kill her more quickly than the disease. The medication was radical; it could destroy the good as well as the bad, but you cannot play with that disease. You cannot sugar-coat it, cherry-flavor it, or pussyfoot around it, because if it's not cured, it will kill you graveyard dead.

God has led me to write about *Dake's Annotated Reference Bible* and the other religious writings I will examine in this book in an effort to eradicate the disease of racism, because we've been pussyfooting around it long enough. It's time for radiation and chemotherapy. I have been cast in the role of doctor, administering the medication. Keep in mind that my point is not to label anyone a racist, but the only thing that any of us can judge anyone by is what we hear or see coming from him or her. Jesus Himself said that **"... a tree is known by its fruit"** (Matthew 12:33).

The section we're going to look at in *Dake's Annotated Reference Bible* is "Notes on Acts of the Apostles." In these notes, Dake lists "30 reasons for segregation of races." It's very important to recognize that, as a social principle, segregation of races has its roots in America's almost 250 years of slavery and, as I pointed out earlier, it is intimately connected to the idea of black inferiority and to the prohibition against interracial marriage. So Dake giving 30 reasons for segregation of races as part of Bible commentary appears to provide powerful support for a social principle that has a long racist history.

The Dake Bible to which I'm referring was not published in 1902, but 1963 — after the start of the Civil Rights Movement that ended legal segregation in the United States. As I write, this edition of Dake's notes has been in print for 37 years. Can you imagine how many people have read those 30 reasons during that time and felt justified in continuing the racist attitudes they learned from their parents across the dinner table or over the backyard barbecue or in the car? How many people have been confirmed in their racism because a Bible commentator said the races ought to be segregated?

These roots of racism have to be pulled up, because racism can never be eliminated until people get it out of their hearts. Racism is not some legal, codified system. It's not white drinking fountains and colored drinking fountains, or white bathrooms and black bathrooms. These are just manifestations. Changing the laws that made segregation legal didn't eliminate racism; it was a crucial first step, but it was only a first step. Racism is *inside*; it is how we think, how we feel. So we have to go inside and dig up the roots. The hundreds of thousands of people who have read Dake's notes have to be told that the justifications for the "segregation of races" are untrue, and that the thoughts and feelings they promulgate are the very opposite of what the Word of God actually teaches us.

I'm going to go through every one of Dake's "30 reasons for segregation of races," because I want to be in complete alignment with the biblical warning, **Abstain from all appearance of evil** (1 Thessalonians 5:22, KJV). The Scripture says **all**, not "some appearances of evil," but **"all appearance of evil"**!

Right from the start, Dake lets us know where he stands. Reason 1 states:

> God wills all races to be as He made them. Any violation of God's original purpose manifests insubordination to Him ([Acts] 17:26; Rom. 9:19-24).[13]

What I infer from this is that Dake is telling us that if you're black, you must stay black, marry black, and in the most intimate ways that Blacks have communion, it should always be with Blacks. Similarly, Whites should remain exclusively with Whites, Reds with

---

[13] Finis Jennings Dake. ed., *Dake's Annotated Reference Bible* (Lawrenceville, Georgia: Dake Bible Sales Inc., 1963, 1971), 159 [in the New Testament]. Finis Jennings Dake was born in 1902 and died in 1987. He was ordained to the New Mexico-Texas district of the Assemblies of God (AG) in 1927, pastored in the Dallas area and then became an evangelist in Oklahoma. In 1932, he became pastor of the Christian Assembly in Zion, Illinois, where he established the Great Lakes Bible Institute, which later merged with Central Bible

Reds, Yellows with Yellows, Browns with Browns. It's very easy to determine where Dake is coming from. All we have to do is go to the Scripture, because if what Dake says is true, the Scripture should substantiate it. We should find verse after verse, Scripture after Scripture, illustration after illustration indicating that God wants the races to remain segregated. We should also find no Scriptures that contradict what Dake says, because God could then be accused of being double-minded.

In order to support his contention, the first Scripture Dake quotes is Acts 17:26:

> **"And He has made from one blood every nation of men to dwell on all the face of the earth, and has determined their preappointed times and the boundaries of their dwellings...."**

I suppose that Dake uses this Scripture to support the idea that the races should be segregated because part of it says, **"He ... has determined their preappointed times and the boundaries of their dwellings...."** There are two reasons why this Scripture *in no way* supports the idea of segregation of black people from white people. The first is that while God did make the boundaries of nations in certain places at the time He originally created them, those boundaries have been changing ever since. Indeed, sometimes, as with Moses leading God's chosen people to the Promised Land, they changed because of God's orders.

Institute. As a result of a controversy involving the violation of the federal Mann Act, which Dake's lawyer referred to as an "unfortunate mistake," Dake's relationship with the AG ended in 1937. Not allowing this to change his life's course, he remained Pentecostal, joined the Church of God in Cleveland, Tennessee, and eventually became independent. He authored popular tracts, books and pamphlets, but is best remembered for the *Dake's Annotated Reference Bible*. See Burgess and McGee, 235-236.

When God made man, He said, **"let them have dominion over ... all the earth...."** (Genesis 1:26). He did not say, "Let the white man have dominion over only this part of the earth for all eternity," "Let the black man have dominion over only this part of the earth for all eternity," "Let the red man have dominion over only this part of the earth for all eternity," "Let the yellow man have dominion over only this part of the earth for all eternity," and "Let the brown man have dominion over only this part of the earth for all eternity." No, God didn't segregate the races into different kinds of men. He said **"man,"** and he gave man **"... dominion over ... all the earth ...,"** not different races segregated forever in different parts of it.

This is related to the second reason the Scripture Dake cites is invalid as a justification for segregation, and this reason is very profound. Far from telling us that the races should be segregated, Acts 17:26 is a statement of unity of all the people in God's creation!

> **"And He has made from one blood every nation of men to dwell on all the face of the earth...."**

The Scripture is telling us that we are all **... made from one blood...**, and therefore whatever nation we may be a member of, we are all related to each other.

The second reference Dake cites is Romans 9, beginning with Verse 19:

> **You will say to me then, "Why does He still find fault? For who has resisted His will?"**
>
> **But indeed, O man, who are you to reply against God? Will the thing formed say to him who formed it, "Why have you made me like this?"**
>
> **Does not the potter have power over the clay, from the same lump to make one vessel for honor and another for dishonor?**
>
> **What if God wanting to show His wrath and to make His power known, endured with much longsuffering the vessels of wrath prepared for destruction,**

and that He might make known the riches of His glory on the vessels of mercy, which He had prepared beforehand for glory,

even us whom He called, not of the Jews only, but also of the Gentiles?

Apparently Dake provides this Scripture to support the previous one he cited. In other words, he seems to be saying that Acts 17:26 is telling us that each *nation* — a term Dake uses to mean race — should stay segregated from all others, and that Romans 9:19-24 is saying that we should not disobey God (**... who are you to reply against God?...**). Dake is right about one thing: We should not question God. The problem is that Dake is so wrong about what the first Scripture means that he's misinterpreted it to mean its direct opposite. If we put these Scriptures together with their true interpretations, they tell us that God has created all of humanity to be brothers, and they ask, Who are we to question God?

The Bible refutes the segregation of races so many times that it's almost laughable to think Dake could imply that integrating the races is a "violation of God's original purpose." Let's see what the Bible says about interracial marriage, the most intimate way that the races can mingle and the target of white-supremacist hate. How about Abraham and Hagar, for example?

We learn about them in Genesis 16:1, when Abraham was still called Abram, and his wife Sarah was known as Sarai:[14]

Now Sarai, Abram's wife, had borne him no children. And she had an Egyptian maidservant whose name was Hagar.

---

[14] God changed Abram's name to Abraham in Genesis 17:5, when He told him he would be "a father to many nations," and Sarai's name was changed to Sarah in Genesis 17:16. Also, God revealed that she would bear Abraham a son and be "a mother of nations...."

Note that Hagar was an Egyptian — not a Hebrew like Abram and Sarai.

Genesis 16:2-4, 15 continue:

So Sarai said to Abram, "See now, the Lord has restrained me from bearing *children*. Please, go in to my maid; perhaps I shall obtain children by her." And Abram heeded the voice of Sarai.

Then Sarai, Abram's wife, took Hagar her maid, the Egyptian, and gave her to her husband Abram to be his wife, after Abram had dwelt ten years in the land of Canaan.

So he went in to Hagar, and she conceived. And when she saw that she had conceived, her mistress became despised in her eyes....

So Hagar bore Abram a son; and Abram named his son, whom Hagar bore, Ishmael.

This is what the Bible tells us, and I haven't found any Scripture that says God objected to the union of Abram, a Hebrew, with Hagar, an Egyptian. This is the second Scripture that disproves Dake's theory (the first being Dake's own reference, Acts 17:26, which, as we've seen, actually tells us about the unity of man rather than prescribing segregation). The biblical principle is, **"... by the mouth of two or three witnesses every word may be established"** (Matthew 18:16), so I could stop here and be sufficient in my proof, but I'm going on to a third Scripture that disproves Dake's theory.

Let's look at Genesis 17:18-21, which talks about Abraham's son born to Hagar, the Egyptian.

And Abraham said to God, "Oh, that Ishmael might live before You!"

16

> **Then God said: "No, Sarah your wife shall bear you a son, and you shall call his name Isaac; I will establish My covenant with him for an everlasting covenant, and with his descendants after him.**
>
> **"And as for Ishmael, I have heard you. Behold, I have blessed him and will make him fruitful, and will multiply him exceedingly. He shall beget twelve princes, and I will make him a great nation.**
>
> **"But My covenant I will establish with Isaac, whom Sarah shall bear to you at this set time next year."**

Abraham's union with Hagar is one of the first interracial marriages recorded in the Bible. Hagar was an Egyptian descendant of Ham, Noah's son who was the father of all the black nations.[15] She became the mother of Ishmael, from whom the Arab nations are descended. Notice in the Scripture that God never criticized Abraham for having a son with Hagar. In fact, God blessed their union. So if interracial marriage doesn't make any difference to God, why should anyone else have a problem with it?

---

[15] It is interesting to note that in his article, "Noah's Second Son: A Lady Day Sermon at King's College Cambridge," anthropologist Sir Edmund Leach begins his inquiry into the origin of man by quoting from Genesis, Chapter 9, which tells of Noah's sons going forth from the ark. Leach points out that the word *Ham* means black. Leach says that at first it referred to the soil of the Nile delta, but it was quickly transferred to mean a color of man's skin. See Leach, "Noah's Second Son: A Lady Day Sermon at King's College Cambridge," *Anthropology Today*, Vol. 4, No. 4, August, 1988, 2-5. The use of the word *Ham* for the delta soil and then for a color of man's skin is particularly appropriate, since it reflects the Lord God's creation of our physical bodies out of the earth. As the Scripture tells us, **And the Lord God formed man of the dust of the ground** (Genesis 2:7).

If, as Dake instructs, "God wills all races to be as He made them," and if, as Dake also says, God "made them" to be segregated, how could God let Abraham have sexual intercourse with an Egyptian, marry her, have a child with her, and bless the child? Is anyone really so dense that he or she cannot see that doesn't make any sense?

What about Moses and his Ethiopian wife, Zipporah? Ethiopia is a black country, which, like Egypt, traces its ancestry to Ham. Indeed, the word *Ethiopian* in Hebrew is *Cushite*. In Genesis 10:6, we find the origin of *Cush* when we read that **the sons of Ham were Cush, Mizraim, Put, and Canaan.** So if Moses, a Hebrew, was white, as we have been told, he still married a black descendant of Ham. Did God have a problem with Moses marrying a black woman?

Numbers 12:1-11 tells us:

Then Miriam and Aaron spoke against Moses because of the Ethiopian woman whom he had married; for he had married an Ethiopian woman.

So they said, "Has the LORD indeed spoken only through Moses? Has he not spoken through us also?" And the LORD heard it.

(Now the man Moses was very humble, more than all men who were on the face of the earth.)

Suddenly the LORD said to Moses, Aaron, and Miriam, "Come out, you three, to the tabernacle of meeting!" So the three came out.

Then the LORD came down in the pillar of cloud and stood in the door of the tabernacle, and called Aaron and Miriam. And they both went forward.

Then He said,

"Hear now My words:
If there is a prophet among you,
I, the LORD, make Myself known to him in a vision;
I speak to him in a dream.
Not so with My servant Moses;
He is faithful in all My house.
I speak with him face to face,
Even plainly, and not in dark sayings;
And he sees the form of the LORD.
Why then were you not afraid
To speak against My servant Moses?"

So the anger of the LORD was aroused against them, and He departed.

And when the cloud departed from above the tabernacle, suddenly Miriam became leprous, as white as snow. Then Aaron turned toward Miriam, and there she was, a leper.

So Aaron said to Moses, "Oh, my lord! Please do not lay this sin on us...."

The Scripture says that **Miriam and Aaron spoke against Moses because of the Ethiopian woman whom he had married**. Moses wasn't just having a sexual relationship with her, he married her; they became man and wife. He was Hebrew, she was a black Ethiopian. God did not get angry with Moses; he got angry with those who criticized Moses!

Let's return to Numbers 12:11:

So Aaron said to Moses, "Oh, my lord! Please do not lay this sin on us, in which we have done foolishly... "

All the racists from that time until now have been fools, acting very foolishly. But that is not all, because the Scripture continues:

So Aaron said to Moses, "Oh, my lord! Please do not lay this sin on us, in which we have done foolishly and in which we have sinned."

The opponents of interracial marriage have sinned. I didn't write this; Aaron said about himself and Miriam, "we have sinned." Numbers 12:12-15 tells us about Aaron's plea to be forgiven:

"Please do not let her be as one dead, whose flesh is half consumed when he comes out of his mother's womb!"

So Moses cried out to the Lord, saying, "Please heal her, O God, I pray!"

Then the LORD said to Moses, "If her father had but spit in her face, would she not be shamed seven days? Let her be shut out of the camp seven days, and afterward she may be received again."

So Miriam was shut out of the camp seven days, and the people did not journey till Miriam was brought in again.

It seems clear that God did not have a problem with the interracial couple. Personally, I don't care either way about interracial marriage. I'm not for it or against it; the only thing I consider important for a good marriage is for a Believer to be wed to another Believer, regardless of skin color. That is because the Bible tells us: **Do not be unequally yoked together with unbelievers** (2 Corinthians 6:14). But for many white people, both Christian and non-Christian, mixing races, especially the black and white races, is the big bugaboo. And that's the problem.

Many people see interracial marriage between white and black people as mixing inferior with the superior. This hatefulness was planted here in 1619, when the first slaves were brought to America, and then as now racial bias has been supported by members of the

Church.[16] I don't understand: If God has no objection to interracial marriage, why should anyone? It seems that if God were upset about the situation, He would have castigated Moses or the Ethiopian woman. He didn't. He castigated the criticizers. Doesn't that tell us something?

There are some white people who say they are against interracial marriage because of "practical considerations." They say it is hard on mixed couples in a society where people still predominantly marry those of their same skin color or ethnicity. They say that their objections have nothing to do with thinking that black people — or other people of color — are inferior or should be kept separate for any reason. These people may even have black friends. They believe their objections have nothing to do with the racist ideas that began in America almost 400 years ago.

Let's presume that people who tell themselves this really are free from bias. *This still doesn't mean that their objections to interracial marriage are correct or that they are not indirectly and unintentionally acting in a racist way.* Why do I say this? Because objections to interracial marriage based on skin color or ethnicity play into racist beliefs, and they validate the continuation of racism and the idea of black inferiority in our society.

Black people may also object to interracial marriage. Whether their objections are based on what they see as "practical considerations" or racist feelings against white people — which are a reaction to white racism — such objections are also against the Word of God.

---

[16] See Oscar Reiss, *Blacks in Colonial America* (North Carolina: McFarland & Company Inc. 1997), 17-21. Reiss explains how ministers of many denominations routinely taught their congregations that slavery was sanctioned by God and that black members were to be submissive and obedient because it was the will of God. Black ministers were only allowed to keep their positions if they upheld these views. Also see Emily Albu, J. William Frost, Howard Clark Kee, Carter Lindberg and Dana L. Robert, *Christianity: A Social and Cultural History* (New York: Prentice Hall Inc., 1998), 448.

Remember, if God has no objection to interracial marriage, why should anyone, of any race?

I've already given you three Scriptures to show why the segregation of races is against the Word of God, but I'm going beyond three witnesses. In the next chapter we're going to look at Salmon and Rahab. And I'm not stopping there, either. I'm going to provide so much Scripture, so much truth, that it will blow the circuits of any racists who may be reading this book. And that's exactly what I want to do.

2

A Revelation From God

 Let's look at what the Bible has to say about Salmon and Rahab. It is bound to shock many people who up to now have been unaware of God's perspective on mixing the races. We first hear about Rahab in Joshua 2:1:

Now Joshua the son of Nun sent out two men from Acacia Grove to spy secretly, saying, "Go, view the land, especially Jericho." So they went, and came to the house of a harlot named Rahab, and lodged there.

Joshua 6:25 goes on to say:

And Joshua spared Rahab the harlot, her father's household, and all that she had. So she dwells in Israel to this day, because she hid the messengers whom Joshua sent to spy out Jericho.

This Scripture lets us know that Rahab and her family (**her father's household**) lived in Israel. Israel was the land of the Hebrews, who, we have been told, are white. Since Rahab was from Jericho, which was in Canaan, she was a Canaanite. This means that she was black, because Canaanites were descended from Ham's son Canaan.

Thus, the Bible tells us that Rahab, a black woman, and all her relatives were dwelling among white people, the Israelites. This did not bother God — which is another direct contradiction of Dake's first reason for segregating the races.

Let's look now at Matthew 1:1-5. These Scriptures tell us about the genealogy of Jesus Christ, the Son of God. Keep this in the center of your mind as we read Verses 1 to 5:

The book of the genealogy of Jesus Christ, the Son of David, the Son of Abraham:

Abraham begot Isaac, Isaac begot Jacob, and Jacob begot Judah and his brothers.

Judah begot Perez and Zerah by Tamar, Perez begot Hezron, and Hezron begot Ram.

Ram begot Amminadab, Amminadab begot Nahshon, and Nahshon begot Salmon.

Salmon begot Boaz by Rahab....

There it is: Rahab, a black woman, is part of the genealogy of Jesus Christ, the Son of God. God has been attempting to get this across to the Church, the white church, which has been the purveyor of racism, century after century. He brings us revelation, and it's absolutely astounding to me how the Church has walked past the revelation with closed eyes and refused to see it.

Let's go back to Matthew 1:1:

The book of the genealogy of Jesus Christ, the Son of David, the Son of Abraham:

Abraham begot Isaac, Isaac begot Jacob....

Notice what is conspicuous in its absence: The Scripture does not say *how* Isaac was begotten by Abraham; it doesn't let us know anything about the woman who begot him.

A Revelation From God

Abraham begot Isaac [it doesn't tell us by whom]**, Isaac begot Jacob** [it doesn't tell us by whom]**, Jacob begot Judah and his brothers** [it doesn't tell us by whom].

Judah begot Perez and Zerah by Tamar [we will get to her next]**, Perez begot Hezron** [it doesn't tell us by whom]**, and Hezron begot Ram** [it doesn't tell us by whom].

Ram begot Amminadab [it doesn't tell us by whom]**, Amminadab begot Nahshon** [it doesn't tell us by whom]**, and Nahshon begot Salmon** [it doesn't tell us by whom].

Salmon begot Boaz by Rahab....

Here's my point: God is *specifically* telling us that **Salmon begot Boaz by Rahab....** Rahab was a Canaanite. Rahab was black. So even if Jesus Christ looked European white, as He has always been portrayed, Jesus Christ had some black "inferior" blood in Him. Now it seems to me that if God were opposed to racial intermixing, He would at least have had enough sense not to put it in His genealogy.

In all probability, Tamar, who the Scripture tells us bore two sons to Judah, was also black. First Chronicles 2:3 tells us that Judah's wife was **Shuah, the Canaanitess**. Earlier, in Genesis 24:3, we have been told that Abraham wanted his son Isaac not to get a wife from the Canaanites, among whom Abraham and his family dwelled. There is no indication that Abraham's family ever left Canaan. Judah was part of Abraham's family and, as we saw, he took his wife Shuah from among the Canaanites. We can infer from the fact that Judah had two sons by his daughter-in-law Tamar (1 Chronicles 2:4) and that there is no record of Judah ever leaving Canaan, that Tamar was probably a Canaanite. If she was, then there are at least two black women in the genealogy of Jesus Christ, and in both instances the Bible has called our attention to these women in a Scripture that, aside from the two women, only mentions men.

25

All of us, of every race, have been lied to. Jesus has some of Ham in Him, because Rahab was a Canaanite. And very possibly Tamar, who is also in the ancestry of Jesus Christ, was also a Canaanite. There's no way racists can weasel out of this. To go back and say that the Canaanites were white would mean that a black man, Ham, had a white son, Canaan. If that were true, then that would mean Canaan was mixed, part black, part white. So Jesus would still have black ancestry. Not only did God make this choice, He went so far as to show everyone who reads the Bible that His own Son had some racial mixture in Him.

I don't know what Dake is talking about when he writes that "God's original purpose" calls for segregation of the races. Think about it again: God included in His plan for the lineage of His Son the marriage of Salmon and Rahab, a marriage between a Shemite and a Canaanite (or Hamite, as descendants of Ham are called). Out of that union came Boaz, an ancestor of David and of Jesus Christ. In the genealogy of His Son, God also included Tamar, who also may well have been black. If God is so opposed to interracial marriage, as Dake and others seem to claim, tell me why Almighty God chose one woman, and perhaps two, of another race to be direct ancestors of our Lord Jesus Christ, the Redeemer of the whole human race?

Another illustration of what seems to have been a mixing of races occurs in 2 Samuel 11. Verse 2 tells us:

> **Then it happened one evening that David arose from his bed and walked on the roof of the king's house. And from the roof he saw a woman bathing, and the woman was very beautiful to behold.**
>
> **So David sent and inquired about the woman. And someone said, "Is this not Bathsheba, the daughter of Eliam, the wife of Uriah the Hittite?"**

The Bible identifies Uriah as a Hittite, and Hittites were black, since they were descended from Heth, the son of Ham's son Canaan.

Because Bathsheba's husband was a Hittite, it is very possible that she was a Hittite. Indeed, all the information the Old Testament gives us about the family of Bathsheba is her union with her black husband; the Old Testament does not link her in any way to any of the people we have been told are white.

In Verses 26 and 27 we find:

When the wife of Uriah heard that Uriah her husband was dead, she mourned for her husband.

And when her mourning was over, David sent and brought her to his house, and she became his wife and bore him a son. But the thing that David had done displeased the Lord.

What displeased the Lord was not that David married Bathsheba; what displeased the Lord was that in order to marry the beautiful Bathsheba, David had her husband Uriah the Hittite killed.[1] So it was murder that displeased the Lord, not the issue of race.

Chapter 12:24 goes on to say:

Then David comforted Bathsheba his wife, and went in to her and lay with her. So she bore a son, and he called his name Solomon. Now the Lord loved him....

It would have been enough to know that David "went in to" Bathsheba, and that she had a son named Solomon, but notice God's superlatives. He tells us **the Lord loved him**. And we know from previous verses that Solomon, this child whom the Lord loved, was born of what the Bible indicates may have been an interracial marriage between David, the Israelite, and Bathsheba. Solomon, their son, who very well may have been part black and part white, is, like Boaz, son of the interracial couple Salmon and Rahab, also part of the genealogy of the Lord Jesus Christ.

---

[1] See Appendix, pages 233-234, for 2 Samuel 11:6-17.

We have seen that in the Old Testament God accepted inter-racial marriage and, in fact, punished Miriam when she spoke against Moses' Ethiopian wife. We have also seen that the New Testament reveals in the genealogy of Jesus Christ at least one and perhaps three ancestors of mixed parentage. What does the New Testament have to say about interracial marriage?

Let's look at Acts 16:1-3:

Then he [Paul] came to Derbe and Lystra. And behold, a certain disciple was there, named Timothy, the son of a certain Jewish woman who believed, but his father was Greek.

He was well spoken of by the brethren who were at Lystra and Iconium. Paul wanted to have him go on with him. And he took him and circumcised him because of the Jews who were in that region, for they all knew that his father was Greek.

Timothy was the offspring of an interracial marriage — between his mother Eunice, a Jew, and his father, whom the New Testament tells us was Greek (Acts 16:1; 2 Tim 1:5). The Israelites and Greeks were considered different races, yet the marriage of Timothy's father and mother must have been acceptable to the Lord because Timothy was used mightily in the formation of the early church.

Again, the only prohibition I can find in the Bible about whom people should marry is not ethnic, but spiritual. I'm repeating this, and I will repeat it again, because I want to establish for all time how untenable racists' lies about the Bible are, so that no one will ever be taken in by them again. God's *only* prohibition regarding marriage is the one I quoted from 2 Corinthians 6:14:

Do not be unequally yoked together with unbelievers....

That's it. Believers should not marry unbelievers. If a white Believer marries a white unbeliever, they are unequally yoked. If a

28

red Believer marries a red unbeliever, they are unequally yoked. The same holds true for black Believers, yellow Believers, and brown Believers. It's about Believers and unbelievers. Color does not matter to God because, out of one blood, God made all men.

3

How God Sees the Races

Having disproved Dake's first reason for segregating the races, we will now look at his second reason:

God made everything to reproduce "after his own kind" (Gen. 1:11-12, 21-25; 6:20; 7:14). Kind means type and color, or he would have kept them all alike to begin with.

When Dake adds the explanatory statement, "Kind means type or color," he grossly misses the mark. In the book of Genesis, the word *kind* appears 18 times. The 18 passages where the word *kind* is used tell us that it means something very different from Dake's supposed definition. Let's read these passages carefully to see what the Bible means by *kind*.

Genesis 1:11-12 states:

Then God said, "Let the earth bring forth grass, the herb that yields seed, and the fruit tree that yields fruit according to its *kind* [all italics mine], whose seed is in itself, on the earth"; and it was so.

And the earth brought forth grass, the herb that yields seed according to its *kind*, and the tree that yields fruit,

whose seed is in itself according to its *kind*. And God saw that it was good.

Genesis 1:21-25 tells us:

So God created great sea creatures and every living thing that moves, with which the waters abounded, according to their *kind*, and every winged bird according to its *kind*. And God saw that it was good.

And God blessed them, saying, "Be fruitful and multiply, and fill the waters in the seas, and let birds multiply on the earth."

So the evening and the morning were the fifth day.

Then God said, "Let the earth bring forth the living creature according to its *kind*: cattle and creeping thing and beast of the earth, each according to its *kind*"; And it was so.

And God made the beast of the earth according to its *kind*, cattle according to its *kind*, and everything that creeps on the earth according to its *kind*. And God saw that it was good.

According to Genesis 6:20:

"Of the birds after their *kind*, of animals after their *kind*, and of every creeping thing of the earth after its *kind*, two of every *kind* will come to you to keep them alive."

Genesis 7:14 tells us:

they and every beast after its *kind*, all cattle after their *kind*, every creeping thing that creeps on the earth after its *kind*, and every bird after its *kind*, every bird of every sort.

Dake says that "kind means type and color." However, as we can see from the above Scriptures, in the book of Genesis, the word *kind*, generally means "species" and *never* means "color." With all due respect to Dake, "type and color" is not an accurate definition of *min* (also spelled *meen* or *miyn*), the Hebrew word for *kind*. *The New Strong's Exhaustive Concordance of the Bible* translates *min* as:

> From an unused root meaning to portion out; a sort, i.e. species: — kind.[1]

The Analytical Concordance to the Bible by Robert Young, who, like James Strong, was a distinguished Hebrew and Greek scholar, also translates the word *kind* from the Hebrew word *min* to mean *species*,[2] as do both *The New Wilson's Old Testament Word Studies* and *The New Brown-Driver-Briggs-Gesenius Hebrew-English Lexicon*.[3]

The Theological Wordbook of the Old Testament by Harris, Archer and Waltke provides a broader and fuller explanation of the term:

> God created the basic forms of life called *min* which can be classified according to modern biologists and

---

[1] James Strong, LL.D, S.T.D., Hebrew Dictionary of the Old Testament, *The New Strong's Exhaustive Concordance of the Bible*, Nelson's Comfort Print ed. (Nashville: Thomas Nelson Publishers, 1995), 77 (4327).

[2] Robert Young, *Young's Analytical Concordance to the Bible* (Peabody, Maine: Hendrickson Publishers), 564.

[3] See William Wilson, *New Wilson's Old Testament Word Studies* (Grand Rapids, Michigan: Kregel Publications, 1987 (revised from 1978), 238, and Briggs, Brown, Driver, *The New Brown-Driver-Briggs-Gesenius Hebrew-English Lexicon* (Oxford, England: J.P. Greene, Sr., 1979), 568.

zoologists as sometimes species, sometimes genus, sometimes family or order.[4]

In his attempt to offer another reason for segregating the races, Dake translates *kind* as "type and color" so that each ethnic and racial group would be defined as a different *kind.* All of the other scholars I've quoted agree that, in fact, *kind* means "species" or sometimes "genus, ... family or order." We can see this borne out in the Scriptures we've examined — the very Scriptures Dake cites to support his false ideas. Grass is a different *kind* from fruit, winged birds are a different *kind* from cattle, cattle are a different *kind* from creeping things. But human beings of all ethnic and racial groups and skin color are all of one *kind*, the species Homo sapiens.

First Corinthians 15:39 sums it up:

All flesh is not the same flesh, but there is one kind of flesh of men, another flesh of animals, another of fish, and another of birds.

Since God clearly states that **there is one kind of flesh of men** — only one — there is no credibility to Dake's second reason for segregating the races. Black people are not a different "kind" from white people — or from people of any other color. We are all humankind.

---

[4] R. Laird Harris, Gleason L. Archer Jr., and Bruce K. Waltke, *Theological Wordbook of the Old Testament* (Chicago: Moody Bible Institute, 1980), 503-504.

4

What the Scriptures Do *Not* Say

According to Dake, Reason 3 is:

God originally determined the bounds of the habitations of nations. ([Acts] 17:26; Gen. 10:5, 32; 11:8; Dt. 32:8).

If this appears familiar, it's because we've seen the thought expressed before in support of Dake's first reason for racial segregation, that it's part of "God's original purpose." Acts 17:26, the first Scripture he cites to prove Reason 3 was also used to support Reason 1.

> **"And He has made from one blood every nation of men to dwell on all the face of the earth, and has determined their preappointed times and the boundaries of their dwellings."**

Once again, when Dake says, "God originally determined the bounds of the habitation of nations," he is pointing out that God originally set up where nations would be and claims that's where God is telling us they are supposed to stay.

Let's look at Dake's second reference, Genesis 10:5, 32:

> **From these the coastland peoples of the Gentiles were separated into their lands, everyone according to his language, according to their families, into their nations....**

> These were the families of the sons of Noah, according
> to their generations, in their nations; and from these
> the nations were divided on the earth after the flood.

Before we discuss these verses, let's read his third reference, Deuteronomy 32:8:

> "When the Most High divided
>   their inheritance to the nations,
> When He separated the sons of Adam,
> He set the boundaries of the peoples
> According to the number of the children of Israel."

Many times, we may not know exactly what something means, but we can find out what it means to a degree by finding out what it does not mean. Again, let's review Deuteronomy 32:8:

> "When the Most High divided
>   their inheritance to the nations,
> When He separated the sons of Adam,
> He set the boundaries of the peoples
> According to the number of the children of Israel."

If what Dake said is correct, this would mean that the way God originally determined "the bounds of the habitation of nations" would have to stay that way forever. If that's true, then the Caucasoid race should have stayed in Europe and not have come to North and South America. Yet Christopher Columbus, Amerigo Vespucci, and later, the Pilgrims—all coming from different lands for different reasons—left their original boundaries and voyaged to the New World either to conquer it or to make a new life for themselves. If, as Dake said, they were supposed to stay in the same place in which God had originally established the boundaries of their nations, we have a problem — no United States of America!

We know white people came here from Europe and that black people were brought here from Africa. But although we aren't absolutely certain precisely where the Native Americans came from, scientific evidence says they came to North America from somewhere else, too, as did the Eskimos.[1] So as I pointed out earlier, groups of people have been changing their boundaries, sometimes for the better, sometimes for the worse, almost since God first created them. Indeed, it was under God's instruction that after leaving Egypt, Moses led God's chosen people to Canaan, which God promised to them.[2]

So again Dake's reasoning is preposterous. He can't use Scriptures about the original boundaries God set as a reason to segregate the races, and then ignore the fact that the entire planet is made up of populations that have moved beyond and away from their original boundaries.

I believe that Dake reveals something about himself in Reason 4:

> Miscegenation means the mixture of races, especially the black and white races or those of outstanding type of color. The Bible even goes farther than opposing this. It is against different branches of the same stock intermarrying, such as Jews marrying other descendants of Abraham (Ezra 9-10; Neh. 9-13; Jer. 50:37; Ezek. 30:5).

---

[1] As anthropologists Joseph H. Greenberg, Christy G. Turner II and Stephen L. Zegura explain, the biological evidence leads to the widely accepted conclusion that the settlement of the Americas had "its origin in migration from Asia via the Bering Strait." See Greenberg, Turner II and Zegura, "The Settlement of the Americas: A Comparison of the Linguistic, Dental, and Genetic Evidence," *Current Anthropology*, Vol. 27, Issue 5, December 1986, 477-497. Also see Stephen A. Flanders, *Atlas of American Migration* (New York: Facts on File, Inc., 1998), 9. The knowledge that mankind migrated to the Americas rather than having originated here was known at least as early as the second decade of the 20th Century. See Alec Hrdlicka, "Transpacific Migrations," *Man*, Royal Anthropological Institute, Vol. 17, February 1917, 29-30.

[2] See Appendix, page 234, for Exodus 3:7-10.

Dake says, "miscegenation means the mixture of races"; perhaps if he had stopped there, the drift of his thinking wouldn't have been quite so obvious. But he adds, "especially the black and white races or those of outstanding type or color." What is so special about the black and white races that he has to single them out as having to be kept apart? What is so special about people of "outstanding type of color"? Why does it always come down to color? And why is there always a special emphasis on black and white?

If Dake does not have racist attitudes towards black people, it seems peculiar to me that he should say "especially the black and white races." If he believes interracial marriage between Blacks and Whites is against God's will, why doesn't he say miscegenation means a mixing of races period, and then quote a Scripture to support that? What is the big deal to white people about Blacks and Whites intermarrying unless they are racially biased against black people? If you make a statement like "especially the black and white races," I don't have to say anything about you — you incriminate yourself.

Since Dake gives Scriptures to back up his statement, we would expect the passages he cites to say something about "especially the black and white races." This seems only reasonable. Indeed, those Scriptures should make color an issue and they should refer specifically to black people and white people, otherwise whoever cited them is perjuring himself.

Let's start with the first Scripture Dake provides, Ezra 9:1-2:

When these things were done, the leaders came to me, saying, "The people of Israel and the priests and the Levites have not separated themselves from the peoples of the lands, with respect to the abomination of the Canaanites, the Hittites, the Perizzites, the Jebusites, the Ammonites, the Moabites, the Egyptians and the Amorites.

"For they have taken some of their daughters as wives for themselves and their sons, so that the holy seed is mixed with the peoples of those lands. Indeed, the

hand of the leaders and rulers has been foremost in this trespass."

Note the phrase **"peoples of those lands."** Does the Bible criticize the Levites for mixing **"holy seed ... with the peoples of those lands"** because of color or ethnicity? No. As the Scripture tells us it is strictly **"with respect to the abomination"** of these other peoples! And what is **"the abomination"**? It is that **"the Canaanites, the Hittites, the Perizzites, the Jebusites, the Ammonites, the Moabites, the Egyptians and the Amorites"** were pagans: They did not worship Jehovah as the Levites did.[3] This is so elementary that it's Bible 101.

Remember, Dake says that miscegenation or intermarrying is prohibited because of color and/or ethnicity. He adds that the Bible "is against different branches of the same stock intermarrying, such as Jews marrying other descendants of Abraham." We'll soon see that this is also not true. As with other Scriptures Dake quotes as proof of what he says about the mixing of races, it is crystal clear that any prohibition against marriage had nothing to do with black and white or any other color — it had to do with Believers and unbelievers. As in Ezra 9:1-2, it had to do with the paganism of the land in which the Israelites found themselves. When we look at the history of Israel, we see that every time the Israelites violated God's Word and got entangled with unbelievers, the unbelievers would always pull them away from Jehovah, and the Israelites would end up worshipping false gods. The law regarding this is the Third Commandment: **"You shall have no other gods before Me"** (Exodus 20:3). From a biblical perspective, it was disobeying this law that got the Israelites in trouble.

---

[3] According to *The New Strong's Exhaustive Concordance of the Bible,* the word *abomination* in Ezra 9:1 literally means "something disgusting, i.e., an abhorrence, especially idolatry or an idol: — abominable (custom, thing) abomination." Strong, 8441.

Let's look at Dake's second reference, Ezra 9:11-12:

"which you commanded by your servants the prophets, saying, 'The land which you are entering to possess is an unclean land, with the uncleanness of the peoples of the lands, with their abominations which have filled it from one end to another with their impurity.' "

What is **"their impurity"**? Again, it is not their color, but their gods.

The passage continues:

"'Now therefore, do not give your daughters as wives for their sons, nor take their daughters to your sons; and never seek their peace or prosperity, that you may be strong and eat the good of the land, and leave it as an inheritance to your children forever.' "

I do not see anything in Verses 1, 2, 11 and 12 about black people and white people. I do not see anything about ethnicity in terms of color. I see a reference to "abominations," which, as we know, in the Old Testament refers to worshipping false gods, idols, the stars, the sun, the moon. But despite the Bible only warning against intermarrying with pagans, Dake says it is against "miscegenation ... especially [between] the black and white races or other outstanding type of color."

Dake's next reference is to Nehemiah, and he cites all of Chapters 9 through 13. Since they are too long to include in their entirety here, for your inspection I'm including them in the appendix of this volume.[4] Although Dake cites Nehemiah 9 through 13 to support his fourth reason for segregating the races, you will not find any references in these chapters to black and white or to the issue of color. But please don't take my word for it in the same way people

---

[4] See Appendix, pages 234-246, for Nehemiah 9-13.

have been taking Dake's word for what he is saying without check-
ing it out. Please read Nehemiah 9 through 13 for yourself.

Dake's third reference, Jeremiah 50:37, tells us:

> **"A sword is against their horses,**
> **Against their chariots,**
> **And against all the mixed peoples who are in her midst;**
> **And they will become like women.**
> **A sword is against her treasures, and they will be**
> **robbed."**

There is nothing in this verse about "black and white," let
alone "especially black and white." Dake cites only Verse 37, but I'd
like you to read the whole chapter, because there is no mention of
black and white in any of it.[5] Jeremiah 50:37 mentions **"mixed
peoples,"** but "mixed" refers to the mixture of Israelite and pagan. It
is not about color.

Dake's next reference is Ezekiel 30:5.

> **"Ethiopia, Libya, Lydia, all the mingled people, Chub,**
> **and the men of the lands who are allied, shall fall with**
> **them by the sword."**

Again, these are Scriptures Dake is using to support his view
that there should be no intermixing of races, "especially black and
white." Yet, like the other Scriptures he has cited, this one says
nothing about "black and white" or skin color. Indeed, the whole
chapter and the chapters before and after it say nothing about "black
and white" or skin color. I reread all of them just to be sure, and I
want you to read them so that you will be sure, too.[6]

Any honest person who reads these Bible references has to
realize that God is not talking about skin color, but once again about

---

[5] See Appendix, pages 246-249, for Jeremiah 50.
[6] See Appendix, pages 249-251, for Ezekiel 30.

Israelites getting involved with the paganism of these other nations. That was the reason for the Israelites' constant strife — they were repeatedly turning away from Jehovah.

Reason 5 of Dake's "30 reasons for segregation of races" is:

> Abraham forbad Eliezer to take a wife for Isaac of Canaanites (Gen. 24:1-4). God was so pleased with this that He directed whom to get (Gen. 24:7, 12-67).

Why did Abraham forbid this? According to Dake, it is because the races should be segregated. What do the Scriptures have to say?

Let's start with Genesis 24:7, which Dake uses to support the second half of his "reason" for segregating the races. Genesis 24:7 states:

> **"The Lord God of heaven, who took me from my father's house and from the land of my family, and who spoke to me and swore to me, saying, 'To your descendants I give this land,' He will send His angel before you, and you shall take a wife for my son from there."**

When we read this Scripture in context, which we will now do, we see that Abraham is giving instructions to his servant about getting a wife for his son Isaac. This was common in biblical times; parents arranged marriages for their children. But so far the Scripture has mentioned nothing about race or skin color, has it?

Genesis 24:1-4 tells us:

> **Now Abraham was old, well advanced in age; and the Lord had blessed Abraham in all things.**
>
> **So Abraham said to the oldest servant of his house, who ruled over all that he had, "Please, put your hand under my thigh,**

> "and I will make you swear by the Lord, the God of
> heaven and the God of the earth, that you will not take
> a wife for my son from the daughters of the Canaanites,
> among whom I dwell;
>
> "but you shall go to my country and to my family, and
> take a wife for my son Isaac."

Dake did not refer to verses 5 and 6, but I will include
them here as they lead into Verse 7, so that you can read them in
sequence.

> And the servant said to him, "Perhaps the woman will
> not be willing to follow me to this land. Must I take
> your son back to the land from which you came?"
>
> But Abraham said to him, "Beware that you do not
> take my son back there.
>
> "The Lord God of heaven who took me from my
> father's house and from the land of my family, and
> who spoke to me and swore to me saying, 'To your
> descendants I give this land,' He will send his angel
> before you, and you shall take a wife for my son from
> there."

In none of these Scriptures do we see one word about not
choosing a Canaanite on the basis of skin color. All we know from
the Scripture is that Abraham said, in effect, "Don't take a wife for
my son from here; get one from there."

Why did Abraham say this? Once again, it is an issue of
Believers and unbelievers. The Canaanites, who at that time possessed the Promised Land, practiced idolatry while Abraham knew
the one true God and worshipped Him alone. It is only natural that
Abraham would want his son to be steadfast in his worship of Jehovah, too, so he arranged to have a wife brought for his son from his

own family — a wife who would be amenable to serving the Lord God Jehovah.

This commitment to seeing that his son remain devoted to the Lord God is evident in Abraham's insistence that his servant bring a wife to his son Isaac rather than allowing Isaac to go to his prospective bride. Abraham knew that traveling outside their camp, Isaac would be subject to the influences of pagans. He obviously did not want his son to be in any way affected by their beliefs ("**... Beware that you do not take my son back there...**") — a fact that Dake completely leaves out of his interpretation.

According to the renowned Bible scholar and commentator Matthew Henry, Abraham saw the wickedness of the Canaanites. He knew by revelation that they were headed for destruction and did not want his son to be snared by them or to suffer reproach because of their evil ways.[7] So Abraham saw to it that Isaac took a wife from his own family. Whether or not Abraham knew by divine revelation that the Canaanites were moving toward destruction is debatable. But what cannot be debated is that Abraham's wish for Isaac reflects — in fact, sets in place — the spiritual principle that the Lord God mandated to His people throughout the Old Covenant and that we've seen stated in 2 Corinthians 6:14: **Do not be unequally yoked together with unbelievers....**

So Abraham's instructions regarding his son's marriage are wholly a spiritual matter; they have nothing to do with differences in skin color. It is interesting to note that Matthew Henry's commentary about the spiritual nature of Abraham's request was available as a resource when Dake wrote his commentary. Indeed, it has been available since the early 18th Century, which means it was available to Church leaders during the time of slavery — yet it was ignored in order to falsify the Scripture and bring in the issue of black and white.

---

[7] *Matthew Henry's Commentary* (Grand Rapids, Michigan: Regency Reference Library, Zondervan Publishing House, 1960), 42.

Dake also cites Genesis 24:12-67 to support his fifth "reason." Since it is very lengthy, rather than include all of it here, I'm including it in the Appendix so that you can read it for yourself.[8] When you do, you will see that these verses are just like the previous verses we read — 24:7 and 24:1-4. They have nothing to do with color; nothing to do with black and white; nothing to do with race or ethnicity as such.

According to Dake, Reason 6 is that:

Isaac forbad Jacob to take a wife of the Canaanites (Gen. 27:46-28:7).

Here, too, by including this as a reason for "segregation of races," the implication is that Isaac didn't allow his son Jacob to take a wife from the Canaanites because of race. Once more, Dake is citing Scripture to show that God's prohibition is a racial issue. Do the Scriptures bear this out?

Genesis 27:46 and 28:1-7 tell us:

And Rebekah said to Isaac, "I am weary of my life because of the daughters of Heth; if Jacob takes a wife of the daughters of Heth, like these who are the daughters of the land, what good will my life be to me?"

Then Isaac called Jacob and blessed him, and charged him, and said to him: "You shall not take a wife from the daughters of Canaan.

"Arise, go to Padan Aram, to the house of Bethuel your mother's father; and take yourself a wife from there of the daughters of Laban your mother's brother.

"May God Almighty bless you,
And make you fruitful and multiply you,

---

[8] See Appendix, pages 251-255, for Genesis 24:12-67.

That you may be an assembly of peoples;
And give you the blessings of Abraham,
To you and your descendants with you,
That you may inherit the land
In which you are a stranger,
Which God gave to Abraham."

So Isaac sent Jacob away, and he went to Padan Aram,
to Laban the son of Bethuel the Syrian, the brother of
Rebekah, the mother of Jacob and Esau.

Esau saw that Isaac had blessed Jacob and sent him
away to Padan Aram to take himself a wife from there,
and that as he blessed him he gave him a charge, saying, "You shall not take a wife from the daughters of
Canaan,"

and that Jacob had obeyed his father and his mother
and had gone to Padan Aram.

The only thing this Scripture says is not to take a daughter
from the daughters of Heth, in the land that Abraham and his family
lived, nor from the daughters of Canaan, but it does not tell us why.
We know from the Bible that the daughters of Heth were pagans, as
we know the Canaanites were. Yet Dake does not even mention this.
He isn't listing "30 reasons for segregation of Believers from pagans"
as it seems he should be, he's listing "30 reasons for segregation of
races" and writing about God's supposed prohibition against
miscegenation, "especially black and white or other type of
outstanding color."

It's interesting to note the full story behind this Scripture that
Dake cites in an attempt to show that God is opposed to interracial
marriage. In order to understand what Rebekah says to Isaac in Verse
46, we have to go back to Genesis 25:21, where Isaac prays for
Rebekah, who was barren, to have a child. The Lord granted his
prayer, but Rebekah apparently had problems during her pregnancy

and inquired of the Lord, **"If all is well, why am I like this?"** (Verse 22). In Verse 23, the Lord tells her that there are two nations in her womb, and that the older one will serve the younger; in other words, that the younger child is the one chosen by God to inherit the promise of Abraham.

Rebekah gives birth to two sons, Esau, the eldest, and Jacob. Verse 28 tells us that **... Isaac loved Esau because he ate of his game, but Rebekah loved Jacob.** From their birth, the two sons were rivals, and the hatred between them only grew. On the day that Isaac was prepared to give the customary blessing to his eldest son, Rebekah deceived him into pronouncing it upon Jacob (Verse 27). Discovering this, Esau vowed to kill Jacob, even though we learn in Genesis 25: 29-34 that Esau had sold his birthright to Jacob, so Jacob rightfully deserved this blessing.

When Rebekah learned of Esau's intent to kill Jacob, Genesis 27:42-46 tells us that she instructed Jacob to prepare to flee to her brother Laban for protection until Esau's anger subsided. It is at this point that the verse Dake cites comes in. Rebekah uses what would have been her husband's own natural desire to have his sons marry as he had (from Abraham's family; indeed, from the house of Laban) in order to get Isaac to go along with her plan. In this way, Rebekah can protect Jacob from Esau and protect Esau from becoming a murderer without having to tell Isaac the whole story. And it worked: Isaac sent Jacob away, which was Rebekah's main goal as a mother.

We can tell from the Scriptures that Isaac's act of sending Jacob away was not motivated by a need to keep his sons from marrying a woman of color. Remember, Esau — who Isaac thought was to inherit the promise — had already crossed the color line (we know that the daughters of Heth, whom he married, were women of color). Apparently Isaac didn't object, since he was still willing to pronounce the promise upon Esau. Isaac's decision to send Jacob away was precipitated by Rebekah's plan to protect both her sons from destruction.

While, as we've seen, none of it has anything to do with skin color, we can see in the Scriptures a confirmation of the precedent not to be unequally yoked with unbelievers. First, we can see how God moves to ensure that this principle is followed in the life of the one who inherits the promise, Jacob. Second, we can see in later Scriptures that God only begins to reveal Himself to Jacob after he has committed to Isaac's command regarding whom Jacob will marry (Genesis 28:10-15). Throughout the Old Testament, God reveals Himself as a jealous God, One who will have no other gods before Him. Jacob's commitment to his father's plan reveals Jacob's commitment to the Lord God. The spiritual focus of this is evident in Esau's futile attempt to regain the blessing by marrying a daughter of Ishmael, who was a daughter of Abraham's lineage (Genesis 28: 8-9). So despite what Dake says, in God's eyes the issue is not color, or even family, but instead your commitment to Him.

5

The Sin of Misrepresenting the Bible

 Dake's Reason 7 for the segregation of the races is:

Abraham sent all his sons of the concubines, and even of his second wife, far away from Isaac so their descendants would not mix (Gen. 25:1-6).

Let's look at Genesis 25:1-6:

Abraham again took a wife, and her name was Keturah.

And she bore him Zimran, Jokshan, Medan, Midian, Ishbak, and Shuah.

Jokshan begot Sheba and Dedan. And the sons of Dedan were Asshurim, Letushim, and Leummim.

And the sons of Midian were Ephah, Epher, Hanoch, Abidah, and Eldaah. All these were the children of Keturah.

And Abraham gave all that he had to Isaac.

But Abraham gave gifts to the sons of the concubines which Abraham had; and while he was still living he sent them eastward, away from Isaac his son, to the country of the east.

All that we know from this Scripture is that Abraham sent his other sons **eastward, away from Isaac**. How can anyone assume that he sent them away because of color? It does not say anything about color. And if the Bible doesn't say that color is the reason Abraham sent his other sons to live in a country to the east — if God does not say that's why — how can a Bible teacher or anyone assume that it was done in order to segregate the races?

The custom at that time was for the son of the first wife to inherit from his father, and Isaac was the son of Abraham's first and principal wife, Sarah. God also made it clear that His Covenant would be fulfilled through Isaac (Genesis 17:19, 21). Isn't it more likely that Abraham sent his other sons eastward in order for Isaac to establish himself without competition or rivalry from his siblings, and so that his siblings could establish themselves away from Isaac? Indeed, this is a lesson that Abraham would have well learned, since Genesis 13 tells us that the land inhabited by Abraham and his nephew Lot was **... not able to support them, that they might dwell together, for their possessions were so great that they could not dwell together....** In order to prevent the strife that was occurring, Abraham and Lot agreed to separate and go to different areas. Abraham was simply applying this principle with his own sons.

According to Dake, Reason 8 is:

> Esau disobeying this law brought the final break between him and his father after life-long companionship with him. (Gen. 25:28; 26:34-35; 27:46; 28:8-9).

Let's look again at the first part of this sentence: "Esau disobeying this law...." Who said that segregating the races was a law? Dake says it, and he says it as if it is a matter of fact: "Esau disobeying this law...." The Bible does not say it is a law; Abraham does not say it is a law; Isaac does not say it is a law; only Dake says it is a law. That is frightening. How many people have picked up a copy of *Dake's Annotated Reference Bible* and read his assertion that it was a *law* to segregate the races, and believed it because they haven't bothered to look any further? Well, we have looked further, and we're going to look even further.

What does the first Scripture Dake cites have to say about this so-called law?

Genesis 25:28 is a verse we've read before. It tells us:

And Isaac loved Esau because he ate of his game, but Rebekah loved Jacob.

Dake says that "Esau disobeying this law brought the final break between him and his father after life-long companionship with him." What does Verse 28 say about color? Nothing. All it says is **Isaac loved Esau because he ate of his game, but Rebekah loved Jacob.** Maybe Dake is using this to establish that Isaac had a close relationship with Esau up to this time. If so, then the next Scripture should state that because Esau broke Dake's so-called law about segregating the races, it brought about a "the final break between him and his father."

The next Scripture Dake cites to support this is Genesis 26: 34-35:

When Esau was forty years old, he took as wives Judith the daughter of Beeri the Hittite, and Basemath the daughter of Elon the Hittite.

And they were a grief of mind to Isaac and Rebekah.

What does this have to do with segregation of the races? It just tells us Esau took his wives from the Hittites and his parents didn't like it. It does not say they didn't like it because the Hittites were black. Why not interpret it to mean that they didn't like it because the Hittites did not have the same beliefs as Isaac and Rebekah, since the Hittites were pagans and were not Believers in Jehovah?

We've also already looked at Dake's next source, Genesis 27:46. It says:

And Rebekah said to Isaac, "I am weary of my life because of the daughters of Heth; if Jacob takes a wife

> of the daughters of Heth, like these who are the daughters of the land, what good will my life be to me?"

As we saw when we analyzed Dake's previous reference to this verse, it doesn't refer in any way to segregating races. It is Rebekah's way of separating her two sons before one murders the other.

The last Scripture that Dake cites to support his eighth reason is Genesis 28:8-9:

> **Also Esau saw that the daughters of Canaan did not please his father Isaac.**
>
> **So Esau went to Ishmael and took Mahalath the daughter of Ishmael, Abraham's son, the sister of Nebajoth, to be his wife in addition to the wives he had.**

There is nothing in this verse either about segregation of the races. There is nothing in any of them. And since there is nothing about segregating the races, there is certainly nothing about it being a law.

Dake's Reason 9 of the "30 reasons for segregation of races" is:

> The two branches of Isaac remained segregated forever.
> (Gen. 36; 46:8-26).

I'd like you to read Genesis 36 for yourself so you can see that none of it says that the races should be segregated, but because it's so long, I'm including it in the Appendix.[1] However, there are two verses — 6 and 7 — we will examine here in light of Dake's statement, which gives us the impression that "the two branches of Isaac" were segregated forever because of their ethnicity or race. To me, this appears categorically dishonest. To show you why, we have to start by answering the question, Why were the two branches separated in the first place?

---

[1] See Appendix, pages 255-257, for Genesis 36.

Genesis 36:6 tells us:

Then Esau took his wives, his sons, his daughters, and all the persons of his household, his cattle and all his animals, and all his goods which he had gained in the land of Canaan, and went to a country away from the presence of his brother Jacob.

Why did Esau do this? Verse 7 gives us an answer:

For their possessions were too great for them to dwell together, and the land where they were strangers could not support them because of their livestock.

Esau did not move far away from his brother Jacob because of skin color or ethnicity, yet these are verses Dake gives us to support one of his 30 reasons. In fact, so far we haven't read a *single* Scripture that says people should be segregated because of race or ethnicity. But we will continue to look, just to see if Dake has any grounds for his claim.

Dake's next scriptural proof is Genesis 46:8-26:

Now these were the names of the children of Israel, Jacob and his sons, who went to Egypt: Reuben was Jacob's firstborn.

The sons of Reuben were Hanoch, Pallu, Hezron, and Carmi.

The sons of Simeon were Jemuel, Jamin, Ohad, Jachin, Zohar, and Shaul, the son of a Canaanite woman.

The sons of Levi were Gershon, Kohath, and Merari.

The sons of Judah were Er, Onan, Shelah, Perez, and Zerah (but Er and Onan died in the land of Canaan). The sons of Perez were Hezron and Hamul.

The sons of Issachar were Tola, Puvah, Job, and Shimron.

The sons of Zebulun were Sered, Elon, and Jahleel.

These were the sons of Leah, whom she bore to Jacob in Padan Aram, with his daughter Dinah. All the persons, his sons and his daughters, were thirty-three.

The sons of Gad were Ziphion, Haggi, Shuni, Ezbon, Eri, Arodi, and Areli.

The sons of Asher were Jimnah, Ishuah, Isui, Beriah, and Serah, their sister. And the sons of Beriah were Heber and Malchiel.

These were the sons of Zilpah, whom Laban gave to Leah his daughter; and these she bore to Jacob: Sixteen persons.

The sons of Rachel, Jacob's wife, were Joseph and Benjamin.

And to Joseph in the land of Egypt were born Manasseh and Ephraim, whom Asenath, the daughter of Poti-Phera priest of On, bore to him.

The sons of Benjamin were Belah, Becher, Ashbel, Gera, Naaman, Ehi, Rosh, Muppim, Huppim, and Ard.

These were the sons of Rachel, who were born to Jacob: fourteen persons in all.

The son of Dan was Hushim.

The sons of Naphtali were Jahzeel, Guni, Jezer, and Shillem.

These were the sons of Bilhah, whom Laban gave to Rachel his daughter, and she bore these to Jacob: seven persons in all.

All the persons who went with Jacob to Egypt, who came from his body, besides Jacob's sons' wives, were sixty-six persons in all.

Where does it say anything in these verses about segregation of the races? All this Scripture does is list the children that these people had. Something is amiss here, as it was in Dake's interpretation of verses 6 and 7, which describe Esau moving to a different land from Jacob, not because of race, as Dake would have us believe, but because the livestock and possessions of each brother **were too great for them to dwell together**. That is an incredible distortion.

Dake's Reason 10 is:

Ishmael and Isaac's descendants remained segregated forever (Gen. 25:12-23; 1 Chr. 1:29).

As with the word *law*, which he used as part of his eighth reason for segregating the races, and which we saw was not part of the Bible, Dake is using very strong language here when he says "segregated forever." Let's see if this time his scriptural support bears out his theory.

Genesis 25:12-23 says:

Now this is the genealogy of Ishmael, Abraham's son, whom Hagar the Egyptian, Sarah's maidservant, bore to Abraham.

And these were the names of the sons of Ishmael, by their names, according to their generations: the first-born of Ishmael, Nebajoth; then Kedar, Adbeel, Mibsam,

Mishma, Dumah, Massa,
Hadar, Tema, Jetur, Naphish and Kedemah.

These were the sons of Ishmael and these were their names, by their towns and their settlements, twelve princes according to their nations.

These were the years of the life of Ishmael, one hundred and thirty-seven years; and he breathed his last and died, and was gathered to his people.

(They dwelt from Havilah as far as Shur, which is east of Egypt as you go toward Assyria.) He died in the presence of all his brethren.

This is the genealogy of Isaac, Abraham's son. Abraham begot Isaac.

Isaac was forty years old when he took Rebekah as wife, the daughter of Bethuel the Syrian of Padan Aram, the sister of Laban the Syrian.

Now Isaac pleaded with the Lord for his wife, because she was barren; and the Lord granted his plea, and Rebekah his wife conceived.

But the children struggled together within her; and she said, "If all is well, why am I like this?" So she went to inquire of the Lord.

And the Lord said to her:

"Two nations are in your womb,
Two peoples shall be separated from your body;
One people shall be stronger than the other,
And the older shall serve the younger."

Where does it say anything in this Scripture about being "segregated forever"? The only time the word *separated* — which is a synonym for *segregated* — is used in this passage, it doesn't refer to Ishmael and Isaac, it refers to the two nations to be born of Isaac and Rebekah, which in the process of birth will be **separated from** [her] **body**.

Dake's next reference, 1 Chronicles 1:29, tells us:

These are their genealogies: The firstborn of Ishmael was Nebajoth; then Kedar, Adbeel, Mibsam....

That's all the Scripture says; it just names Ishmael's sons. Even though none of the Scriptures Dake cites prove his assertion that "Ishmael and Isaac's descendants remained segregated forever," nor do they say anything about race or ethnicity, Dake uses them to support his tenth reason for segregating the races. I'm not saying Dake was a racist. But regarding what we've read of Dake's commentary up to now, God in Heaven knows you would have to hire someone to help you misunderstand so much, and you would have to pay him overtime.

Dake's Reason 11 is:

Jacob's sons destroyed a whole city to maintain segregation (Gen. 34).

Before we examine this statement, I want to reiterate that I am delving into this commentary not to attack anyone, but to identify beliefs that might in any way contribute to color and ethnic prejudice. Racism is not genetically transmitted, it's attitudinal, and if we are not made aware of the biased messages that are sent and received, they can fool us, and we can become perpetuators of racism ourselves. Because of the sheer number of notes Dake has put into his *Annotated Bible*, his work has an appearance of authority and scholarship, an appearance that it must be right. That is what makes his "30 reasons for segregation of races" so dangerous — because taken at face value they look as if they are backed up by the Bible. It's only by examination that we can see that nowhere does the Bible support segregation based on skin color or ethnicity.

Let's look at Genesis 34. From Dake's notes, we would expect it to say that "Jacob's sons destroyed a whole city to maintain segregation." It's a lengthy passage, but it's so important that I want to examine it here in full.

Genesis 34 tells us:

> **Now Dinah the daughter of Leah, whom she had borne to Jacob, went out to see the daughters of the land.**
>
> **And when Shechem the son of Hamor the Hivite, prince of the country, saw her, he took her and lay with her, and violated her.**
>
> **His soul was strongly attracted to Dinah the daughter of Jacob, and he loved the young woman and spoke kindly to the young woman.**
>
> **So Shechem spoke to his father Hamor, saying, "Get me the young woman as a wife."**
>
> **And Jacob heard that he had defiled Dinah his daughter. Now his sons were with his livestock in the field; so Jacob held his peace until they came.**
>
> **Then Hamor the father of Shechem went out to Jacob to speak with him.**
>
> **And the sons of Jacob came in from the field when they heard it; and the men were grieved and very angry, because he had done a disgraceful thing in Israel by lying with Jacob's daughter, a thing which ought not to be done.**
>
> **But Hamor spoke with them, saying, "The soul of my son Shechem longs for your daughter. Please give her to him as a wife.**
>
> **"And make marriages with us; give your daughters to us, and take our daughters to yourselves.**

"So you shall dwell with us, and the land shall be before you. Dwell and trade in it, and acquire possessions for yourselves in it."

Then Shechem said to her father and her brothers, "Let me find favor in your eyes, and whatever you say to me I will give.

"Ask me ever so much dowry and gift, and I will give according to what you say to me; but give me the young woman as a wife."

But the sons of Jacob answered Shechem and Hamor his father, and spoke deceitfully, because he had defiled Dinah their sister.

And they said to them, "We cannot do this thing, to give our sister to one who is uncircumcised, for that would be a reproach to us.

"But on this condition we will consent to you: If you will become as we are, if every male of you is circumcised,

"then we will give our daughters to you, and we will take your daughters to us; and we will dwell with you, and we will become one people.

"But if you will not heed us and be circumcised, then we will take our daughter and be gone."

And their words pleased Hamor and Shechem, Hamor's son.

So the young man did not delay to do the thing, because he delighted in Jacob's daughter. He was more honorable than all the household of his father.

And Hamor and Shechem his son came to the gate of their city, and spoke with the men of their city, saying:

"These men are at peace with us. Therefore let them dwell in the land and trade in it. For indeed the land is large enough for them. Let us take their daughters to us as wives, and let us give them our daughters.

"Only on this condition will the men consent to dwell with us, to be one people: if every male among us is circumcised as they are circumcised.

"Will not their livestock, their property and every animal of theirs be ours? Only let us consent to them and they will dwell with us."

And all who went out of the gate of his city heeded Hamor and Shechem his son; every male was circumcised, all who went out of the gate of his city.

Now it came to pass on the third day, when they were in pain, that two of the sons of Jacob, Simeon and Levi, Dinah's brothers, each took his sword and came boldly upon the city and killed all the males.

And they killed Hamor and Shechem his son with the edge of the sword, and took Dinah from Shechem's house, and went out.

The sons of Jacob came upon the slain, and plundered the city, because their sister had been defiled.

They took their sheep, their oxen, and their donkeys, what was in the city and what was in the field,

and all their wealth. All their little ones and their wives they took captive; and they plundered even all that was in the houses.

> **Then Jacob said to Simeon and Levi, "You have
> troubled me by making me obnoxious among the in-
> habitants of the land, among the Canaanites and the
> Perizittes; and since I am few in number, they will
> gather themselves together against me and kill me. I
> shall be destroyed, my household and I."**

> **But they said, "Should he treat our sister like a harlot?"**

Here is a Bible scholar telling us the Bible says, "Jacob's
sons destroyed a whole city to maintain segregation." After reading
it, do you think it says that?

Dake went to a Bible institute, he was a pastor and a Bible
teacher; he was not a youth still in junior high or high school or the
first year of college. When a man publishes an annotated reference
Bible and puts it out to educate the public, he is supposed to know
what he is talking about or he is a danger to society. Dake wrote that
"Jacob's sons destroyed a whole city to maintain segregation," and
he refers us to Genesis 34 to back this up. But in all of Genesis 34,
the word *segregation* is not used even once. The word *separation* is
not used even once.

I read Genesis 34 publicly on *Ever Increasing Faith* television for everyone all over the United States to hear. I had the junior
high, high school and first-year college students who were in our
congregation that day render a verdict. Not one of them said that the
passage was about segregation or separation. This passage tells us
clearly that Jacob's sons destroyed that city because their sister was
violated there. It was not about race; it was about rape. Her brothers
were taking revenge. As the Scripture clearly states: **The sons of Jacob
came upon the slain, and plundered the city,** *because their sister had
been defiled* [italics mine]. Indeed, Jacob's sons defend their actions
to their father by asking him, **"Should he** [Shechem] **treat our sister
like a harlot?"**

How does a Bible scholar read this Scripture and say it is
about segregation when children and teenagers can see that it's not?
Something is wrong. And this is the kind of writing and speaking

that has perpetuated racism within the Church. Ever since *Dake's Annotated Reference Bible* was published, his notes have been read and believed. This has given many white people justification to maintain a racially prejudiced point of view, a belief that black people should be separate from white. Any support of segregation of Blacks from Whites also supports the idea of black inferiority, because these biases are so closely intertwined. As a result, Dake's notes on "30 reasons for segregation of races" also serves to undermine the self-esteem of African Americans by leading black people to think that biblically speaking, white racists must be correct, that we must be inferior. If you read notes in a Bible that seem to say this, you can draw the conclusion that these notes represent God's teaching. But they do not.

Let's look at Dake's Reason 11 again:

Jacob's sons destroyed a whole city to maintain segregation.

My next point about this is so crucial that I want to make it step by step. First, note that by using the word *maintain*, Dake is saying that racial segregation already existed at that time. Second, as we've noted, he is saying that Jacob's sons killed and plundered in order to preserve this segregation of races. Stop and think about what this means: Dake is actually creating a verbal picture of Jacob's sons destroying a whole city to assure that what Dake calls the "law" of segregation of races is not broken. By doing this, Dake is giving the impression that wherever we find racial segregation in our own world, it is rightfully fulfilling biblical law. And by citing Scripture to back this up, and by interpreting it the way he does, there is even the appearance that the Bible condones violence to "maintain segregation." This is why I said that something is wrong.

And that is an understatement.

6

What God Is Really Saying

According to Dake, Reason 12 is:

God forbad intermarriage between Israel and all other nations (Ex. 34:12-16; Dt. 7:3-6).

Take note of the subtlety operating here. Remember, Dake's overall title for this commentary is "30 reasons for segregation of races." Therefore, every one of his 30 reasons has to do with segregation of races. This means when he states "God forbad[e] intermarriage between Israel and other nations," the implication is that God forbad[e] "intermarriage" with "other nations" because of race. If that were true, I wouldn't criticize his interpretation. But is it true?

Let's look at Dake's first reference. Exodus 34:12-16 says:

> **"Take heed to yourself lest you make a covenant with the inhabitants of the land where you are going, lest it be a snare in your midst.**
>
> **"But you shall destroy their altars, break their sacred pillars and cut down their wooden images**
>
> **"(for you shall worship no other god, for the LORD, whose name is Jealous, is a jealous God),**
>
> **"lest you make a covenant with the inhabitants of the land, and they play the harlot with their gods and make**

sacrifice to their gods, and one of them invites you and you eat of his sacrifice,

"and you take of his daughters for your sons, and his daughters play the harlot with their gods and make your sons play the harlot with their gods."

I don't see anything in these verses of Exodus 34 that has to do with race. Once again, this Scripture, like many we've seen before, is telling us about false gods and how Israel could become entrapped by them through involvement **with the inhabitants of the land where** [they were] **going**. There is nothing about race or color.

The second Scripture Dake cites is Deuteronomy 7. Keep in mind that Dake says, "God forbad[e] intermarriage between Israel and all other nations." Again I ask the question, Why did God do this? Dake's implication is that it's because of race.

Deuteronomy 7:3 tells us:

"Nor shall you make marriages with them. You shall not give your daughter to their son, nor take their daughter for your son."

Verses 4 to 6 answer my question about why God says this:

"For they will turn your sons away from following Me to serve other gods; so the anger of the Lord will be aroused against you and destroy you suddenly.

"But thus you shall deal with them: you shall destroy their altars, and break down their sacred pillars, and cut down their wooden images, and burn their carved images with fire.

"For you are a holy people to the Lord your God; the Lord your God has chosen you to be a people for Him- self, a special treasure above all the peoples on the face of the earth."

There isn't a single word in this passage about race. It's the same issue as it always has been and always will be with God in any of the Scriptures concerning prohibition of "intermarriage": The prohibition is against Believers being yoked with unbelievers; it has nothing to do with the color of anyone's skin. If we hadn't read the Scriptures ourselves, maybe we would have believed that God forbade Israel intermarrying because of race. But God never forbade Israel or anyone from intermarrying because of race.

According to Dake, Reason 13 is:

Joshua forbad the same thing [intermarriage between nations] on sentence of death (Josh. 23:12-13).

Dake is implying here that through Joshua God said that in order to preserve the segregation of races, if Israel intermarried with other nations, the people of Israel would die.

Although Dake refers us to Joshua 23:12-13, I think it would be profitable to begin by reading Joshua 23:6-7:

"Therefore be very courageous to keep and to do all that is written in the Book of the Law of Moses, lest you turn aside from it to the right hand or to the left,

"and lest you go among these nations, these who remain among you. You shall not make mention of the name of their gods, nor cause anyone to swear by them; you shall not serve them nor bow down to them,"

When it says, **"you shall not serve them nor bow down to them,"** what is the Scripture referring to? Their color or their gods? The fact that the Bible specifically mentions **"their gods"** and doesn't say one word about anyone's skin, let alone skin color, makes the answer obvious and beyond question.

If possible, the next passage makes the intent of God's warning even clearer:

"but you shall hold fast to the Lord your God, as you have done to this day.

"For the LORD has driven out from before you great and strong nations; but as for you, no one has been able to stand against you to this day.

"One man of you shall chase a thousand, for the LORD your God is He who fights for you, as He promised you.

"Therefore take careful heed to yourselves, that you love the LORD your God.

Now let's read verses 12 and 13:

"Or else, if indeed you do go back, and cling to the remnant of these nations—these that remain among you—and make marriages with them, and go in to them and they to you,

"know for certain that the LORD your God will no longer drive out these nations from before you. But they shall be snares and traps to you, and scourges on your sides and thorns in your eyes, until you perish from this good land which the LORD your God has given you."

Dake's use of these Scriptures to support segregation of races is, in a word, insupportable. The issue in the Bible is not race or color; it's the same as it always is — idol worship. Yet Dake says the reason for God's prohibition against "intermarriage" is race. Once again, this is dangerous. I have spoken with Finis Jennings Dake's family,[1] and they assured me that he was not a racist, and I cannot say that he was. But I believe I can say without contradiction that the notes in his *Annotated Reference Bible* smack of racism to me.

---

[1] See Chapter 9 for the letters the Dake family wrote to me about Finis Dake, about my commenting publicly on *Dake's Annotated Reference Bible,* and for a recounting of our subsequent communication.

Our nation is in great trouble because of the division between black people and white people; the Church is in deep trouble because of the division between black people and white people. Black people did not start this division. We have been victims of it. White people started it, and because white people have the power in this society, white people have to fix it.[2] What we black people must do is learn not to be victims of it, not to let our self-image be determined by those who are prejudiced against us. Whatever race we are — black, white, red, yellow, brown — we have to recognize racist attitudes for the lies they are, and to remember that God has told us that we are all made **...in** [His] **image ... likeness...** (Genesis 1:26), and that our bodies, in all their variety of colors, shapes and sizes, are the same **... dust of the ground...** (Genesis 2:7).

Dake's Reason 14 is:

God cursed angels for leaving their own "first estate" and "their own habitation" to marry the daughters of men (Gen. 6:1-4; 2 Pet. 2:4; Jude 6-7).

Since this, too, is under the heading, "30 reasons for segregation of races," Dake is saying that God cursed the angels because they crossed over the race line to marry. What do the Scriptures tell us?

Genesis 6:1-4, Dake's first reference, states:

Now it came to pass, when men began to multiply on the face of the earth, and daughters were born to them,

---

[2] See Volume 1 of *Race, Religion & Racism* for the historical roots of racism in the United States, how it has benefited white society economically and how the government can help make amends for the exploitation of Blacks.

> that the sons of God saw the daughters of men, that
> they were beautiful; and they took wives for themselves
> of all whom they chose.
>
> And the LORD said, "My Spirit shall not strive with
> man forever, for he is indeed flesh; yet his days shall
> be one hundred and twenty years."
>
> There were giants on the earth in those days, and also
> afterward, when the sons of God came in to the daugh-
> ters of men and they bore children to them. Those were
> the mighty men who were of old, men of renown.

Notice the phrase **sons of God**. In the first chapter of the Book of Job, we'll see these words used again. In the Old Covenant, the phrase **sons of God** does not mean that these "sons" have accepted Jesus as their Savior and Lord; those of us who have been born again call God "our Father," and we are called "His children." But in the Old Testament, **sons of God** does not refer to human beings.

Here is how we can tell that whoever the Bible identifies as **sons of God** are other than people like we are. Verse 4 tells us:

> There were giants on the earth in those days, and also
> afterward, when the sons of God came in to the daugh-
> ters of men....

The Bible wouldn't have to say **daughters of men** unless it was distinguishing them from **the sons of God**. By making this distinction, the Bible is saying that the women were **daughters of men** — in other words, daughters of human beings — and the men, being **sons of God**, were something other than human. In fact, the sons of God were angels.

Dake next cites 2 Peter 2:4 and Jude 6-7 from the New Testament.

2 Peter 2:4 tells us:

For if God did not spare the angels who sinned [these are the angels that we read about in the verses in Genesis], **but cast them down to hell and delivered them into chains of darkness, to be reserved for judgment....**

Jude 6-7 says:

And the angels who did not keep their proper domain [the original *King James* says "their first estate"], **but left their own abode** [the original *King James* says "habitation"], **He has reserved in everlasting chains under darkness for the judgment of the great day;**

as Sodom and Gomorrah, and the cities around them in a similar manner to these, having given themselves over to sexual immorality and gone after strange flesh, are set forth as an example, suffering the vengeance of eternal fire.

Dake is right in one respect: The Scriptures do refer to angels, but what do they have to do with segregation of races? That is the vital point, and again he is off the mark. Since he is using these passages to support segregation of races, he is saying that angels are a racial or an ethnic group and that God cursed them for getting involved with daughters of men, whom Dake is implying are members of another racial or ethnic group. But angels are spirits and women are human beings, and neither is a racial or an ethnic group.

Now you may wonder, "How can angels, who are spirits, become involved with women who are flesh and blood?" That is a good question. But remember you are also a spirit, because you are made in the image and likeness of God. In order to live here on earth, you have to have a physical body — in other words, a house. So we are spirits, we have souls, and we live in bodies.[3]

---

[3] See Volume 1, Part II, Chapter 3, of *Race, Religion & Racism* for a discussion of the spirit, soul and physical body.

Even knowing that we are spirits inside our physical bodies, you may still wonder: How can angels come to earth and have sexual relations with humans since they are spirits and not born from a physical mother and father?

Let's look at Hebrews 13:2:

Do not forget to entertain strangers, for by so doing some unwittingly entertained angels.

This tells us that apparently angels can take on human form. That's why Paul tells us to be careful, because when a stranger comes to our door, we cannot know if he or she is a human or an angel. It's because angels can assume human form that they were able to leave "their first estate" (heaven) and become involved with women here in the earth-realm. But Dake does not say God cursed the angels for doing this; he says God cursed them because they violated the segregation of races. And that simply does not compute.

7

The Real Abomination

Dake's Reason 15 is:

Miscegenation caused Israel to be cursed (Judges 3:6-7; Num. 25:1-8).

As we've noted, miscegenation means interracial marriage. It could be a Caucasian marrying an Asian, an Asian marrying a Native American, a Black marrying a Hispanic, a Hispanic marrying an Arab.

In America, from the days of slavery, the word *segregation* has always meant separating black people from white people. Here Dake is using another word, *miscegenation*, that in America has rarely been used outside the context of Blacks and Whites. In fact, in Reason 4, Dake defined miscegenation as "the mixture of races, especially the black and white races." My question is, if a person has no trace of racial or color prejudice in his thinking, why use terminology that is so loaded with racial overtones? Why not just say "interracial marriage"? Why say "miscegenation"?

If we interpret Dake's statement about miscegenation literally, it means that Israel was cursed because of interracial marriage. If Dake is right about this curse and the reason for it, then every person of one racial or ethnic group who marries someone of another racial or ethnic group would be cursed. If it's a curse for Israel, it has to be a curse for everyone, because God created everyone else as well as Israel, and if everyone is not cursed for doing what Israel did, God would be violating His own Word. Since Romans 2:11 tells us that God is no respecter of persons (**For there is no partiality with God**), if He is going to curse Israel for interracial marriage, He has to curse all other nations for interracial marriage, too.

Let's read the Scripture Dake gives us to show us that Israel was cursed because they were involved in miscegenation.

Judges 3:6-7 says:

> **And they took their daughters to be their wives, and gave their daughters to their sons; and they served their gods.**
>
> **So the children of Israel did evil in the sight of the LORD. They forgot the LORD their God and served the Baals and Asherahs.**

Nothing in this Scripture tells us that God condemned the children of Israel for interracial marriage — it says God condemned them for intermarriage with pagans.

Let's looks at the next Scripture Dake cites to prove Israel was cursed for mixing the races.

Numbers 25:1-8 tells us:

> **Now Israel remained in Acacia Grove, and the people began to commit harlotry with the women of Moab.**
>
> **They invited the people to the sacrifices of their gods, and the people ate and bowed down to their gods.**
>
> **So Israel was joined to Baal of Peor, and the anger of the LORD was aroused against Israel.**
>
> **Then the LORD said to Moses, "Take all the leaders of the people and hang the offenders before the LORD, out in the sun, that the fierce anger of the LORD may turn away from Israel."**

71

So Moses said to the judges of Israel, "Every one of you kill his men who were joined to Baal of Peor."

And indeed, one of the children of Israel came and presented to his brethren a Midianite woman in the sight of Moses and in the sight of all the congregation of the children of Israel, who were weeping at the door of the tabernacle of meeting.

Now when Phinehas the son of Eleazar, the son of Aaron the priest, saw it, he rose from among the congregation and took a javelin in his hand;

and he went after the man of Israel into the tent and thrust both of them through, the man of Israel, and the woman through her body. So the plague was stopped among the children of Israel.

I don't see anything in this Scripture about Israel being cursed and I don't see anything in it about a problem with miscegenation or interracial marriage. What I do see is that verses 1 and 2 say:

Now Israel remained in Acacia Grove, and the people began to commit harlotry with the women of Moab.

They invited the people to the sacrifices of their gods. And the people ate and bowed down to their gods.

Israel didn't bow down to ethnicity and it didn't bow down to miscegenation. Israel **bowed down to their gods**.

The Bible even tells us in Verse 3 that this is the problem:

So Israel was joined to Baal of Peor and the anger of the LORD was aroused against Israel.

The Bible is as clear as can be: **The anger of the Lord was aroused against Israel** because the children of Israel bowed down to the false gods of Moab and Baal of Peor, not because anyone married out of his or her ethnic group.

Dake's Reason 16 is:

This was Solomon's sin (1 Kings 11).

By saying "*This* [italics mine] was Solomon's sin," Dake is apparently implying that "Solomon's sin" is the same as the one mentioned in the previous reason. So it seems Dake is saying the sin was miscegenation. Does the Scripture he cites support this?

1 Kings 11:1-2 tells us:

> **But King Solomon loved many foreign women, as well as the daughter of Pharaoh: women of the Moabites, Ammonites, Edomites, Sidonians, and Hittites —**
>
> **from the nations of whom the Lord had said to the children of Israel, "You shall not intermarry with them, nor they with you...."**

If we stop reading here, Dake's statement might appear justifiable. From these verses, it would seem God is saying that the children of Israel (and Dake is asserting that, by implication, all other people as well) should not marry outside of their own ethnic group. But if God said the children of Israel should not intermarry with certain people — and the Scripture tells us He did — we know there had to be a very good reason for it, because the people God told Israel not to intermarry with were people He created. So we're left with the question, What was God's reason for the prohibition?

For clarification, let's look at Verses 2 and 3:

> **"... Surely they will turn away your hearts after their gods." Solomon clung to these in love.**
>
> **And he had seven hundred wives, princesses, and three hundred concubines; and his wives turned away his heart.**

How many times have we seen the same misinterpretation? The issue in this Scripture is not skin color or mixing of ethnic groups, it is other gods.[1]

1 Kings 11:4-10 says of Solomon:

… and his heart was not loyal to the LORD his God, as was the heart of his father David.

For Solomon went after Ashtoreth the goddess of the Sidonians, and after Milcom the abomination of the Ammonites.

Solomon did evil in the sight of the LORD, and did not fully follow the LORD, as did his father David.

Then Solomon built a high place for Chemosh the abomination of Moab, on the hill that is east of Jerusalem, and for Molech the abomination of the people of Ammon.

And he did likewise for all his foreign wives, who burned incense and sacrificed to their gods.

So the LORD became angry with Solomon, because his heart had turned from the LORD God of Israel, who had appeared to him twice,

and had commanded him concerning this thing, that he should not go after other gods; but he did not keep what the LORD had commanded.

---

[1] It's important to note that the people who worshiped other gods didn't do so because they were defective; they worshiped other gods of their own free will — and of their own free will they could have turned from false gods to worship the One True God.

These are some of the Scriptures Dake gives to support his contention that Israel and Solomon were cursed because of miscegenation or interracial marriage. Read the rest of 1 Kings 11,[2] and you will see that it never brings up miscegenation or interracial marriage as a sin; it talks about the punishment God carried out against Solomon because Solomon turned his heart away from Him and turned instead to false gods.

There are white people and black people who believe that the races should not mix because they have been misled into believing that "It's against God" or "It's against the Bible." Again, I'm not promoting interracial marriage. I'm already married, so it's of no concern to me one way or the other personally. My point is, why should it matter to anyone when it doesn't matter to God? Why are people so upset about it if God is not?

We found by reading the Scriptures that Solomon's sin was not miscegenation, but idol worship. Yet for years this Bible commentator has taught through his Bible that Solomon got into trouble with God because of miscegenation. That is simply not true. It's a lie that needs to be exposed and rooted out.

Dake's Reason 17 returns to the same familiar theme:

> This was the sin of Jews returning from Babylon (Ezra 9:1-10:2, 10-18, 44; 13:1-30).

Once more Dake is saying that "the sin" is miscegenation or mixing of the races. And once more I say that the only people to whom interracial marriage is important are racists. No one else cares. Notice that in making interracial marriage a "sin," Dake is saying that anyone who is reading this who is part of an interracial couple is in sin. When we read the Scriptures he cites, again we would expect them to state that interracial marriage is a sin.

Ezra 9:1 tells us:

---

[2] See Appendix, pages 257-260, for I Kings 11.

When these things were done, the leaders came to me, saying, "The people of Israel and the priests and the Levites have not separated themselves from the peoples of the lands, with respect to the abominations of the Canaanites, the Hittites, the Perizzites, the Jebusites, the Ammonites, the Moabites, the Egyptians, and the Amorites."

What does the Bible call our attention to in this passage? That **"the people of Israel and the priests and the Levites have not separated themselves from the peoples of the lands, with respect to the abominations."** We know from our previous readings that **"the abominations"** refers to worshipping false gods. And the Scripture *specifically* points us to **"the abominations"** as being the area of concern when it says that the Jews had **"not separated themselves from the peoples of the lands, *with respect to the abominations* [italics mine]."** Why would the Scripture specify that the separation should have been **"with respect to the abominations"** if separation of races was the problem? Why would the Bible leave out separation of races if it was, as Dake asserts, a "law"?

Ezra 9:2-14 says:

"For they had taken some of their daughters as wives for themselves and their sons, so that the holy seed is mixed with the peoples of those lands. Indeed, the hand of the leaders and rulers has been foremost in this trespass."

So when I heard this thing, I tore my garment and my robe, and plucked out some of the hair of my head and beard, and sat down astonished.

Then everyone who trembled at the words of the God of Israel assembled to me, because of the transgression of those who had been carried away captive, and I sat astonished until the evening sacrifice.

The Real Abomination

At the evening sacrifice I arose from my fasting; and having torn my garment and my robe, I fell on my knees and spread out my hands to the LORD my God.

And I said: "Oh, my God, I am too ashamed and humiliated to lift up my face to You, my God; for our iniquities have risen higher than our heads, and our guilt has grown up to the heavens.

"Since the days of our fathers to this day, we have been very guilty, and for our iniquities we, our kings, and our priests have been delivered into the hand of the kings of the lands, to the sword, to captivity, to plunder, and to humiliation, as it is this day.

"And now for a little while grace has been shown from the LORD our God, to leave us a remnant to escape, and to give us a peg in His holy place, that our God may enlighten our eyes and give us a measure of revival in our bondage.

"For we were slaves. Yet our God did not forsake us in our bondage; but He extended mercy to us in the sight of the kings of Persia, to revive us, to repair the house of our God, to rebuild its ruins, and to give us a wall in Judah and Jerusalem.

"And now, O our God, what shall we say after this? For we have forsaken Your commandments,

"which you commanded by Your servants the prophets, saying, 'The land which you are entering to possess is an unclean land, with the uncleanness of the peoples of the land, with their abominations which have filled it from one end to another with their impurity.

'Now therefore, do not give your daughters as wives for their sons, nor take their daughters to your sons; and never seek their peace or prosperity, that you may be strong and eat the good of the land, and leave it as an inheritance to your children forever.'

"And after all that has come upon us for our evil deeds and for our great guilt, since You our God have punished us less than our iniquities deserve, and have given us such deliverance as this,

"should we again break Your commandments, and join in marriage with the people committing these abominations? Would you not be angry with us until You had consumed us, so that there would be no remnant or survivor?"

Once again, the problem was not the people as such, but their abominations. And, of course, if we want to stay away from the abominations that people choose to practice, we stay away from those people. The dealer on the corner dispenses the abominations of crack, heroin, and cocaine. If I want to stay away from the abominations of crack, heroin, and cocaine, I stay away from the person who is peddling these drugs. We have to stay away from those whose abominations get us in trouble; this is what the Scripture is warning us about.

The next Scripture Dake cites, Ezra 9:15-10:2, tells us:

"O Lord God of Israel, You are righteous, for we are left as a remnant, as it is this day. Here we are before You, in our guilt, though no one can stand before You because of this!"

Now while Ezra was praying, and while he was confessing, weeping, and bowing down before the house of God, a very large assembly of men, women, and children gathered to him from Israel; for the people wept very bitterly.

And Shechaniah the son of Jehiel, one of the sons of Elam, spoke up and said to Ezra, "We have trespassed against our God, and have taken pagan wives from the peoples of the land; yet now there is hope in Israel in spite of this."

Notice that in the latter part of Ezra 10:2 it says:

"... [We] have taken pagan wives...."

Why doesn't the Bible say "wives of the land" or "wives of another ethnic group"? Because that is not what God wanted to say. The word *pagan* is used to tell us that the problem was with pagan worship, not with the people. It's like the example I gave before: If you want to stay away from drugs, you stay away from the drug dealer.

So far, we haven't seen anything in any of these verses about miscegenation as such being "the sin of the Jews returning from Babylon."

Let's look now at Ezra 10:10-18:

Then Ezra the priest stood up and said to them, "You have transgressed and have taken pagan wives, adding to the guilt of Israel.

"Now therefore, make confession to the LORD God of your fathers, and do His will; separate yourselves from the peoples of the land, and from the pagan wives."

In other words, separate yourself from the dope dealers.

Then all the assembly answered and said with a loud voice, "Yes! As you have said, so we must do.

"But there are many people; it is the season for heavy rain, and we are not able to stand outside. Nor is this the work of one or two days, for there are many of us who have transgressed in this matter.

"Please, let the leaders of our entire assembly stand; and let all those in our cities who have taken pagan wives come at appointed times, together with the elders and judges of their cities, until the fierce wrath of our God is turned away from us in this matter."

Only Jonathan the son of Asahel and Jahaziah the son of Tikvah opposed this, and Meshullam and Shabbethai the Levite gave them support.

Then the descendants of the captivity did so. And Ezra the priest, with certain heads of the fathers' households, were set apart by the fathers' households, each of them by name; and they sat down on the first day of the tenth month to examine the matter.

By the first day of the first month they finished questioning all the men who had taken pagan wives.

And among the sons of the priests who had taken pagan wives the following were found of the sons of Jeshua the son of Jozadak, and his brothers: Maaseiah, Eliezer, Jarib, and Gedaliah.

Notice that over and over again the Bible does not just say "wives," or even "foreign wives" to indicate wives of a different nationality from Israel, but *"pagan* [italics mine] **wives,"** indicating, in case we still haven't gotten it, that the problem was paganism.

Let's go now to Dake's third reference, Ezra 13:1-30.

The fact is, there is no Ezra 13!

8

Seeing Through Misinterpretation to Truth

According to Dake, Reason 18 is:

God commanded Israel to be segregated (Lev. 20:24; Num. 23:9; 1 Ki. 8:53).

As we saw before, when God told the people of Israel to do something or not to do something, He had a reason for it. So if He "commanded Israel to be segregated," we must analyze the Scriptures to see what the reason is. Let's see if the Scriptures Dake refers us to provide the answer.

Leviticus 20:24 says:

> **But I have said to you, "You shall inherit their land, and I will give it to you to possess, a land flowing with milk and honey." I am the LORD your God, who has separated you from the peoples.**

This Scripture tells us God separated Israel from other nations but it doesn't explain why. If we had not disproved Dake's prior "reasons" for segregating races, we might believe that God commanded Israel to be segregated because of what Dake called "Israel's sin" and "Solomon's sin," the same "sin" for which Dake said "Israel was cursed": miscegenation. But did God really separate Israel to prevent interracial marriage?

The next Scripture Dake cites, Numbers 23:9, states:

For from the top of the rocks I see him,
And from the hills I behold him;
There! A people dwelling alone,
Not reckoning itself among the nations.

There is still no clarification of why God separated Israel from other nations.

Dake's next reference, 1 Kings 8:53, says:

"For You separated them from among all the peoples
of the earth to be Your inheritance, as You spoke by
Your servant Moses, when You brought our fathers
out of Egypt, O Lord God."

This passage gives us the answer. It has nothing to do with miscegenation, race, ethnicity or skin color. The Scripture is as plain as day: God separated Israel from other peoples so they would be His inheritance. Of course we know from history that God chose Israel to be the channel through which He brought His Word to humankind. He separated Israel out and gave them His law. This was the reason that "God commanded Israel to be segregated."

It is unbelievable to me that God's Word can be so misinterpreted in commentary that instead of conveying a spiritual truth — that Israel was separated from other nations to be God's spiritual inheritance — it conveys the false impression that God separated Israel from other peoples because of race, ethnicity and skin color. How could God, who shows no partiality (Acts 10:34), have possibly separated Israel from other nations because of skin color or ethnicity? How could God, who has told us that we are made of one kind of flesh (1 Corinthians 15:39) and one blood (Acts 17:26), have possibly separated Israel from other nations because of skin color or ethnicity? How could a biblical scholar possibly believe that was why God separated Israel?

82

Dake's Reason 19 is:

Jews recognized as a separate people in all ages because of God's choice and command (Mt. 10:6; Jn. 1:11). Equal rights in the gospel gives no right to break this eternal law.

Dake talks here not only about a "law," but about what he calls an "eternal law." Since *eternal* means lasting forever, Dake is saying that "because of God's choice and command," Jews will always be separated from others; this means they can never mix with any other ethnic group.

Dake's first scriptural reference, Matthew 10:6, says:

"But go rather to the lost sheep of the house of Israel."

If we read the context of this verse, we find that Jesus spoke these words as he sent out His disciples. What do Jesus' Words have to do with the "eternal law" that Israel should be separated?

Dake's second reference, John 1:11, tells us:

He came to His own, and His own did not receive Him.

Remember, Dake is citing this as proof that:

… Equal rights in the gospel gives no right to break this eternal law [of separation of Israel].

If Dake's assertion were right, it would mean that the Jews (Israel) would be separated forever from all other Believers. It would mean that even though I am in Christ, any Jewish Believer would be separated from me and from the rest of the Believers. Dake says this is an "eternal law." If he's right, no one else can ever be included in the group of Jewish Believers, because Jews have to be separated. If he's right, the Jews have to stay with the Jews, whether they are in Christ or not, because this is a command and choice of God; it is an "eternal law" that cannot be broken.

Let's look at John 10:1-16, a Scripture that Dake has not cited but that addresses precisely this point.

In John 10:1-16, Jesus says:

> "Most assuredly, I say to you, he who does not enter the sheepfold by the door, but climbs up some other way, the same is a thief and a robber.
>
> "But he who enters by the door is the shepherd of the sheep.
>
> "To him the doorkeeper opens, and the sheep hear his voice; and he calls his own sheep by name and leads them out.
>
> "And when he brings out his own sheep, he goes before them; and the sheep follow him, for they know his voice.
>
> "Yet they will by no means follow a stranger, but will flee from him, for they do not know the voice of strangers."
>
> Jesus used this illustration, but they did not understand the things which He spoke to them.
>
> Then Jesus said to them again, "Most assuredly, I say to you, I am the door of the sheep.
>
> "All who ever came before Me are thieves and robbers, but the sheep did not hear them.
>
> "I am the door. If anyone enters by Me, he will be saved, and will go in and out and find pasture.
>
> "The thief does not come except to steal, and to kill, and to destroy. I have come that they may have life, and that they may have it more abundantly.

"I am the good shepherd. The good shepherd gives His life for the sheep.

"But a hireling, he who is not the shepherd, one who does not own the sheep, sees the wolf coming and leaves the sheep and flees; and the wolf catches the sheep and scatters them.

"The hireling flees because he is a hireling and does not care about the sheep.

"I am the good shepherd; and I know My sheep, and am known by My own.

"As the Father knows Me, even so I know the Father; and I lay down My life for the sheep.

"And other sheep I have which are not of this fold; them also I must bring, and they will hear My voice; and there will be one flock and one shepherd."

Who is Jesus talking about in this passage? I surmise that the **"sheepfold"** is Israel, because at the time Jesus spoke there were no Christians, since no one had been born again. Jesus also said, **"And other sheep I have which are not of this fold...."** These **"other sheep,"** then, must have been of another sheepfold besides Israel. Once we realize that Israel is the sheepfold over which He is the shepherd at the time He is speaking, we recognize that Jesus is talking about the day coming when He will bring *all* His sheep together, when there will be only one sheepfold and one shepherd. We know this because Jesus Christ is the Head of the Body, the Church, and the Church is one Body with one head, and that Body is made up of people from all nations — not just Israel.

Dake's Reason 20 is:

Segregation between Jews and all other nations to remain in all eternity (Isa. 2:2-4; Ezek. 37; 47:13-48:35;

Zech. 14:16-21; Mt. 19:28; Lk. 1:32-33; Rev. 7:1-8; 14:1-5).

We know from disproving Dake's previous reason, which is also based on the supposed separation of the Jews from all other nations, that his reasoning here is also invalid. But let's analyze it separately.

Since in Reason 20 Dake again uses the word *eternity*, if he's right it would mean that the Jews will be segregated from all other nations in the Kingdom Age, when time will end and the present earthly kingdoms of men will be replaced with the Kingdom of God, over which Jesus Christ will reign. Dake gives us a multitude of Scriptures to validate his assertion. Once more, there is absolutely nothing in any of the Scriptures he cites about Israel being segregated from other races "in all eternity." Because Dake gives so many references that do not prove his point, I'm not including them all in this chapter, but I have included them in the Appendix so you can see for yourself.[1] However, there is one verse he cites, Matthew 19:28, that I would like to look at here, because it perfectly sums up how off base Dake is in his so-called proof. Remember, Dake is citing this Scripture to substantiate his twentieth reason for segregation of the races, that "Segregation between Jews and all other nations [is] to remain in all eternity."

Matthew 19:28 tells us:

So Jesus said to them, "Assuredly I say to you, that in the regeneration, when the Son of Man sits on the throne of His glory, you who have followed Me will also sit on twelve thrones, judging the twelve tribes of Israel."

What does this Scripture have to say about Jews being segregated from all other nations for eternity? Nothing, even though

---

[1] See Appendix, pages 261-268, for Isaiah 2:2-4; Ezekiel 37; 47:13-48:35; Zechariah 14:16-21; Luke 1:32-33; Revelation 7:1-8; 14:1-5.

it's one of the Scriptures Dake provides to prove his point. In Matthew 19:28, Jesus is telling the Apostles that in the Kingdom Age they will be with Him, and they will judge Israel, which, in essence, had the first right of refusal on God's plan of redemption, since He brought Jesus into the world through them. Because God made His plan known to Israel first, Israel will be judged for rejecting Jesus. But Israel as a nation will not be separated from other nations forever; individual Jews along with individual Gentiles who accept Jesus Christ will be together as the people of God. Indeed, He desires that no man should perish or spend eternity apart from Him. This is why 2 Peter 3:9 tells us that God **... is longsuffering toward us, not willing that any should perish but that all should come to repentance.**

Not only is Dake's interpretation incorrect, once again he is implying that the Bible is talking about segregating races, when in fact it is presenting a spiritual matter that has nothing to do with race.

According to Dake, Reason 21 is:

All nations will remain segregated from one another in their own parts of the earth forever ([Acts] 17:26; Gen. 10:5,32; 11:8-9; Dt. 32:8; Dan. 7:13-14; Zech. 14; Rev. 11:15; 21:24).

As we've already noted, all anyone has to do is look at the world today to know this statement is untrue. And all of the many Scriptures Dake refers us to say the same thing about this subject — nothing! Don't take my word for it, I could have made a mistake; I didn't, but you won't know that unless you read it for yourself.[2] As an example of how fallacious his thinking is, let's look at one of his references, Revelation 11:15. It says:

Then the seventh angel sounded: And there were loud voices in heaven, saying, "The kingdoms of this world

---

[2] See Appendix, pages 268-271, for Acts 17:26; Genesis 10:5, 32; 11:8-9; Deuteronomy 32:8; Daniel 7:13-14; Zechariah 14; Revelation 21:24.

have become the kingdoms of our Lord and of His
Christ, and He shall reign forever and ever!"

As you can see, there isn't a single word in this verse about
"all nations being segregated from one another in their own parts of
the earth forever." Indeed, the Scripture is not about segregation, it
is about unity through Jesus Christ.

Dake's Reason 22 is:

Certain people in Israel were not even to worship with
others (Dt. 23:1-3; Ezra 10:8; Neh. 9:2; 10:28; 13:3).

As with the previous two reasons, I'm not going to include
here all of Dake's many references, because they continue to follow
the pattern of saying nothing to validate his reason for segregating
races.[3] Let's look at one of the Scriptures he cites, Nehemiah 13:3,
to see just how far off the mark he is:

So it was, when they had heard the Law, that they separated all the mixed multitude from Israel.

What does this verse have to do with proving Dake's point?
If we do not think about it or do further reading of the Scriptures, we
might be left with the impression from Dake that Israel was to separate
from **all the mixed multitude** because "certain people in Israel were
not even to worship with others." But Nehemiah 13:3 doesn't tell us
why **all the mixed multitude** [was separated] **from Israel**. To find out, let's
look at the Scriptures Dake does not give us, Nehemiah 13, verses 1 and
2, which lead into and explain Verse 3.

Nehemiah 13:1-3 says:

---

[3] See Appendix, page 271, for Deuteronomy 23:1-3; Ezra 10:8;
Nehemiah 9:2; 10:28.

On that day they read from the Book of Moses in the hearing of the people, and in it was found written that no Ammonite or Moabite should ever come into the assembly of God,

because they had not met the children of Israel with bread and water, but hired Balaam against them to curse them. However, our God turned the curse into a blessing.

So it was, when they had heard the Law, that they separated all the mixed multitudes from Israel.

Now we know why the mixed multitudes were separated from Israel: not because of race, but because they mistreated Israel. Once again, it is dishonest of Dake to lead us to believe otherwise; it is misrepresenting the Bible, it is misrepresenting the Word of God.

Dake's Reason 23 is:

Even in heaven certain groups will not be allowed to worship together (Rev. 7:7-17; 14:1-5; 15:2-5).

We will analyze only three verses here, too, but I would like you to read the others for yourself, because none of them computes.[4] Revelation 15:2-5 tells us:

And I saw something like a sea of glass mingled with fire, and those who have the victory over the beast, over his image and over his mark and over the number of his name, standing on the sea of glass, having harps of God.

They sing the song of Moses, the servant of God, and the song of the Lamb, saying

---

[4] See Appendix, pages 271-273, for Revelation 7:7-17; 14:1-5.

> **"Great and marvelous are Your works,**
> **Lord God Almighty!**
> **Just and true are Your ways,**
> **O King of the saints!**
> **Who shall not fear You, O Lord, and glorify Your**
>   **name?**
> **For You alone are holy.**
> **For all nations shall come and worship before You,**
> **For Your judgments have been manifested."**
> **After these things I looked, and behold, the temple of**
> **the tabernacle of the testimony in heaven was opened.**

I don't see anything in this passage validating that "even in heaven, certain groups will not be allowed to worship together." But these are Scriptures Dake uses to support his claim. In fact, there is nothing in these verses indicating that any group who serves God will be left out. It is a vision of heaven, of **"those who have the victory over the beast, over his image and over his mark and over the number of his name."** It has nothing to do with racial or ethnic groups or skin color; it has nothing to do with division in heaven; it is about what is waiting in heaven for all those who through the Lord have been saved.

I think by now we have a very clear picture of what is going on in Dake's notes. He starts out with a proposition he apparently believes in, that races should be segregated. He backs up his so-called reasons with scriptural references. Sometimes these Scriptures are about separation of peoples, sometimes they are not — but even when they are, the basis for that separation is *never* race, ethnicity or skin color; almost always it is about the separation of Believers from unbelievers; sometimes it is separation based on reprisal or revenge.

Often Dake's misinterpretations are so obvious that nobody who reads the Scriptures could miss them; other times, they require thought. But for the readers who don't check the Scriptures or don't stop to reflect on them, Dake's "reasons" may look like facts; worse, they may look as if they have come from God. It is only by analyzing them as we are doing that we can see the truth, and see that although Dake's "reasons" are given as Bible commentary, they have nothing to do with the Word of God.

With his next reason, Dake moves into a whole new range of reasons, which we might categorize as animal, vegetable or mineral.

According to Dake, Reason 24 is:

> **Segregation was so strong in the O.T. that an ox and an ass could not be worked together (Dt. 22:10).**

Dake is using this to support segregating races, but what does segregating races have to do with oxen and asses? Let's see if the Scripture Dake refers us to sheds any light on the matter. Deuteronomy 22:10 says:

> **"You shall not plow with an ox and a donkey together."**

No, it's definitely about oxen and asses. If Dake wants to talk about races, let him talk about races, not about animals that are clearly not part of the human race. As absurd as Reason 24 is, we have to pay attention to it and expose it for the untruth it is, because it is the kind of supposed biblical justification that has been passed on for centuries from father to son, from pulpit to pulpit, from congregation to congregation, from denomination to denomination in order to support the separation of races.

For his next reason, Dake returns to an old theme, miscegenation. Reason 25 is:

> **Miscegenation caused disunity among God's people (Num. 12).**

This is so grossly incorrect that it is pitiful. Indeed, when I read something like this, it causes me to be suspicious of anything else that the person may have written. Dake refers us to the whole twelfth chapter of Numbers, but we are not going to include all of it here because it's unnecessary to prove the fallacy of Dake's statement.

We're going to examine several verses of Numbers 12, however, some of which we've read before, so that we can understand exactly what is going on in this passage, and see that it does not support the point Dake is trying to make, that "miscegenation caused disunity among God's people." (Remember, that's "God's people"!)

Numbers 12:1 tells us:

> **Then Miriam and Aaron spoke against Moses because of the Ethiopian woman whom he had married; for he had married an Ethiopian woman....**

No one was upset about Moses marrying the Ethiopian woman but Miriam and Aaron. It wasn't "God's people"! The congregation wasn't even involved.

Numbers 12:2-10 says:

> **So they** [Miriam and Aaron] **said, "Has the Lord indeed spoken only through Moses? Has He not spoken through us also?" And the LORD heard it.**
>
> **(Now the man Moses was very humble, more than all men who were on the face of the earth.)**
>
> **Suddenly the LORD said to Moses, Aaron, and Miriam, "Come out, you three, to the tabernacle of meeting!" So the three came out.**
>
> **Then the LORD came down in the pillar of cloud and stood in the door of the tabernacle, and called Aaron and Miriam. And they both went forward.**
>
> **Then He said,**
>
> **"Hear now My words:**
> **If there is a prophet among you,**
> **I, the LORD, make Myself known to him in a vision;**
> **I speak to him in a dream.**

Not so with My servant Moses;
He is faithful in all My house.
I speak with him face to face,
Even plainly, and not in dark sayings;
And he sees the form of the LORD.
Why then were you not afraid
To speak against My servant, Moses?"

So the anger of the LORD was aroused against them
[Miriam and Aaron, not against Moses for marrying that
black woman], **and He departed.**

And when the cloud departed from above the taber-
nacle, suddenly Miriam became leprous, as white as
snow. Then Aaron turned toward Miriam, and there
she was, a leper.

I encourage you to read the rest of the chapter, which I am
including in the Appendix.[5] There is nothing in it that says that God
identifies miscegenation as causing disunity among His people. God
identifies criticism as the problem. To show us how much God was
opposed to Miriam and Aaron involving themselves in Moses'
business, Miriam was struck with leprosy. So the Bible is telling us
that the best thing for us to do is *not* to criticize.

Dake's Reason 26 is:

Stock was forbidden to be bred with other kinds (Lev.
19:19).

We have now been presented with another animal reason. Is
the Scripture Dake cites this time any more supportive of his point
than the one he cited last time?

Leviticus 19:19 tells us:

---

[5] See Appendix, page 273, for Numbers 12:11-16.

**" 'You shall keep My statutes. You shall not let your
livestock breed with another kind. You shall not sow
your field with mixed seed. Nor shall a garment of
mixed linen and wool come upon you.' "**

The Scripture talks about livestock, plants and products that
come from plants. Once again, it has nothing to do with segregation
of races.

According to Dake, Reason 27 is:

Sowing mixed seed in the same field was unlawful (Lev.
19:19).

Since Dake refers us to the same verse we just reviewed, we
don't have to analyze it again. Let's confine ourselves to his reasoning:
"Sowing mixed seed in the same field was unlawful." What does
that have to do with the segregation of the races?

Reason 28 is:

Different seeds were forbidden to be planted in vineyards (Dt. 22:9).

For this reason, which again appears to be related only to
vegetables and fruits, not human beings, Dake provides one Scripture.
Deuteronomy 22:9 says:

**"You shall not sow your vineyard with different kinds
of seed, lest the yield of the seed which you have sown
and the fruit of your vineyard be defiled."**

After reading it, we are left with the same question: What
does it have to do with the segregation of races?

Dake's Reason 29 is:

Wearing garments of mixed fabrics forbidden (Dt. 22:11;
Lev. 19:19).

We have already read the two Scriptures Dake cites in connection with prior reasons. And we are still left to wonder, what does mixed fabric have to do with segregating races?

We have now reached Dake's final reason. Given his track record to this point, we would expect that it, too, would not be substantiated. But we might be wondering what the nature of it will be: Will it attempt to be powerful and comprehensive in order to give strong support to his idea that the races should be segregated?

The answer is yes.

According to Dake, Reason 30 is:

> Christians and certain other people of a like race are to be segregated (Mt. 18:15-17; 1 Cor. 5:9-13; 6:15; 2 Cor. 6:14-18; Eph. 5:11; 2 Th. 3:6-16; 1 Tim. 6:5; 2 Tim. 3:5).

Dake gives numerous Scriptures to support this. We're going to focus on only one of them here.[6] But before we do, I have a question about Reason 30: Since when are Christians a race? Aren't Christians people of *all* races who have accepted Christ as their Savior and Lord?

This is how far some people will go to support the idea of segregation of races. They will use the word *race* or the concept of race where it has no application at all, even when their words go against the teachings of God. As I said before, *Dake's Annotated Reference Bible* seems so authoritative. That's why God led me personally to go through every single "reason" and reference that Dake gives. I could not have done any less and still have fulfilled my mission. Again, I'm not trying to find fault with the man; I'm focusing on the so-called truths that he as a Bible teacher has taught. For years, his Bible with his commentary has been in circulation. People have believed what he wrote, and as a result they think they have a legitimate biblical base for the racism their parents, aunts, uncles

---

[6] See Appendix, pages 273-275, for Matthew 18:15-17; 1 Corinthians 5:9-13; 6:15, 2 Corinthians 6:14-18; 2 Thessalonians 3:6-16; 1 Timothy 6:5; 2 Timothy 3:5.

and friends may have taught them, and for the prejudiced garbage they have heard about "those people over there." Dake's notes can be used to support these beliefs. He gives "30 reasons for segregation of races" — and not one single Scripture he cites supports any of his contentions.

Let's read Ephesians 5:11. It says:

And have no fellowship with the unfruitful works of darkness, but rather expose them.

What does that have to do with races or nations? Nothing. Is Dake saying that Christians should not have fellowship with those who do not follow God, or that white people should be segregated from black, red, yellow and brown people? Or that integration is an unfruitful work of darkness? I don't really know what he's saying. What I do know is that even though this Scripture has nothing to do with segregating the races, it is a very important warning. God is telling us, **have no fellowship with the unfruitful works of darkness, but rather expose them.**

Racism is an unfruitful work of darkness. And it is my mission to expose it. Exposing it is the only way to end the deadly combination of distorted religion and racism that has come straight from Hell.

9

When Will the Church Wake Up?

In the January, 1992, edition of *Dake's Annotated Reference Bible*, several changes have been made in the "30 reasons for segregation of races." It's interesting to examine what these changes are.

The first change is the title: Now it's called "30 reasons nations separated," so "segregation" has been changed to "separated" and "races" has been changed to "nations." The other changes are in the wording of some of the "reasons." Below are the "30 reasons nations separated" with a comparison of how the words have been changed from "30 reasons for segregation of races":

1. God wills all races to be as He made them. Any violation of God's original purpose is not consistent with His will ([Acts] 17:26; Rom. 9:19-24) ["Is not consistent with His will" has replaced "manifests insubordination to him."]

2. God made everything to reproduce "after his own kind" (Gen. 1:11-12, 21-25; 6:20; 7:14). *Kind* means type and color or all things would be alike. God wants variety in his creation of trees, plants, fish, animals, and mankind. God loves all nations and calls "good" the races he created. [The reason remains the same and *kind* is still defined as "type and color." The phrase "or all

97

things would be alike" and the commentary that follows it
has replaced "He would have kept them all alike to begin
with."]

3. God originally determined the bounds of the habitations of nations ([Acts] 17:26; Gen. 10:5, 32; 11:8;
   Dt. 32:8). Nations were one until worship of a strange
   god forced God to choose the nation of Israel as His
   inheritance, to separate nations, and to set bounds.
   [The first statement remains the same; the commentary that
   begins with "Nations were one…" has been added.]

4. Miscegenation means the mixing of races, especially
   those of widely different type or color. The Bible even
   goes farther than opposing this. It is against different
   branches of the same stock intermarrying such as Jews
   marrying other descendants of Abraham (Ezra 9-10;
   Neh. 9-13; Jer. 50:37; Ezek. 30:5). [The words "especially those of widely different type or color" have replaced
   "especially the black and white races, or those of outstanding type or color."]

5. Abraham forbad Eliezer to take a wife for Isaac of the
   Canaanites (Gen.24:1-4). God was so pleased with
   this that He directed whom to get (Gen. 24:7, 12-
   67). ["The" has been added before "Canaanites."]

6. Isaac forbad Jacob to take a wife of the Canaanites
   (Gen. 27:46-28:7). [This remains the same.]

7. Abraham sent all his sons of the concubines, and even
   of his second wife, far away from Isaac so their descendants would not mix (Gen. 25:1-6). [This remains
   the same.]

8. Esau disobeying this law brought grief to his father
   and mother after lifelong companionship (Gen. 25:28;
   26:34-35; 27:46; 28:8-9). [The comment about disobeying the so-called law against intermarriage between two "nations" remains the same; "brought grief to his father and

mother after a lifelong companionship" has replaced "brought the final break between him and his father after a life-long companionship."]

9. Two branches of Isaac remain separate forever (Gen. 36; 46:8-26). ["The" has been deleted before "two branches"; "remain separate forever" has replaced "remain segregated forever."]

10. Ishmael's and Isaac's descendants remain separate forever (Gen. 25:12-23; 1 Chr. 1:29). ["Separate forever" has replaced "segregated forever."]

11. Jacob's sons destroyed a whole city to maintain separation (Gen. 34). ["Separation" has replaced "segregation."]

12. God forbad Israel to intermarry (Ex. 34:12-16; Dt. 7:3-6). [Previously this read: "God forbad intermarriage between Israel and all other nations."]

13. Enemies remained in the land as a penalty for this (Josh. 23:12-13). [This replaces "Joshua forbad the same thing on sentence of death," though the Scripture cited remains the same.]

14. God cursed angels who left their "own habitation" for the daughters of men (Gen. 6:1-4; 2 Pet. 2:4; Jude 6-7). ["Their own first estate," which used to precede "their own habitation," has been deleted.]

15. Intermarriage caused a curse on Israel (Judg. 3:6-7; Num. 25:1-8). [Previously this read: "Miscegenation caused Israel to be cursed."]

16. This was Solomon's sin (1 Ki. 11). [This remains the same.]

17. This was a sin of Jews returning from Babylon (Ezra 9:2; 10:2, 10, 44; Neh. 13). [Previously, the Scriptural references were: Ezra 9:1-10:2, 10-18, 44: 13:1-30. Ezra 13, which was cited in 1963 but which does not exist, has been changed to Nehemiah 13.]

18. God told Israel to be separated (Lev. 20:24; Num. 23:9; 1 Ki. 8:53). [Previously this read, "God commanded Israel to be segregated."]

19. Jews are recognized as a separate people in all ages because of God's choice (Mt. 10:6; Jn 1:11). [After "God's choice" the phrase "and command" has been deleted. Also deleted is, "Equal rights in the gospel gives no right to break this eternal law."]

20. Separation between Jews and all other nations to remain in eternity (Isa. 2:2-4; Ezek. 37; 47:13-48:35; Zech. 14:16-21; Mt. 19:28; Lk. 1:32-33; Rev. 7:1-8; 14:1-5). ["Separation" has replaced "segregation" and "in eternity" has replaced "in all eternity."]

21. All nations will remain separated on earth forever ([Acts] 17:26; Gen. 10:5, 32; 11:8-9; Dt. 32:8; Dan. 7:13-14; Zech. 14; Rev. 11:15; 21:24). [Previously this read, "All nations will remain segregated from one another in their own parts of the earth forever."]

22. Certain people in Israel were not to worship with others (Dt. 23:1-3; Ezra 10:8; Neh. 9:2; 10:28; 13:3). [The word "even" has been removed after "were not."]

23. In heaven a specific group will have a new song that no man can learn but the 144,000 (Rev. 14:1-5). [Previously this read: "Even in heaven certain groups will not be allowed to worship together." While Revelation 14:1-5 is still cited, 7:7-17 and 15:2-5 have been deleted.]

24. An ox and an ass could not be worked together (Dt. 22:10). [Previously this read: "Segregation was so strong in the O.T. that an ox and an ass could not be worked together."]

25. Intermarriage caused disunity among God's people (Num. 12). ["Intermarriage" has replaced "miscegenation."]

26. Stock was forbidden to be bred with other kinds (Lev. 19:19). [This remains the same.]

27. Sowing mixed seed in the same field was unlawful (Lev. 19:19). [This remains the same.]

28. Different seeds were forbidden to be planted in vineyards (Dt. 22:9). [This remains the same.]

29. Wearing garments of mixed fabrics forbidden (Dt. 22:11; Lev. 19:19). [This remains the same.]

30. Christians and certain people of the same race are to be separate (Mt. 18:15-17; 1 Cor. 5:9-13; 6:15; 2 Cor. 6:14-18; 2 Th. 3:6, 14; 1 Tim. 6:5; 2 Tim. 3:5). ["Separate" has replaced "segregated." Reference to Ephesians 5:11 has been deleted, and 2 Thessalonians 3:6, 14 has replaced 2 Thessalonians 3:6-16.][1]

It is curious to note that after making these modifications and taking such great pains to change "segregation" to "separation," there are still 19 references that use the word *segregation* in the Complete Concordance Encyclopedic Index section of the same Bible. As for the changes to the "30 reasons" section, I'd like you to judge for yourself whether you think the "30 reasons nations separated" have been sufficiently corrected from "30 reasons for segregation of races."

An awesome incident happened as I began to teach about Dake's 1963 Bible in my church as part of the series on *Race, Religion & Racism* on which this book is based. Even before the teachings went to the public via television, the Dake Publishing Company heard about what I was doing, and sent me a letter and a copy of their latest Bible. It appears to me that the letter was sent with the

---

[1] *Dake's Annotated Reference Bible* 1992, 159 [in the New Testament].

hope of forestalling me from teaching on the Dake Bible. Read it and see what you think.

February 18, 1998

Dr. Frederick K.C. Price:

We are writing this letter to you personally, to your congregation, and to your television audience. We wish to express our sincere regrets and apologies for any commentary in *The Dake Annotated Reference Bible* that has been interpreted as being supportive of slavery, racism, or discrimination. Neither Finis Dake nor any member of the Dake family would ever want to contribute to the oppression of African Americans or any other race of people.

As a new convert, Finis Dake often attended a Black church and was baptized there. He frequently preached in Black churches throughout the country, and Blacks attended the churches that he pastored as well. He held in highest esteem his many African-American brothers who dedicated their lives to the ministry of the Gospel and the full experience of the Holy Spirit. Furthermore, we know that people of color throughout the world have played a vital role in winning many souls to Christ, though most of them have not been publicly recognized.

Dr. Dake was neither a racist, nor proud. In fact, in the early 1930s he wrote a booklet entitled *One Hundred Fifty Jawbreakers for Anglo-Saxons,* refuting the Anglo-Saxon theory which supports the notion of white supremacy. This publication is inconsistent with the idea that his reference notes on racial separation were intended to advocate white supremacy. In addition, his notes on Colossians 3:11-12 clearly state that "as a new creation in Christ there is no distinction made in rights and privileges because of race, sex, color, or position in life."

From our hearts, we are certain that Dr. Dake never intended for his reference notes to be used to support racism of any kind. Yet we very clearly see how his thirty reasons for the separation of the nations can be interpreted as advocating racism, and we agree that racism has no place in the body of Christ, or anywhere else. Please accept this letter as a public statement from the entire Dake family that we ask for forgiveness.

Dr. Dake's reference notes were based on his understanding of the Word of God. However, we do not wish the Dake notes to offend anyone through confusion about this sensitive topic. Therefore, we have labored to omit all racially insensitive references. We have enclosed a new Dake Bible, printed in January of 1997, for your use. We hope that you will agree that the changes it contains demonstrate our commitment to reach out with an open heart to help heal the pains of racial injustice. The Dake Bible has blessed hundreds of thousands of people all over the world, and we want it to continue to promote spiritual growth, healing and reconciliation.

You mentioned in your sermon last Sunday that radiation treatments to cure cancer, if not administered properly, can be just as deadly as the cancer itself. The Dake family agrees that racial prejudice in the body of Christ is, and has been, a cancerous schism to our fellowship and a hindrance to the witness of His name. However, like the radiation treatments you mentioned, the public airing of these problems could be just as dangerous as the evil of racism itself.

Therefore, we ask that you would consider meeting with us and with other Christian leaders so that we can seek to resolve these issues in ways that will be of the greatest benefit to the body of Christ, to our ministries, and to the thousands and even millions of souls who can come to the Lord once they see that we are truly united in love as our Lord commanded.

We have gone to great lengths to change the Dake notes so that they will not offend any ethnic or racial group. We will go to even greater lengths to have full reconciliation and forgiveness between ourselves and our Christian brothers and sisters regarding this issue. We feel confident that you will join us in this endeavor. Therefore, we wait to hear from you as soon as possible, so that the details of such a conference can be arranged.

Dr. Price, none of us can undo our personal, familial, or national histories. But we can direct the present and the future. As you seek God's direction in the weeks to come, we urge you to prayerfully consider this letter as a public appeal for forgiveness and healing. You are in a position to speak life or death, to build up or destroy, to extend mercy or withhold it.

Your humble servants,

Derrick Germaine	Finis J. Dake, Jr.
General Manager	Dake Publishing
Dake Publishing	
Annabeth Dake Germaine	Finette Dake Kennedy
Dake Publishing	Dake Publishing

Cc: Creflo Dollar, Kenneth Copeland, Dr. Oral Roberts, Kenneth Hagin, Marilyn Hickey, Dr. Bill Winston, Dr. A.R. Bernard, Dr. Raleigh Washington, Dr. Steve Land, Dr. Sondra A. O'Neile, Keith Butler, Jerry Savelle, Jesse Duplantis, E.V. Hill, T.D. Jakes, Joyce Meyer, John Avanzini, Norvel Hayes, Benny Hinn, John Osteen, James Robinson, Mark Rutland, and Christian ministers and bookstores throughout the country.

On February 25, 1998, I responded to their letter.

To the Dake Family:

Greetings in the wonderful name of Jesus.
In response to your faxed letter dated February 18, 1998, I must say, I was surprised, to say the least, to have re-

ceived a letter from you. I don't know what I've done to deserve this honor.

It is true that I am in the process of teaching a series entitled "Race, Religion & Racism" in my church and ultimately to the body of Christ at large. God gave me this assignment about seven years ago. For the last three years I have been doing extensive research on the subject. We have a horrendous problem of racism in the church, which no one else seems to want to address in depth. This is my task. In order to destroy racism in the church, we must locate its roots and pull them out of the ground of the heart of the church. It is a fact that must be admitted that White Christians (people) — **not all, but far too many** — hold negative attitudes and opinions about African Americans. Where do attitudes and opinions come from? From observation, association and teaching. Racial and color prejudice (racism) is not genetically transmitted, nor is it passed through the blood. It is socially transmitted from father to son, from father to son and on and on it goes. The major transmitters of racism have been the teachings in the home by parents and teachings in the church by religious leaders, both preachers and teachers, both from the pulpit and the printed page.

The Lord has led me to go back to the past and pull up the roots that have produced the present situation! I have never said nor inferred that Dr. Dake was a racist. After all, I have never met him. I operate on the basis of two biblical principles among many others: Matthew 12:33 [KJV], "Either make the tree good, and his fruit good; or else make the tree corrupt, and his fruit corrupt; for the tree is known by his fruit," and 1 Thessalonians 5:22, "Abstain from all appearance of evil." No human is omniscient enough to know what is in the heart or mind of another human, until they speak, write or act. Based upon that, the Holy Spirit has led me to research volumes of material, both secular and Christian, to find the roots of racism and dig them up.

The notes in the "Dake Annotated Reference Bible" are a case in point. The notes in the 1963 edition on the "30 Reason for Segregation of Races," is a prime example of the **appearance** of evil. Racism is evil, ungodly and satanically inspired. If in fact Dr. Dake was not a racist or racially and color prejudiced, he leaves himself wide open for the title, with his note #4, which states: "Miscegenation means the mixture of races, especially the black and white races...." The KKK, skinheads and racists in general love to see that statement coming from a Bible teacher in a Bible! Let's be fair about this, there is absolutely nothing in the Bible from Genesis to Revelation about Blacks and Whites not mixing; we find it only in the minds of racists. Then, in note #11, Dr. Dake says, "Jacob's sons destroyed a whole city to maintain segregation (Gen. 34)." Based on **appearance**, this is a gross distortion of the truth. Jacob's sons didn't destroy the city because of **race**, but because of **rape**! And what's so amazing is that you sent me a 1997 edition of your Bible, wherein you discontinued the use of the "30 Reasons" as such, but included, "separation for Messiah's line:" and then still left under #7, "maintain separation (Gen. 34)." The reason hasn't changed, not even in 1997. It was because of **rape**, not **race**!

Do you have any idea of how many people have bought and studied the Dake Bible from 1963 to 1998 (**35 years**)? How many people have read the notes I have referred to and concluded that what their fathers and mothers, yes, even pastors have taught them must be true about Blacks and Whites? These are roots that **appear** to be racist and racially prejudiced. We, as the Body of Christ, and I, mandated by the Holy Spirit, must pull up these roots and show by the Scriptures that they are not to be believed. People who have these Bibles must be informed that these particular notes must be discarded.

In your letter you mentioned, "We wish to express our sincere regrets and apologies for any commentary in

'The Dake Annotated Reference Bible' that has been interpreted as being supportive of slavery, racism or discrimination." To me this issue is not personal; however, I would be the first to say to you, apologies accepted! But the fact of the matter still stands, the notes are already printed and have been circulating for the past 35 years. It has to be fixed! I see two ways by which this can possibly be done. First, when automobile manufacturers — Ford, General Motors, etc. — find a flaw in their product, they do a recall at their expense. In other words, they fix or replace the faulty part. Are you willing to do that? Thirty-five years of printed material — that's a lot of "parts." Second, someone has to point out the faulty parts, so that people can avoid them. That is a part of my assignment with the series "Race, Religion & Racism."

Please know that I am not targeting Dake's Bible as the only **apparent** racially motivated publication. I have over 300 pages of notes on the "Religion" section alone, from Dake's Bible to the Mormons to Islam. This is not personal; it's principle.

You mentioned in your letter about meeting with you. If you think it would be beneficial to meet with me, you are cordially invited to do so.

Thank you for writing and for your concern (it is my concern also) for the Body of Christ.

In the Service of the King
Frederick K.C. Price, Ph.D.

Another letter from the Dake family followed.

March 3, 1998

Dear Dr. Price:

Thank you for your quick response to our letter, and for your gracious acceptance of our apologies. We are also grateful for your willingness to meet with us.

We are in agreement with you that the sin of racism in the church must be dealt with. And we trust that you have seen our willingness to do all we can toward this end, as God leads us.

We feel that the changes in our 1997 printing reflect a sincere effort on our part to remove offensive stumbling blocks. Yet perhaps our work is not done. It may very well be that God would use you to assist us in finishing what we've started.

We recognize that God has given you a position of leadership in the body of Christ. Therefore, we are open to hear your perspective on the issues that concern us so deeply.

We would indeed like to meet with you, to listen respectfully to all of your objections and concerns regarding the 1997 printing of the Dake Bible. We have no desire to debate these matters or to defend ourselves in the proposed meeting. We simply want to hear you fully. Afterwards, we will give thoughtful, prayerful consideration to all of your concerns. With prayer and godly counsel, we're confident that we will find God's direction for our ministry.

So, Dr. Price, we accept your cordial invitation to meet with you. Please let us know when would be the best time, so that we can coordinate our schedules.

Sincerely,

Derrick Germaine	Finis J. Dake, Jr.
General Manager	Dake Publishing
Dake Publishing	
Annabeth Dake Germaine	Finette Dake Kennedy
Dake Publishing	Dake Publishing

This is where we are at the time of this writing. The publishers of the Dake Bible assured me in their letter that they had deleted statements that would be offensive to certain ethnic groups. They sent me their most recent Bible so I could see that they had made an effort to correct the past. I accepted that with thanks and told them I was open to meeting with them to discuss further changes. They have never met with me. They have also never responded to my suggestion that the way to correct the past is for them to recall their original Bible and acknowledge to the public that it was faulty because of the misinterpretations that appear to support racism.

Their apology is accepted, their good intentions are noted. But what was done in the past needs to be uprooted. It's right that the Dakes should want to publish correct Bible commentary, but someone still has to take responsibility for all the years that the 1963 *Dake's Annotated Reference Bible* — which was unscriptural and incorrect — has influenced people and helped to perpetuate racism because it gives the impression that the Bible supports the segregation of races. That's why I talked about it in my series; that's why I'm writing about it in this book.

I thank God that in the 1997 edition there is a further modification of the commentary. But as part of their notes on separation, they have left a statement almost intact from the 1963 and 1992 editions that represents all that was wrong with the "30 reasons."

In the 1997 notes on the Book of Acts, the "30 reasons" section has been changed so that the heading now reads: "Separation in Scripture (17:26)." Under this heading, there are the subheadings "Separation for Messiah's Line," "Separation in Israel," "Miscellaneous Separation" and "Christian Separation."

Under "Separation of Israel," there is the statement:

Jacob's sons destroyed a whole city to maintain separation (Gen. 34).

I have a problem with this. How can people be so diligent that they delete the original "30 reason for segregation of races" and leave the worst reason of all exactly as it appeared in the original text? I call it the worst reason because it has no scriptural support (as we've seen,

Jacob's sons did not "destroy a whole city to maintain separation," they destroyed the city because of the rape of their sister) and because of its possible interpretation by racists since it appears to condone violence as a means "to maintain separation."

It bears repeating that there are people, primarily white Christians, who believe that what Dake's commentary says is biblically correct. They must be told that it is incorrect.

The preface of the 1997 edition of *Dake's Annotated Reference Bible* states:

> In the preparation of this work ... the aim has been to prove the teachings of the side-columns with plain Bible references; and now, the reader is invited to see for himself what these related passages actually say on any given subject of the notes.

This is an invitation to do what I'm doing. The publishers are telling me to examine the Scriptures referred to in these notes. Over the years I have learned to check up on everything; I don't trust anyone, not even myself. But in this case, they are inviting me to "see for [myself] what these related passages actually say on any given subject of the notes," so my analysis is in line with their instructions.

I want to be very clear: I am no more interested in attacking Dake's successors than I am in attacking Dake. I want to get to the root of why people have racist ideas. Why do white people think that they're superior and that black people and people of other racial and ethnic groups are inferior? As Christians, they could not have gotten that idea from the Holy Spirit because, as we have been seeing, it is not in the Word of God.

So where do racist attitudes come from? They are taught by precept and example. The reason I'm dwelling on what members of the Church have taught is because what we believe today is so often predicated on what our forebears have been exposed to in the past, and a segment of the white Christian Church has been contributing to this teaching for hundreds of years. I know it stings to recognize this, and I hate that it does, but we have to tell the truth. If we don't stop this disease, it will continue to spread until it destroys the whole body. We have to get rid of it, and we have to do it now. It has already spread too far. And the only way to stop it is to identify and root out whatever is not, according to the Scriptures, true, noble, just, pure, lovely, and of good report (Philippians 4:8).

In respect to this, there was another influential Bible commentator, Cyrus Ingerson Scofield, whose reference Bible, first published in 1909 and revised in 1917,[2] has been read by millions of readers,[3] and has been called "the single most important publication affecting millenarian ideas to the present time."[4]

As part of his notes, Scofield states:

> A prophetic declaration is made that from Ham will descend an inferior and servile posterity.[5]

---

[2] *The Scofield Reference Bible* was later published in a *New and Improved Edition* in 1917. See Stanley M. Burgess and Gary B. McGee, 771.

[3] Burgess and McGee, 247.

[4] Henry Warner Bowden, *Dictionary of American Religious Biography*, 2nd ed. Rev. and enl., s.v., "Scofield, Cyrus Ingerson" (Westport, Connecticut: Greenwood Press, 1993), 477. Cyrus Ingerson Scofield was born in 1843 and died in 1921. Scofield fought in the Confederate army and was a lawyer before converting to Christianity in 1879. After working as a volunteer with the St. Louis YMCA and studying the Bible with a well-known minister, he was chosen to be a pastor in Dallas where he became fascinated with the Bible. According to J. William T. Youngs, Scofield "never learned the original tongues of the Bible, and he rejected higher criticism as leading to apostasy. He held that every word of the Bible — even as translated into English — was divinely inspired." His aim in compiling *The Scofield Bible* was to aid his followers in finding what he considered biblical truths through his notes on various topics. J. William T. Youngs, *The Congregationalists, Denominations in America*, No. 4 (Westport, Connecticut: Greenwood Press, 1990), 298.

[5] Cyrus Ingerson Scofield, ed., *The Scofield Reference Bible* (New York: Oxford University Press, Revised 1917), 16.

This is not from the first chapter of the Bible of the Grand Wizard of the KKK! It is written by a Bible teacher whose writing has taught millions of Christians. And what is he teaching them? That "a prophetic declaration is made that from Ham will descend an inferior and servile posterity." There it is: the word *inferior*. This is a major — perhaps *the* major — root of the idea many white people hold that black people are inferior. Even today many white people think this, and because of writings such as Scofield's, they believe they are biblically justified.[6]

I'll go with whatever the Bible says, if the Bible says it. But I'm not going with racist garbage that a man who purports to be a Bible scholar comes up with out of his prejudiced imagination. It should not be in print unless it can be proven with the Book from which he claims he got it. I'm focusing on this because it is exactly how racism has been perpetuated. We've seen what Charles Carroll wrote in 1902 in *The Tempter of Eve*; we've seen what Scofield wrote in his *Scofield Reference Bible* in 1917; we've seen what Dake wrote in his *Annotated Reference Bible* in 1963, and what it still contained in 1997. People have believed these things in the Church — in the Church! — where Galatians 3:28 tells us there is neither slave nor free, male nor female, Jew nor Gentile. But there *is* black and white? Apparently, that is in between the verses. But what kind of justification is that? We ought to be able to find support for what these Bible teachers and scholars tell us *within* the verses of Scripture that are being commented on. Otherwise, these teachers and scholars ought to be arrested for lying and given 25 consecutive life terms.

---

6 Indeed, in Chapter 1 we looked at Old Testament scholar Stephen L. McKenzie's comment on this same Scripture, Genesis 9, and its misinterpretation of some verses as referring to the so-called curse of Ham, which was used to subordinate black people, not only in the time of slavery, but today. In fact, McKenzie called attention to what he called Dake's "racist explanation" of it. Stephen L. McKenzie, 3-4.

Scofield states:

> A prophetic declaration is made that from Ham will de-
> scend an inferior and servile posterity.

When we read Genesis 9:24-25, the verse Scofield cites in reference to his statement, we should find something about Ham's descendants being "inferior." If we don't, Scofield has no business putting it into his commentary, because he has no business putting into the Scripture something that God did not put into it. As God warns us in Deuteronomy 4:2, **"You shall not add to the word which I command you, nor take from it...."**

Genesis 9:24-25, Scofield's supposed source, says:

> **And Noah awoke from his wine, and knew what his younger son had done unto him. And he said, cursed be Canaan; a servant of servants shall he be unto his brethren.**

This passage does not mention the word *inferior*. Although it has often been used to justify the supposed "curse of Ham," by which racists mean black skin and an inferior position to Whites, the Scripture doesn't even say that Ham was cursed. This is how lies have been promulgated. It's been so-called Christian leaders, teachers in the Church, who have perpetuated this polluted thinking. Scofield said "inferior"; God never said "inferior." And yet people have believed the lie of inferiority. The Klan believes it. Many white people who consider themselves Christians and are not in the Klan believe it. And many black people believe they are inferior because this garbage has been presented to them as truth all their lives. That's why many can't cope with life, because they have believed this thinking, believed that it is the will of God when it is really the will of these supposed Bible teachers.

Let's read Scofield's statement once again:

> A prophetic declaration is made that from Ham will de-
> scend an inferior and servile posterity.

At the very least, I think I'm safe in saying that a pronouncement like this certainly seems to vindicate racism. Again, I return to the Bible, which tells us to avoid all appearance of evil. To avoid all appearance of racism, Scofield should not appear to be supporting the racist doctrine of black inferiority, which has been used to support the racist doctrine of racial segregation and the racist condemnation of interracial marriage. It should not appear to lend scriptural support to beliefs that have no scriptural basis but are founded only on fear, ignorance, ethnic pride and an attitude of white superiority.

We are the inheritors of what our forefathers have done, whether good or bad, right or wrong. My purpose in bringing this out is not to cause division but to cause healing. The sickness of racism can never be healed if it's never addressed openly and honestly. That is why I'm doing my best to illuminate where these lies came from.

We can see that some of them came from so-called Christian ministers. The lies began in 1619 with the start of slavery in America. That is why it was justifiable to enslave a whole race of people — because some of those who were supposed to know the Bible interpreted it as saying that people of the enslaved race were inferior, that they were only animals and could therefore be treated any way you liked. Kill them, beat them, rape them. What difference does it make? There were ministers telling the slave owners in 1619, 1719, and 1819 what *Scofield's Reference Bible* told white Christians in 1909 and 1917, and what it continued to tell people for decade after decade after decade: that the descendants of Ham are "servile and inferior." In 1963, Dake wrote about "30 reasons for segregation of races"; in 1992 his commentary was modified to be included under "30 reasons nations separated"; in 1997 it was changed and put under the heading "Separation in Scripture," which still includes the vile and false statement that "Jacob's sons destroyed a whole city to maintain separation."

Our nation is in the shape it's in because the Church has not done what God commissioned it to do. It has been perpetuating its own program and its own thoughts and its own prejudices, and these have been the program, thoughts and prejudices of the white majority. It's unfortunate, but this majority has been in control, so it has set the pattern and the tone. Now the Church must learn to think as God thinks and to see as God sees.

1 Samuel 16:6-7 tells us:

So it was, when they came, that he looked at Eliab and said, "Surely the Lord's anointed is before Him!"

But the Lord said to Samuel, "Do not look at his appearance or at his physical stature, because I have refused him. For the Lord does not see as man sees; for man looks at the outward appearance, but the Lord looks at the heart."

The Church has not done this. The Church has looked at the outside and never taken the time to look at the heart. If it had looked at the heart, it never would have allowed segregation of the races, let alone allowed some Church leaders to support it.

10

Expressions of Racism

 To show you how strong racial prejudice and prejudice against interracial marriage are among some white people today, I want to share a letter that I received from a couple while I was teaching the series entitled "Race, Religion & Racism" in my church.

The husband writes:

Dear Pastor Price: My wife and I are the mixed couple from Buffalo who wrote you recently. Below you will find a letter written to my wife two days before our wedding date, 6/18/88.

The wife adds:

Pastor Price, this letter was very disturbing to me as a new wife-to-be. However, at the time I chose to keep this letter to myself and the Lord and not tell anyone else until ten years later.

Below is the letter that the wife received two days before her wedding.

Dear [name withheld]:

We have just heard who you are marrying on Saturday and are <u>VERY, VERY, SORRY</u> to hear it. Have you taken leave of your senses to marry a black one? Oh, [name withheld], think what kind of life you will have ahead of you. Is it that you are so desperate just to be married that you would cross the color line? What if you have children by this man? What kind of future do they have? Whites belong with whites and blacks belong with blacks. Give it serious thought before Saturday comes and then it is too late.

Contempt for black people drips from almost every word of this letter. The writer doesn't even refer to the woman's fiancé as a "black *man*"; he or she calls him "a black one." When I read this to my congregation, someone exclaimed, "Unbelievable!" Unfortunately, it is believable. Look what the pens of the white Bible scholars whose work we have examined have written about black people: Carroll wrote that black people were "animals," that we are "the beast of the field"; Scofield that black people are "inferior"; Dake that miscegenation — "especially whites and blacks" — is against God's will.

The letter this woman received before her wedding is typical of thousands and thousands of situations in our country in which so-called Christians warn their family members or friends against the supposed wrongness of interracial marriage. It's not just a collection of individual situations, however; it's a pervasive attitude. If you ever start to think the issues I'm talking about aren't real, or that they only come into play with radical white-supremacist groups, remember this letter. And remember that Bible scholars and teachers have been the prime perpetrators of this garbage.

Have you taken leave of your senses to marry a black one? Think what kind of life you will have ahead of you. Is it that you are so desperate just to be married that you would cross the color line?

In relation to this letter, I'd like to look at the commentary in a Bible produced by a man whose name is a household word: Jimmy Swaggart. Since the notes I'm about to quote are in a *Jimmy Swaggart Bible*, apparently he okayed them and was in harmony with them.

In the section on Leviticus, under the heading "contribution that women made," reference is made to an Israelite woman named Shelomith, who had married an Egyptian and whose son blasphemed the Lord and was put to death. The notes in the *Jimmy Swaggart Bible* state that Shelomith:

> Indirectly suffered the consequences of the law that God gave to Moses.[1]

Under the next heading, "Significance Today," the commentary is:

> Although common in this twentieth century, mixed marriages are unlawful in God's plan and produce heartache and tragedy. Throughout the Old Testament accounts of family lineage, we find that whenever there was a marriage between people of mixed races there was also a disturbed situation. The offspring were affected to an even greater degree.[2]

Let's focus on the core statement in these notes:

> Mixed marriages are unlawful in God's plan....

This is a bold-faced lie. It's not Bible, it's racist! Let's look at the passage in Leviticus so that you will see for yourself that there is not one word about mixed marriages being "unlawful in God's plan."

Leviticus 24:10-16 states:

> **Now the son of an Israelite woman, whose father was an Egyptian, went out among the children of Israel;**

---

[1] Lynette Goux, "Women of the Bible," *Jimmy Swaggart Ministries Bible*, edited by Marvin Solum, B.A. M.Div., M.R.E., Th.D. (Dallas: Heritage Publishers Inc., 1983. Licensed by Jimmy Swaggart Ministries, Baton Rouge, Louisiana), xix.

[2] Goux, "Women of the Bible," *The Jimmy Swaggart Ministries Bible*, xix-xx.

and this Israelite woman's son and a man of Israel fought each other in the camp.

And the Israelite woman's son blasphemed the name of the Lord and cursed; and so they brought him to Moses. (His mother's name was Shelomith the daughter of Dibri, of the tribe of Dan.)

Then they put him in custody, that the mind of the Lord might be shown to them.

And the Lord spoke to Moses, saying,

"Take outside the camp him who has cursed; then let all who heard him lay their hands on his head, and let all the congregation stone him.

"Then you shall speak to the children of Israel, saying: 'Whoever curses his God shall bear his sin.

'And whoever blasphemes the name of the Lord shall surely be put to death. All the congregation shall certainly stone him, the stranger as well as him who is born in the land. When he blasphemes the name of the Lord, he shall be put to death.' "

The Scripture then continues to name other sins and their punishments, including murder (Verse 17) and disfigurement of a neighbor (Verse 18); Verse 20 is the Scripture that contains the famous phrase "**... eye for eye, tooth for tooth ....**" But *nowhere* does it mention interracial marriage as a sin. How could the Scripture make it any clearer that what is "unlawful in God's plan" is blaspheming the name of the Lord?

The Church is full of hypocrisy. How many ministers smile at black people and take our money and think we're inferior? We're not good enough, but our dollars are. People have been angry that I'm addressing this. They tell me I shouldn't talk about it, that it's going to cause division in the Church, that I'm not acting out of love. My answer is that I am acting out of love. I'm telling the truth and telling the truth is love. If telling the truth were going to divide the Body of Christ, then Jesus lied to us when He said **"...the truth shall make you free."** [John 8:32]

The truth is that the white part of the Church is responsible for perpetrating and tolerating racist, or what appear to be racist, interpretations of the Bible, and it needs to face it, admit it and fix it. The white part of the Church cannot just say, "We apologize. Let's forget it." It has to fix it. Otherwise, it would be like me backing out of my driveway with my wife and two kids while you come barreling around the corner driving 90 miles an hour, hitting my car, turning it over seven times, and then, when I'm lying in the street bleeding, my wife's head cracked on the sidewalk, both of my kids dead, my car totaled, you screech to a halt, run back to see what's happened, see me lying there bleeding to death, and say to me, "I'm so sorry that I hit you. Would you please accept my apology?" Then you get in your car and drive off. Yes, your apology is accepted, but clearly it is not enough.

The Church needs to admit that it is pervaded by racism and it needs to eliminate it. Recently, I even found an example of racism in the *Ever Increasing Faith Study Bible* that we use in our church. It's not in the commentary on Scripture, so it isn't presented as a teaching, it's in the topical index, but it teaches people anyway. Under the heading "Abominations — things utterly repulsive," under the subheading "Applied to perverse sexual relations," the editors include "racial intermarriage."[3] Then it cites Ezra 9:1-14. We have already looked at this passage in Dake's commentary. The issue in Ezra 9:1-14 is not interracial marriage, it is intermarriage between Believers

---

[3] "Topical Index to the Bible: From Genesis to Revelation," *The Holy Bible: New King James Version* (Nashville: Thomas Nelson Inc., 1982), "Abominations — things utterly repulsive"; Reference "B," "Racial Intermarriage," 6.

and unbelievers, Jews and pagans; the abominations referred to are the abominations of idol worship.

It's horrifying how the so-called inferiority of black people has become interwoven into the thinking of white society. It's equally horrifying how racist misinterpretations of the Bible have become interwoven into the thinking of the Church. They appear again and again. What does the topical index tell readers when it lists "racial intermarriage" under "Abominations — things utterly repulsive"? It tells them the lie that interracial marriage is utterly repulsive to God.

We have written to the publishers of *The Ever Increasing Faith Study Bible*, Thomas Nelson Publishers, and asked them to admit their error and to correct it in future printings.

Examine the Bible you use. You may find that the commentary or other added sections are polluted by racist beliefs. The more we look, the more we find, and the more we find, the clearer it becomes how pervasive these attitudes are in our society and the way they have become so pervasive. Remember the letter the young woman received two days before her wedding, asking her, "Have you taken leave of your senses to marry a black one?" Who knows how much support that letter writer found for his or her bigoted point of view in the commentary and notes of a Bible? How many so-called Bible scholars have stopped to ask themselves why if God, who can create and sustain a universe, had wanted to prohibit interracial marriage, He wouldn't have just come out and said so? Wouldn't He have just directly stated, "I don't want any races to ever mix because of their color"?

The misuse of authority on the part of some white people within the Church has spawned such books as *Message to the Black Man in America*, in which Elijah Muhammad writes:

> The Bible is now being called the Poison Book by God Himself, and who can deny that it is not poison? It has poisoned the very hearts and minds of the so-called Negroes so much that they can't agree with each other. From the first day that the white race received the Divine

Scripture they started tampering with its truth to make it
suit themselves, and blind the black man. It is their nature
to do evil, and the Book can't be recognized as the pure
and Holy Word of God.[4]

This is someone on the outside looking at the track record of
the Church. And the track record of the Church opened the door for
this. But white people have not changed the Scriptures. The Bible is
just as it was when it came from the original writers. The Scriptures
say the same thing that they have always said. There's not a thing in
the world wrong with the Bible. Contrary to what Elijah Muhammad
writes, the Bible is not a poison book. The poison comes from the
pens of some of those who attempt to interpret it; it comes from the
warped, prejudiced attitudes that are reflected in these interpretations.
The poison comes from people, not from the Book. Just because
someone drives up in a Ford, robs a bank, kills everyone and drives
off with the money doesn't mean there's something wrong with Fords.
You don't get rid of the whole Ford Motor Company just because
some criminals used a Ford in a getaway. So don't throw away the
Bible and Christianity just because some people have misused it.
Read the Bible right and use it right!

We have looked at the following verses, but the principle
they put forth is so important that I would like to look at them again
in light of Elijah Muhammad's criticism.

1 Samuel 16:6-7 says:

**So it was, when they came, that he looked at Eliab
and said,**

"Surely the Lord's anointed is before Him!"

---

[4] Elijah Muhammad, *Message to the Black Man in America* (Chicago:
Muhammad Mosque of Islam No.2, 1965), 94.

But the Lord said to Samuel, "Do not look at his appearance or at his physical stature, because I have refused him. For the Lord does not see as man sees; for man looks at the outward appearance, but the Lord looks at the heart."

If the white man had changed the Bible as some have alleged, this Scripture would not be telling us God looks at the heart and not the outward appearance. It would be telling us God looks at the color of a man's skin and makes a judgment based on that. If the white man had changed the Bible, 1 Corinthians 15:39 would not say there is one kind of flesh of men, and Acts 17:26 would not say we are made from one blood. If the white man had changed the Bible, Moses would have been struck with leprosy for marrying the Ethiopian woman instead of Miriam for criticizing the marriage. And if the white man had changed the Bible, there would certainly be no black ancestors in the genealogy of Jesus Christ.

To put it simply, if the white man had changed the Bible, he would have made it fit all of his racist actions. He hasn't changed it; he has just misinterpreted it. All we have to do is read it to know that God doesn't look at anybody's outward appearance, God always looks at our hearts.

I find myself wondering about the white people around the world, especially in America, and especially in the Church in America, who claim they're saved but are still racist in their attitudes. Do they really know God? Because if they have the nature of God, they ought to see like God, act like God, think like God and talk like God, for they are supposed to have God's Spirit in them. And there is no racism in God. So what is it doing in them?

Maybe these people are just members of a denomination; maybe they are just religious. But they certainly couldn't have the Spirit of God in them, because the Spirit of God does not have any racism in Him. Therefore, He couldn't inspire it in them.

So if you have racism in you — I'm saying *if*, I'm not assuming that you do — then maybe you don't have the Spirit of God in you. It's just food for thought, serious thought.

We have just read in 1 Samuel that **"the Lord does not see as man sees,"** that **"man looks at the outward appearance, but the Lord looks at the heart."** Since the Scripture tells us this and the Bible expositors and publishers tell us something very different, is it possible that the Bible expositors and publishers have learned that God has altered His attitude since 1 Samuel? Maybe He used to not look at the outward appearance but He has changed His perspective and now looks at the outward appearance? If this were so, we ought to be able to find something in the Bible that tells us this.

Malachi 3:6, which is a long way from 1 Samuel, says:

"For I am the Lord, I do not change."

This means that if God did not look at the outward appearance in 1 Samuel, He doesn't look at the outward appearance in Malachi. But some might say, "Brother Price, 1 Samuel is in the Old Testament and Malachi is in the Old Testament." Let's look in the Book of Hebrews, which is in the New Testament. When Jesus walked the earth, He said, **"I and my Father are One"** (John 10:30). He also said, **"... I always do those things that please Him"** (John 8:29). He even went so far as to say, **"I speak to the world those things which I heard from Him"** (John 8:26). We read in 1 Samuel that God says He doesn't see as man sees. That is the racists' problem: If we blindfolded all the racists, we wouldn't have the problem of racism; it's what they *see* that causes the problem, because they always look at the outside, they never look at our hearts, they never consider our character.

Hebrews 13:8 states:

Jesus Christ is the same yesterday, today, and forever.

This tells us that God still looks at the heart and not at the outward appearance. So if you look at the outward appearance, you don't know God. You may know some things about God, but you don't know Him yet, because if you knew Him and were born of His

Spirit, you would have His nature and God would not have raised you to be a racist.

Church, we have a serious problem! People are shouting and singing and having concerts and thinking they are going to sing their way into heaven. Think again. If they think the Lord Jesus Christ is coming back for this racist, prejudiced, lying Church, they aren't using the brains God gave them. We have to fix this. We can't pray it away; we have to confront it directly. Confrontation is always unpleasant, it can even be traumatic, but it has to be done. The sooner we do it and get it over with, the more quickly we can be rid of it and go on to something better. Then we can shout and sing and dance. But until then, we have to fix it. And people will never fix it until someone challenges them. That is why I am writing this book.

In *Beyond the Rivers of Ethiopia*, Dr. Mensa Otabil makes a very vital point:

> Because of the role organized religion has played in the domination of the black race, there is a cry in many quarters for us to go back to our ancestral religions and totally reject the Bible. That is not the way out! When a man is bitten by a snake, it takes an anti-snakebite serum prepared from a snake to bring healing and restoration to that person. I totally believe that if the Bible was misused and misapplied to bind our people, we would need an Anti-Oppression Serum prepared from the revealed Truth in God's word to bring healing, liberty and restoration to us.[5]

I agree 100 percent — because that is the biblical principle. We have a record of it in the Book of Numbers, Chapter 21. We can only cure the problem by taking the truth of God's Word and using it to destroy the lie. That is my mission.

---

[5] Dr. Mensa Otabil, *Beyond the Rivers of Ethiopia* (Bakersfield, California: Pneuma Life Publishing, 1993), 21.

Numbers 21:1-9 tells us:

The king of Arad, the Canaanite, who dwelt in the South, heard that Israel was coming on the road to Atharim. Then he fought against Israel and took some of them prisoners.

So Israel made a vow to the Lord, and said, "If You will indeed deliver this people into my hand, then I will utterly destroy their cities."

And the Lord listened to the voice of Israel and delivered up the Canaanites, and they utterly destroyed them and their cities. So the name of that place was called Hormah.

Then they journeyed from Mount Hor by the Way of the Red Sea, to go around the land of Edom; and the soul of the people became very discouraged on the way.

And the people spoke against God and against Moses: "Why have you brought us up out of Egypt to die in the wilderness? For there is no food and no water, and our soul loathes this worthless bread."

So the Lord sent fiery serpents among the people, and they bit the people; and many of the people in Israel died.

Therefore the people came to Moses, and said, "We have sinned, for we have spoken against the Lord and against you; pray to the Lord that He take away the serpents from us." So Moses prayed for the people.

Then the Lord said to Moses, "Make a fiery serpent [this is the "anti-snakebite serum"], **and set it on a pole;**

and it shall be that everyone who is bitten, when he looks at it, shall live."

So Moses made a bronze serpent, and put it on a pole; and so it was, if a serpent had bitten anyone, when he looked at the bronze serpent, he lived.

The people asked Moses to pray to the Lord to take the serpents away. God didn't take the serpents away; instead, He prepared for them an anti-snakebite serum from the venom of the fiery serpent. He told Moses to make a bronze replica of the snake and set it on a pole, so that when anyone who had been bitten would look at it, that person would be healed.

Thus, God used the same thing to heal people that had originally brought the judgment, but only if the people were obedient. When they looked at the bronze serpent, it represented turning from the government of self to the government of God. This was their salvation.

It would be a grievous mistake to throw the Bible away. Instead, let's make an anti-snakebite serum from the truth revealed in it.

In *Sex and Race, Volume 1,* historian J.A. Rogers says:

The first attempt to found a doctrine of race, based on physical appearance, came with the introduction of Negro slavery in Virginia. Prior to that, "race" was used chiefly as meaning a contest. The King James Version of the Bible uses it only in this sense. Shakespeare also uses it in the sense of "family." But the American slave-holders, finding themselves forced to explain how the teachings of Christ could be reconciled with the cruelties of slavery, set their lackeys, the theologians, who were the "scientists" of that time to find an explanation. Turning to the Bible, the leading "scientific" authority of that period, the servile divines, discovered that Cain had taken a wife from the land of Nod.[6]

In the story of creation, there were then only three people on the planet, Adam, Eve and Cain. Who were the people living in the land of Nod? According to Rogers, this is what the slaveholders and the ministers at that time believed:

> They were pre-Adamites! And pre-Adamites could be no other than Negroes, that is, people who had no part or lot in the creation by God. Moreover, Cain was wicked and low and could have been counted on to marry a Negro. Abel, "the righteous" and respectable would have lived with her in concubinage. Yes, there could be no doubt, whatever, that the people of the land of Nod were Negroes.[7]

It was with interpretations and beliefs such as these that the slaveholders, ministers and the Founding Fathers of this nation could claim to be Christians and also justify slavery. This is the kind of garbage our theology has been built on, and unfortunately this kind of thinking is still alive in our country today.

In the spring of 1996, I received a letter from Joseph Jennings, who has a wonderful ministry to young people. In his letter, he related a very interesting story, part of which occurred because he is black.

> Dear Dr. Price,
>
> Last year I was in Fort Pierce, Florida, in numerous schools. After speaking in a local high school, a crying

---

6 J.A. Rogers, *Sex and Race: Negro-Caucasian Mixing in All Ages and All Lands*, Vol. 1, 9th edition (St. Petersburg, Florida: Helga M. Rogers, 1967), 22.

7 Rogers, 22.

teenage boy walked up and told me that I had just saved his life. During my presentation he had heard me say that he could make it, that there "was hope." I was amazed and asked him what had affected him in such an emotional way? He said that Saturday was Prom Night and afterwards he was going home to a loaded .38 revolver and blow his brains out. He wanted to commit suicide, but he changed his mind.

Afterwards, I was featured in a variety of positive TV news programs, newspaper articles, and radio broadcasts. But the one that really amazed me was the radio ministry of [a white supremacist] who, as a result of that attempted suicide story, featured Joseph Jennings on his message of the week, "How Can a Nigger Tell a White Man He Can't Kill Himself?"

I'm sure the teenager's parents were glad they never taught their son that black people were inferior. This young man might not have been saved from suicide if he had been taught to think that black people were inferior and that their opinions were invalid. Apparently, this never occurred to the white supremacist.

Besides his radio program, the white supremacist had a recorded message that he changed weekly. In Joseph Jennings' letter to me, he wrote that when he called and listened to the white supremacist's message for the week, he was "absolutely astounded" by it. He recommended that I call myself. I did, and this is what I heard:

"Hi. White pride. White pride. It's great to be white. White men fight back. White pride makes the difference.

"Hello, boys and girls. I'm glad you called. It was good of mommy and daddy to teach you how to use a phone so you can call Mr. Wizard. Thank you. It's a wonderful day in my neighborhood because my neighborhood is still all white. Is your neighborhood all white? Is your school all white? I went to an all-white school after my parents saw what a school full of niggers was like. Are there niggers in your school, boys and girls? Can you say nigger? I'm sure you can. Go on, try it. Say nigger. Nigger. That's it. Very good. They call me Mr. Wizard. Can you say wizard? Sure you can. Say wizard. Very good. When your mommy and your daddy love you they protect you from niggers. They put you in a really good private school for white children, so you can learn and become someone important. Mr. Wizard knows you can't learn much when you're ducking niggers all day in school. Niggers are very mean, aren't they? And they smell bad, too. That's because niggers don't like soap. Tell your mommy and daddy you want to go to a good, fun, safe, all-white school. Tell them you don't like the niggers. Tell them to call Mr. Wizard if they say no. They won't say no because your parents love you. If mommy and daddy make you go sit with the niggers, they probably don't care about you. Those kinds of mommies and daddies are stupid. Well, boys and girls, I see by the old clock on the wall that we're out of time. But I'll be back with more of Mr. Wizard's Neighborhood real soon. Be good."

When I hear or read something like this, I have several reactions. The first is to dismiss it as vile, dumb and ignorant, which it is. The second is to realize how abominable it is that anyone is trying to pass these views to children. The third is that as abominable as white supremacists are, at least they are honest enough to let me know where they stand. Some "Christians," who say they operate by truth and by the Bible, won't come out as honestly and state racist views openly so we can hear them, but they hold these views privately. Not everyone, of course, not even the majority; but too many who think of themselves as Christians are secret racists, hiding like snakes. They won't use the word *nigger*. They won't proclaim themselves white supremacists. But they will tell us that we're cursed because we're black, and that our blackness itself is a curse, because, they tell us, "God cursed Ham!"

You may tend to laugh at "Mr. Wizard" with his radio "ministry" and recorded message and tell yourself, "Those are just the opinions of an uneducated bigot." But it's not as simple as that. "Mr. Wizard" has been educated — by racists, just as he is attempting to educate a future generation of racists. He didn't invent the word *nigger*. Nor did he invent all the observations he made about so-called niggers. "They don't like soap." Where did that come from? "They smell bad." Where did that come from?

I've had the privilege of traveling all over the world, and I can tell you smell doesn't have a color. I was in a foreign country with my wife and a white couple picked us up in their car to take us to the meeting at which I was going to speak. I was almost asphyxiated in that vehicle from the foul odor coming from that couple! But although smell has nothing to do with color, our nation has talked about it as if it does. It has done this to justify its behavior. "We can enslave you because you don't like soap and you smell bad." "We can lynch you because you don't like soap and you smell bad."[8] "We can segregate you because you don't like soap and you smell bad." "We can pay you less because you don't like soap and you

---

[8] Between 1882 and 1900, more than 3,000 African-American citizens were lynched. A vast majority of these were in the South. The grounds given for lynching included charges of insulting whites and having bad manners. See Gayle K. Berardi and Thomas W. Segady, "The Development of African-American Newspapers in the American West: A Sociohistorical Perspective, *Journal of Negro History*, Vol. 75, Issue 3/4, Summer/Autumn, 1990, 99. Berardi and Segady cite Ethel R. Dennis, *The Black People of America* (New York,1970), 169, as the source for this statistic. "By 1893, the lynching of Blacks in the South had become such an everyday event that Atticus G. Haygood, a prominent white Methodist bishop and a concerned observer of Southern race relations, complained that the killing of black people 'is not so extraordinary an occurrence to need explanation; it has

smell bad."[9] "We can tell white people not to marry you because you don't like soap and you smell bad."

Let me show you how the word *nigger* has been passed down from generation to generation. In his book, *Boys in the Hoods*, Johnny Lee Clary, a former Imperial Wizard of the KKK who is now a true Christian and preacher of the Gospel, makes an all-important statement about racism. It illustrates the fundamental point I made repeatedly as I taught the series "Race, Religion & Racism": Racism is not in the genes, it's not in the blood, it's in the house where children are raised.

Clary writes:

One day when I was five years old, I was sitting in a car with my father in front of a grocery store in Del City,

---

become so common that it no longer surprises.'" See W. Fitzhugh Brundage, *Lynching in the New South: Georgia and Virginia, 1880-1930* (Chicago: University of Illinois Press, 1993), 8. For more information about the lynching of black people, also see Ralph Ginzburg, *100 Years of Lynching* (New York: Lancer Books, 1962). Related to lynching is the racial bias exhibited in America regarding the hanging of African Americans. For example, according to Harriet Frazier, former professor of criminal justice at Central Missouri State University, "Rape in Missouri was punishable by hanging. For decades, however, death sentences for rape were given only to black men convicted of assaulting white women." See Rich Montgomery, "Photo Exhibit Resurrects Grim History of Missouri," Knight-Ridder/Tribune News Service, March 1, 2000.

[9] The National Urban League reports that "In the 1990s, after nearly 50 years of civil rights activities and affirmative action programs, Blacks earned 59% of what Whites earn." Further, the 1990 Census indicated that black per capita net worth was $9,359 versus $44,980 for Whites. See Claud Anderson, *Black Labor, White Wealth* (Bethesda, Maryland: PowerNomics Corporation of America Inc., 1994), 13. Dr. Anderson cites the U.S. Census Bureau's 1990 data, the National Urban League's 1988 and 1992 reports on the state of black America, and a 1990 published report from the Joint Center for Economic Studies.

Oklahoma, a small town outside of Oklahoma City. The year was 1964 [not 1619, not 1776, not 1865, but 1964], and it was the first time in my life that I had seen a black person.

As a black man walked out of the store, I sat amazed and shocked. Turning to my father, I exclaimed, "Look, Daddy! A chocolate covered man!"

My father looked at me and replied, "Son, that is not a chocolate covered man. That's a 'nigger.' Say 'nigger,' son; say, 'nigger.'"

Innocent and unsuspecting, I blared out the window of the car, "Nigger, nigger, nigger!"

My dad laughed hilariously, jabbing his cigar into his mouth and blowing a puff of smoke in the air.

That incident marked the day when the first seed of racism was planted in my heart.[10]

This is exactly why I say that it's necessary to go back to the past so that we can identify and uproot whatever is inconsistent with the Word of God.

In an article entitled *Grace and Race,* Maurice I. Irvin, who is white, states:

> Dr. Billy Graham has said, "Of all people, Christians should be the most active in reaching out to those of other races" (*Christianity Today,* October 4, 1993). However, few white evangelicals *reach out.* Rather, we stay within our white circles and ignore those who are "different."

---

[10] Johnny Lee Clary, *Boys in the Hoods* (Bakersfield, California: Pneuma Life Publishing, 1995), ix.

In a 1994 article in *Focus on the Family* magazine, Glen Kehrein points out that a few years ago, Bill Moyers did a television special called "Crisis in America: The Vanishing Black Family." After laying out the tremendous problems of the black underclass, Moyers assembled a panel of experts to suggest "solutions." Incredibly, no one represented the church because it was perceived as a non-player in the arena of race relations.[11]

It's pitiful that the panel didn't include any representatives of the Church because the perception was that the Church doesn't care about this area, that it doesn't have anything to say about it. Or is the perception that the Church has done so much to contribute to the perpetuation of racism, how could it possibly contribute to its cure?

The article goes on to say what the writer, from his perspective as a white person, sees as the problem in the Church:

> Most seriously, many white Christians are quite satisfied with a lack of interracial interaction, particularly with African Americans, because we are to some degree racist in heart.
>
> Most of us will deny this stoutly, but in fact many of us never have allowed the Lord to expose and root out our prejudices. A few months ago, a group of evangelical leaders publicly acknowledged that "racism continues to exist within the church in the form of systemic and structural discrimination, segregation and stereotyping," and these leaders called these things "ungodly injustices."

The article further states:

---

[11] Maurice Irvin , "Grace and Race," *Alliance Life: A Biweekly Publication of the Christian and Missionary Alliance*, Vol. 130, No. 14, August 9, 1995, 6,12.

Prejudice, discrimination and segregation clearly are contrary to the teaching of God's Word. Redemption makes every believer, whatever his race, a brother or sister in Christ (Ephesians 2:14-15). We are part of one Body (Ephesians 4:4-5). Galatians 3:26-28 teaches that cultural and racial distinctions are not to be carried over into the life of the church.

Jesus told us to love others. He rebuked racial prejudice with the parable of the Good Samaritan. He modeled racial tolerance in John 4 by deliberately traveling through Samaria and by ministering to a Samaritan woman. Jews looked upon Samaritans with much the same disdain as whites have tended to feel towards blacks in America. And what could be clearer than the admonition of Romans 15:7: "Accept one another, then, just as Christ accepted you, in order to bring praise to God" (NIV). The parable of the Good Samaritan also teaches that neutrality is not an option.

This has been one of the major problems with racism in the white segment of the Church. Even though the majority of white people are not racist — and thank God they're not — the problem is their silence. Many who are not racist have said nothing to friends, relatives and coworkers who are racists about racism being wrong, so these people feel justified in perpetuating their racism. That's what Irvin is talking about when he says:

The parable of the Good Samaritan also teaches that neutrality is not an option.

Irvin concludes:

We cannot remain on "the other side" of our communities and ignore people who need our help. First John 3:17 rebukes the Christian who sees a brother in need but has no pity on him. Romans 12:13 says, "Share with

God's people who are in need," and Black Christians are God's people.

We cannot be neutral in regard to racism; we can only be for it or against it.

As Jesus said in Matthew 12:30: **"He who is not with Me is against Me, and he who does not gather with Me scatters abroad."**

11

The Necessity of Recognition

 In his article "Changing Habits of the Heart," Chris Rice, who happens to be white, has some interesting things to say about the possibilities for improving the relationship between the races in the Church, and what it will take to bring this about.

Truces are being signed, flags of surrender waved, promises made, forgiveness requested and granted, and peace pipes passed as never before. Thirty years ago many whites stood on the sidelines while black believers suffered for the sake of justice. But today it seems we may be heading into a new era of racial harmony that could go down as one of the Church's finest hours.

But if we keep old habits, "reconciliation" will become a cheap cliché, and this new enthusiasm just a temporary fad. What will ensure that the seeds God is patiently sowing do not get choked by the tendency to retreat to our old ways?

Four changes in habit could help reconciliation go the distance.

1. Theological Shift: Action follows thinking. Addressing racial division and separation in the Church is not

137

optional — it is fundamental to who we are. Reconciliation is a non-negotiable responsibility that must begin to be reflected in our theology.

2. Relational Shift: Nothing will give reconciliation a surer foothold in the Church than one-to-one friendships of genuine trust formed across racial lines, especially between leaders. Why would children, students and congregations take "optional" risks and sacrifices that their parents, teachers and pastors aren't willing to take? Leaders only will be able to guide others as they experience this trust in their own lives.

3. Paradigm Shift: The biblical model of reconciliation is being challenged fiercely by three competitors. "Homogeneous church" models — with two extremes being white homogeneity and black Afrocentrism — preach a gospel that "saves" but is too weak to reconcile. Jesus never settled for that. "Integration," meaning whites with a sprinkling of minorities, is still the most popular concept of race relations. But integration has been a one-way street that ultimately costs whites very little. Reconciliation cannot be forced and will be evidenced by friendships, common mission and mutual submission extending beyond Sunday morning.

4. Resource Shift: Churches, denominations, campus groups, periodicals, radio and TV programs, associations and action groups must put weight behind what we believe. A commitment to reconciliation will add a whole new dimension to already complicated decisions such as selecting leaders, planting churches (thousands more specifically interracial churches need to be planted), hiring staff, building networks and choosing priorities. But if racial reconciliation is to become a sign by which Christians are identified, it is time we unleashed the resources of the Church in an all-out invasion against racial segregation. God is once again tearing down the walls of separation. This

> time, let's create some habits of the heart to ensure
> our witness of reconciliation lasts long after the
> honeymoon is over.[1]

I applaud Rice for this fine, timely and insightful article. But I'd like us to focus on his use of the word *reconciliation* in reference to black people and white people. This is a term we have been hearing in the Church today. I would certainly not say anything negative concerning anyone's efforts to make reconciliation a reality in our troubled times. However, I would like to suggest that reconciliation, even though it is a very worthy endeavor, is totally out of place right now in our society, because reconciliation is not the issue. Let me clarify what I mean.

In *Webster's New International Dictionary*, we find that the first definition of *reconcile* is:

> To cause to be friendly again; to restore to friendship; to
> bring back to harmony; as, to reconcile persons who
> have quarreled.[2]

This definition pinpoints why I disagree with the idea of reconciliation between Blacks and Whites. *Webster's* says *reconcile*

---

[1] Chris Rice, "Changing Habits of the Heart," *Alliance Life*, 9. Note that from a theological point of view, according to *Vine's Expository Dictionary of Old and New Testament Words*, reconciliation is the English translation of the Greek word *katallasso*. *Vine's* explains: *Katallasso* "with regard to the relationship between God and man, the use of this and connected words shows that primarily 'reconciliation' is what God accomplishes, exercising His grace towards sinful man on the ground of the death of Christ in propitiatory sacrifice under the judgment due to sin," 2 Corinthians 5:19. See W.E. Vine, *Vine's Expository Dictionary of Old and New Testament Words* (Nashville: Thomas Nelson Publishers, 1984, 1996), 513-514.

[2] *Webster's New International Dictionary*; Second Edition, Unabridged (Springfield, Massachusetts: G and C Merriam Co. Publishers, 1960), 2080.

means "to restore friendship." Reconciliation cannot work between black people and white people because in this nation and in the Church, we have never been friends.

According to *Webster's*, the first definition for *friend* is:

> One who entertains for another such sentiments of esteem, respect, and affection that he seeks his society and welfare.[3]

"Esteem"? "Respect"? "Affection"? "Seeks his society and welfare"? Does any of this describe the American society's or the Church's feelings for and behavior towards black people? This is why I say that although reconciliation is being put forth by people of good intentions and good hearts — people who want to do what's right — it is the wrong concept for the needs of our time. Only equals can be reconciled. You cannot reconcile a dog and a man. They are not equals. And black people in America and in the Church have never been accepted as equals by the society as a whole and by the Church as a whole. We have been accepted as inferiors. And you cannot reconcile an equal with an inferior. The first step toward a good relationship between Blacks and Whites is not reconciliation, but *recognition*. We need the Church, the white church, to accept once and for all that when the Bible says in Acts 17:26: **"And He has made from one blood every nation of men..."** God is making it very clear that like all other people, we are equal with white people.

This is a hard pill for some to swallow. "Equal with a nigger?!" some will say to themselves. Racist beliefs have been part of some people's thinking for so many generations that they run deep. When is the white church going to start believing the Bible when it tells us in Galatians 3:28, **"There is neither Jew nor Greek, there is neither slave nor free, there is neither male nor female; for you are all one in Christ Jesus"**? When is the Church going to start practicing

---

[3] *Webster's*, 1009.

that from the inside? When is the Church really going to change its habits of the heart?

If the majority of the Church and society had respected black people and considered us friends, they never would have made us ride in the back of the bus. We would have ridden in the front of the bus with them. And I would never make my friend come to my house and drink out of a water fountain marked "Colored Only." My friends drink out of the same fountain I drink out of; they eat at the same table I eat at. Why did they have a "colored" restroom and a "white" restroom? Why did they make black children go to a run-down building they called a school and give them an inferior education?[4] Why

---

[4] There has been a long history of America offering inferior education to Blacks. African Americans' desire for education following the Civil War is evident in the fact that as educational opportunities for Blacks became somewhat available between 1870 and 1910, black people's overall literacy rate rose from 20 percent to 70 percent. Indeed, between 1880 and 1910, about 1,876 African-American newspapers were known to be in existence. By 1910, the literacy rate for African Americans was almost 90 percent in the West, twice what it was in the South during the same period. See Gayle K. Berardi and Thomas W. Segady, "The Development of African-American Newspapers in the West; A Sociohistorical Perspective," 86-111. Despite black people's desire for education, in the latter part of the 19th Century, black schools in Missouri, for example, were in dilapidated quarters and were frequently moved to new locations, forcing black students to walk long distances, often passing white schools closer to their homes. Until 1890, most black schools were not given names like white schools but were numbered — Colored School No. 1, Colored School No. 2 — and their teachers were paid about half of what teachers in white schools were paid. Black students were also given old books. Still, until 1905 when Missouri law made education compulsory, there were more black children enrolled in schools in St. Louis than there were white children of a similar economic status. See Amy Stuart Wells and Robert L. Crain, *Stepping Over the Color Line: African-American Students in White Suburban Schools* (New Haven, Connecticut: Yale University Press, 1997), 76-79.

In the year 2000, public education for black and other minority children in low-income families — which is the majority of black and other minority children — was still inferior. According to Kati Haycock

were black people given inferior medical treatment, even when it could cost them their lives?[5] Why were black people the subjects of

---

and M. Susana Navarro, "Into the education of poor and minority children, we put less of everything we believe makes a difference. Less experienced and well-trained teachers. Less instructional time. Less rich and well-balanced curricula. Less well-equipped facilities. And less of what may be most important of all: The belief that these youngsters can really learn. All in all, we teach poor and minority students less." See Haycock and Navarro, "A Report From the Achievement Council," *Unfinished Business: Fulfilling Our Children's Promise* (Oakland, California: Inkworks Press, 1990), 3-4. In 1905, reviewing Charles Carroll's book *The Negro A Beast*, Edward Atkinson commented: "The fact [is] now recognized that the only safe foundation for the government of the people by the people is the public school." Lamentably, as far as black and other minority children are concerned, today, almost 100 years after Atkinson wrote this statement, equal public education has yet to be provided. See Edward Atkinson, "The Negro A Beast," *The North American Review*, August 1905. For more information about the discrepancies between white and black education, see Charles Wollenberg, *All Deliberate Speed: Segregation and Exclusion in California Schools, 1855-1975,* (Berkeley: University of California Press, 1976). Also see *The Education Watch, Vol. II, 1998* (Washington, D.C.: The Education Trust, Inc., 1998), 10-17, which was created to promote high academic achievement for all students, primarily focusing on the schools and colleges most frequently neglected: those educating low-income, African American, Latino and Native American students. According to *The Education Watch*, though students are entitled to the same education, the reason they don't get it is because, "We teach different students different things." Students from low-income families are generally automatically enrolled in vocational courses; only a little more than 28 percent are placed in college preparatory courses. But more than 65 percent from high-income families are routinely enrolled in college preparatory classes. A second reason for the educational disadvantage among minority students is that some of them get lower quality instruction, i.e. lack of reading and math resources, poor teachers.

[5] In her book on the life of physician Charles R. Drew, Spencie Love quotes from a 1948 report by the National Committee on Segregation in the nation's capital, pointing out the "disproportionate disease and death rates of Washington's black citizens." This is only one example reflecting the inferior medical treatment historically offered to black people in America, but it is typical of what happened to Blacks in the

experiments that harmed their health without them even knowing the experiments were being done on them?[6] Esteem? Respect? Affection? I don't think so.

The white church is largely responsible for the problems of racism in the United States because the white church is the majority of society. The biblical principle is, **"For everyone to whom much is given, from him much will be required"** (Luke 12:48). And much has been given to the Whites in America!

South and, in a less formalized manner, in many places outside the South. The report attributed the greater death and disease rate among Blacks in Washington not only to the poorer living conditions of the city's segregated black citizens but also to limited medical and hospital care. The hospital facilities available to black residents were inferior, the report noted, and did not come close to meeting black patients' "greater need" of them. The report pointed out that Freedmen's and Gallinger's, the two hospitals that served the bulk of black patients, operated on inadequate budgets, and the segregated accommodations for black patients offered fewer beds and other significant resources. The report further noted that the color line was rigidly maintained when black beds were full, even when white beds were available. In 1945, for example, a young black woman had been forced to deliver her baby on the sidewalk on a cold winter morning after being refused admission to one of the private church-supported white hospitals. See Spencie Love, *One Blood: The Death and Resurrection of Charles R. Drew* (Chapel Hill: University of North Carolina Press, 1996), 173. Drew was the first doctor to set up a blood bank after evidence from the research he was conducting at Columbia University showed that blood plasma could supplant whole blood transfusions. Drew died tragically at 45 years old when he dozed off while driving from Washington to Tuskegee, Alabama, and his car ran off the highway in North Carolina. There seems to be little substance to reports that he was denied prompt and efficient medical attention because of his race.

[6] One such experiment, the Tuskegee Study, was revealed in 1972, after 40 years of deception. This study constituted the longest non-therapeutic experiment on human beings in medical history. Such government agencies as the United States Public Health Service, the Alabama State Department of Health and the Veterans Hospitals, along with several practicing physicians in Macon County, Alabama — even the Tuskegee Institute, a black college founded by African-American educator and author Booker T. Washington — conspired to keep 399

In 1906, God gave the Church the opportunity to unify itself, to bring all Christians of every ethnicity and color together as one to make a statement to the world. That year, He visited this planet in Los Angeles, at a place called Azusa Street, through a black, one-eyed preacher named William J. Seymour. This coming of the Holy Spirit, which gave rise to the Pentecostal church, was called the "Azusa Revival" or "Awakening." People came from all over the globe to experience it. God was moving in a mighty way. But how did white Christians react? Because a black man, William Seymour, was the point man for this Awakening, instead of remaining together in esteem, respect, affection and friendship with African Americans, in a short time white Christians in essence said, "We're not going to mix with black people and have congregations and churches with them. We're going to have our own Pentecostal churches." And that is exactly what they did.[7]

---

black men suffering from syphilis not only ignorant of their disease but also untreated. None of these men was ever told that he was part of a study; they were all simply left to suffer and informed that they had "bad blood," a term used to describe any number of physical ailments. One of the most shocking and inhumane aspects of this study is that a chief coordinating physician, Dr. Raymond Vonderlehr, was said to have encouraged the continued observation of these men "with the idea of eventually bringing them to autopsy."

Racist attitudes helped to establish and sustain the study. Many of the white doctors were convinced that syphilis was more prevalent among Blacks than Whites. Some even referred to their black patients — if these subjects of experiment can actually be called "patients" — as "ignorant and stupid." Apparently, none of the doctors was bothered by ethical questions, even though the doctors were denying these black men treatment with salvarsan or mercury in the 1930s and penicillin after it was discovered in the 1940s. It was viewed as perfectly acceptable to lie and watch them slowly disintegrate. What is equally astounding is how the Tuskegee Institute allowed itself to become part of such a deception of its own people in order to succeed in a white-dominated society. For more information on this medical study that produced nothing of any enduring scientific value, see James H. Jones, *Bad Blood: The Tuskegee Syphilis Experiment* (New York: Free Press, 1981).

[7] Seymour, the son of emancipated slaves, was born in the bayou country of Louisiana in 1870. As a young man, he was a member of the all-black Methodist Episcopal Church. Upon moving to Cincinnati, Ohio,

The Necessity of Recognition

This isn't the only example of segregated churches. Many white churches wouldn't let black people into their congregations.

---

he joined the Evening Light Saints, who taught holiness, divine healing, racial equality, and the outpouring of the Holy Spirit before the Second Coming of Christ. Shortly thereafter, he contracted smallpox and was left blind in one eye. Seymour was so eager to learn about glossalalia (speaking in unknown languages; also called speaking in tongues), which Pentecostal leader Charles Parham touted as the evidence of having received the true baptism of the Holy Spirit, that he sat outside segregated classes taught by Parham. When Seymour shared this knowledge in a small church in Los Angeles that he had just come to pastor, the doors of the church were locked in rejection of this teaching. Not discouraged, Seymour continued in private homes until a member of his prayer group spoke in tongues. Word quickly spread that an outpouring of the Spirit had hit. To accommodate the crowds, Seymour moved his Apostolic Faith Mission to Azusa Street.

It has been said that at the Azusa Street Revival, "The color line was washed away in blood." Nearly every account of the revival that sparked the American Pentecostal Movement notes that at Azusa, all people — Blacks, Whites, Asians, Indians — worshipped freely together. Never in history had any such multiracial group surged at one time into one single church. This alone was miraculous, but for all of them to come together under the leadership of a black man made this revival particularly noteworthy. Such unity was not to last long. With the onslaught of visitors came prominent would-be pastors who played on Seymour's ethnicity and doctrinal differences to establish their own churches. It was not long before new denominations were formed, the most notable being the white-dominated Assemblies of God that was founded in 1914, less than two years after Charles Parham, whose segregated Bible classes Seymour had once sat outside, declared that the free intermingling of worship between the races at Azusa was "an awful shame." By 1916, the American Pentecostal Movement had divided into three major doctrinal camps, and by the early 1930s each of these had split along racial lines. This pattern of racism set such a precedent that in 1948, when the Pentecostal Fellowship of North America was formed for the distinct purpose of demonstrating to the world the fulfillment of Christ's prayer for unity, only white organizations were invited to join. And by 1965, it remained exclusively white. See Timothy E. Fulop and Albert J. Raboteau, eds., *African-American Religion: Interpretive Essays in History and Culture* (New York: Routledge, 1997), 297-309. See also Mircea Eliade, ed. *The Encyclopedia of Religion* (New York: Macmillan Publishing, 1987), Vol. 16, 232. For more information on the Azusa Street Revival, see L.

Why do you think there are black Baptists and black Methodists and other black churches? Because white people would not let us worship with them. This is history![8]

If we do not understand the past, we cannot uproot it, and if we don't uproot it, we will continue to perpetuate the attitudes of the past in the future. However well meaning people are, when they talk about reconciliation, they are missing the point: We cannot reconcile because we have never been equals, we have never been one, we have never been friends. I've said this before, but I must say it

---

Grant McLung, Jr., ed., *Azusa Street and Beyond: Pentecostal Missions and Church Growth in the Twentieth Century* (South Plainfield, New Jersey: Bridge Publishing, 1986). According to Microsoft Encarta Encyclopedia, Online Deluxe, "Black and white denominations within the U.S. Pentecostal Church voted in 1994 to create a national multiracial association."

[8] While both the Baptist and Methodist churches were initially against slavery, their members were not opposed to practicing segregation. Blacks were made to sit in galleries or in the back pews, sometimes even outside. In one instance, Richard Allen, Absalom Jones, William White and other black members of the St. George Methodist Episcopal Church in Philadelphia were dragged from a church service while they were on their knees in prayer. They had mistakenly taken seats in a section of the church reserved for Whites only. This incident has traditionally been regarded as the catalyst for the formation of the African American Methodist Episcopal Church and subsequent similar Protestant denominations. In other cases, Whites simply withdrew their membership from a church once the black membership became too large, leaving the black members to sustain themselves as a separate church. Occasionally, black churches, particularly those of the Baptist faith, rose up independently to meet the needs of black people that were being ignored by the established white churches. See Albert J. Raboteau, *Slave Religion: The "Invisible Institution" in the Antebellum South* (New York: Oxford University Press, 1978), 131, 137-138, 142-145. See also Joseph R. Washington, Jr., *Black Religion: The Negro and Christianity in the United States* (Boston: Beacon Press, 1966), 186-201. For more information regarding the splitting of the Protestant Church, see Milton C. Sernett, *Black Religion and American Evangelicalism: White Protestants, Plantation Missions, and the Flowering of Negro Christianity, 1787-1865* (Metuchen, New Jersey: Scarecrow Press Inc. and the American Theological Library Association, 1975).

again because it is something that the dominant white society and the Church still do not accept and act on: We *are* equal, and we must be recognized as equal. We have not just become equal, we have always been equal; the problem has been that the society and the Church have not wanted to recognize this. Yes, even in chains before the slave master we were equal in the eyes of God.

We know Acts 17:26 tells us: **"And He has made from one blood every nation of men...."** I don't understand how God could make out of one blood all the nations of the earth and somehow, when black people and white people intermarry, just because of the pigmentation of skin, black skin is seen as polluting that one blood that everyone has. How is it that the blood of black people is seen as inferior blood? I invite the foremost hematologist to explain this to me.

Esteem? Respect? Affection? Jim Crow was how Whites respected us.[9] Until comparatively recently, our country required black

---

[9] In Chapter 1, we looked generally at how the South used Jim Crow laws to subjugate black people after the Emancipation Proclamation and Civil War. Professor James H. Dormon reports that the origin of the term *Jim Crow* can, perhaps, be traced to the early 19th Century. He states that in the late 1820s, a stereotype of the Negro began to emerge on the American stage as a character known as Jim Crow. First introduced by Thomas Dartmouth Rice, this "comic rustic song and dance figure" was enormously popular among white audiences and quickly inspired imitators. The Jim Crow character was presented as a type of human not to be taken seriously; he was certainly not to be afforded any form of equality with white people. In this way, entertainment was effectively used to reinforce the racism of the day. See James H. Dormon, "Shaping the Popular Image of Post-Reconstruction American Blacks: The 'Coon Song' Phenomenon of the Gilded Age," *American Quarterly*, Vol. 40, Issue 4, December, 1988, 450-451.

With the Jim Crow character vivid in the minds of the Southern audience, it's no wonder that when the former slave states were looking for ways to maintain control of the recently freed slaves, they reverted to this popular stereotype that lent support to the image of black people as unworthy and incapable of equality with Whites.

Historians also refer to "cradle-to-grave segregation," which resulted from the various Jim Crow laws that segregated everything from children's playgrounds to cemeteries. In fact, in one Southern

men to fight its wars so that it could continue Jim Crowism. Even while we were fighting, they segregated us. We were not good enough to fight side by side with white people for their freedom, but we could fight by ourselves for their freedom.[10] And when we came

---

town, a black man found himself in trouble when his horse drank from the same trough as horses owned by white people. See Gayle K. Berardi and Thomas W. Segady, "The Development of African-American Newspapers in the American West: A Sociohistorical Perspective," *Journal of Negro History*, Vol. 75, Issue ¾, Summer/ Autumn, 1990, 100.

   Because segregation became so intimately entwined with everyday life, much of our nation's social and economic history is reflected in the Jim Crow laws. For example, in the 1920s, when women began to bob their hair and become patrons at barber shops, Atlanta passed an ordinance forbidding Negro barbers to serve women or children under 14 years of age. With the emergence of taxicabs, Mississippi passed a law in 1922 requiring Jim Crow cab service. This law soon spread to other prominent Southern cities such as Birmingham and Atlanta, where signs were required to be painted in contrasting colors on cabs, identifying which race the cab served. Only white drivers could drive white people and black drivers black people. In the 1930s, federal law stepped in to hinder the circulation of Hollywood films showing interracial boxing because Jim Crow laws in many states prohibited the races from competing in athletic events. For more information about Jim Crow laws, see C. Vann Woodward, *The Strange Career of Jim Crow* (New York: Oxford University Press, 1974), 116-117.

[10] African Americans have fought in every war this country has engaged in, beginning with the American Revolution. But it was not until 1866 that congressional legislation was passed permitting the first enlistment of African Americans into the regular army. This in no way meant that black men were assured of equal treatment in the armed services. For a brief history of African Americans serving in the U.S. military and how they were segregated from the white military regiments, see Debra Newman Ham, ed., *The African American Odyssey* (Washington, D.C.: Library of Congress, 1998), 83-103. Ham notes that in addition to being segregated from the white fighting units in World War I, attempts were made by the U.S. government to segregate black soldiers from the local civilians where they were stationed. When the French government requested American soldiers to fill vacancies in their front line of defense, the all-black 369th Regiment was sent. But while

back, they still wouldn't let us live in the same neighborhoods as white people.[11] I want this to sink in, because we're looking for the

---

serving in France, the American Expeditionary Forces distributed a circular entitled, "Secret Information Concerning Black American Troops," which told French civilians to "avoid all social contacts and any attempts to integrate black soldiers into activities beyond military operations." As if this was not horrendous enough, the summer after World War I ended, more than 70 African Americans were lynched, several of them by veterans still in uniform. See C. Vann Woodward, 114-115. During World War II, African-American soldiers were still not integrated with white soldiers or treated as their equals. Segregation was the policy, and any exceptions to the "rule" were markedly few. Strict segregation was enforced both on the base and off, with white commanding officers adhering to the racist practices of local authorities. While black soldiers comprised about 9 percent of all draftees, the majority were inducted into the Army and assigned non-combat duties, such as cooking and cleaning. Throughout the war, only one black man, Ensign Dennis Nelson, commanded an integrated logistical support unit, only one gained admission to the Naval Academy, and only one black officer reached the rank of lieutenant.

For information on the role African Americans played in the Vietnam War, see Wallace Terry, ed., *Bloods: An Oral History of the Vietnam War* by Black Veterans (New York: Ballantine, 1985).

[11] A shameful example of this occurred in 1924, when, according to Wells and Crain, "The National Association of Real Estate Boards adopted an article in its code of ethics stating that a real estate agent should never introduce into a neighborhood 'members of any race or nationality ... whose presence will clearly be detrimental to property values in the neighborhood.' " Then the National Association of Real Estate Boards made it possible for state commissions to revoke the licenses of any agents who violated this code. Wells and Crain, *Stepping Over the Color Line*, 40.

The National Association of Real Estate Boards adopted this article six years after black soldiers had served in World War I and just three years after the terrible violence of the Red Summer of 1921 — so named because of the bloodshed perpetrated by white people against Blacks in cities across America, from Tulsa, Oklahoma, to Chicago, to Washington, D.C. For more about the destruction of Tulsa's Black Wall Street and the Red Summer, see Scott Ellsworth and John Hope

root systems so that we can get racism out of our systems. The reason many white people do not respect us today is because, based on the root systems of the past, they think they are better than we are. I know of situations where a white person has married a black person and even in their relationship, the white spouse thinks he or she is better than the black spouse. Unfortunately, this kind of thinking is also still present in the Church.

Although religious writing is my primary focus in this book, I have included some other relevant secular writing, too, in order to present a fuller picture of society. People in society go to church; people in society also claim to be Christians. How can we separate our Christianity from public service? We can't. Separating our Christianity from anything that we do is hypocritical; we must be the same in public as we are in private.

In this context, let's look at the Dred Scott case, one of the most significant cases to be decided by the United States Supreme Court in terms of white attitudes towards black people. The Supreme Court's decision reflected the thinking of many white people, particular Southerners, in mid–19th Century America.

Franklin, *Death in a Promised Land* (Baton Rouge: Louisiana State University Press, 1982) and Cedric J. Robinson, *Black Movements in America* (New York: Routledge, 1997), 116-117.

As 70 black men were lynched following World War I, there was also violence against African Americans during and following World War II, this time specifically related to Whites not wanting to live near Blacks. Wells and Crain report that "during World War II, a rash of anti-black violence erupted in cities around the country as defense industry jobs drew white workers off the farms, creating a shortage of housing and severe overcrowding in the cities for blacks and whites alike. White homeowners and tenants increasingly resorted to violence as Blacks encroached upon their neighborhoods. In Chicago, for instance, Whites assaulted 46 black homeowners between May 1944 and July 1946. And from 1945 through the 1950s, large-scale riots over the black occupation of previously all-white neighborhoods broke out in Chicago and Detroit, with lesser disturbances in St. Louis, New York and Philadelphia. The violence subsided as segregated suburbia blossomed, allowing many Whites to flee the cities rather than stay and fight for their urban neighborhoods." See Wells and Crain, 40.

In 1846, Dred Scott and his wife Harriet appealed to the Supreme Court for their freedom. They had filed a suit because, even though they were held as slaves in Missouri, their master, John F.A. Sanford, had transported them into free territory in Illinois and in other parts of the U.S. territory in which the Missouri Compromise of 1820 had prohibited slavery. The Lower courts had supported the rights of Sanford to take his slaves anywhere he wanted, so Dred and Harriet Scott brought their case to the Supreme Court, the highest court in the land.[12] Remember, we're talking about this in the context of esteem, respect, affection, friendship.

What did the Supreme Court say when it finally gave its decision eleven years later? Out of nine judges, seven voted to deny Dred and Harriet Scott their freedom. In addition, the Supreme Court decided that being of African descent meant that they and all black people in America — even freed slaves and children born to freed slaves — were not actually citizens of America, and therefore did not have the rights of citizens.

In *History of the United States From the Compromise of 1850*, historian James Ford Rhodes says:

> Two days after the inauguration of Buchanan, Chief Justice Taney delivered the opinion of the court. He stated that one of the questions to be decided was: "Can a Negro whose ancestors were imported into this country and sold as slaves become a member of the political community formed and brought into existence by the Constitution of the United States, and as such become entitled to all the rights, and privileges, and immunities, guaranteed by that instrument to the citizen...?" The answer is no. Negroes "were not intended to be included under the word *citizens* in the Constitution, and therefore can claim none of the rights and privileges which

---

[12] See "Scott v. Sanford (The Dred Scott Decision)," in *Landmark Documents on the U.S. Congress*, Raymond W. Smock, ed. (Washington, D.C: Congressional Quarterly, 1999), 185-186.

that instrument provides for and secures to the citizens of the United States."

"Moreover, in the opinion of the Court, the legislation and histories of the times, and the language used in the Declaration of Independence, show that neither the class of person who had been imported as slaves, nor their descendants, whether they had become free or not, were then acknowledged as part of the people, nor intended to be included in the general words used in that memorable instrument. It is difficult, at this day, to realize the state of public opinion in relation to that unfortunate race which prevailed in the civilized and enlightened portions of the world at the time of the Declaration of Independence, and when the Constitution was framed and adopted. But the public history of every European nation displays it in a manner too plain to be mistaken.

"They had for more than a century before been regarded as beings of an inferior order, and altogether unfit to associate with the white race, either in social or political relations; and so far inferior that they had no rights which the white man was bound to respect, and that the Negro might justly and lawfully be reduced to slavery for his benefit."[13]

Esteem? Respect? Affection?

Rhodes goes on to comment about the way slaves were treated in slave states and about how black people were viewed not just by Southern slaveholders, but by some other Americans, including the majority of the Supreme Court.

[A slave was] bought and sold, and treated as an ordinary article of merchandise and traffic, whenever a

---

[13] James Ford Rhodes, *History of the United States From the Compromise of 1850* (Chicago: University of Chicago Press, 1966), 219-221.

profit could be made by it. The opinion was at that time fixed and universal in the civilized portion of the white race. It was regarded as an axiom in morals as well as in politics, which no one thought of disputing, or supposed to be open to dispute; and men in every grade and position in society daily and habitually acted upon it in their private pursuits, as well as in matters of public concern, without doubting for a moment the correctness of this opinion.

Citing the famous clause of the Declaration of Independence which asserted "that all men are created equal," the chief justice [please take note, this is the Chief Justice of the highest court of the land] said: "The general words above quoted would seem to embrace the whole human family, and if they were used in a similar instrument at this day would be so understood. But it is too clear for dispute that the enslaved African race were not intended to be included, and formed no part of the people who framed and adopted this Declaration."[14]

---

[14] Rhodes, 219-221. The Dred Scott Decision was one of the most important legal pronouncements affecting Blacks during both the antebellum and postbellum periods. As a result of the decision, Whites understood that, at least legally, black Americans had no rights that Whites were bound to respect. For a brief, but excellent account of the famous, or infamous, Dred Scott case, see *Dred Scott v. Sandford, A Brief History With Documents*, by Paul Finkelman (Boston: Bedford Books, 1997). Also see, *The Dred Scott Case: Its Significance in American Law and Politics* by Don E. Fehrenbacher (New York: Oxford University Press, 1978). The consensus of the judges in the Supreme Court was clearly a victory for the Southern states' advocacy of slavery. But, ironically, the Dred Scott Decision also served as a wake-up call to the North. Northern states, which did not want slavery to spread to their states, both for moral reasons and because they saw slavery as a feudal institution which would jeopardize their own industrial future,

Let's look at black people from the viewpoint of the primary author of the Declaration of Independence, Thomas Jefferson. Although Jefferson is rightly acknowledged for his attempt to insert in the Declaration of Independence a clause that

---

realized that with the Court's decision to legalize slavery nationwide, the Northern policy of nonintervention would no longer work. With Congress now having to protect slavery in the West, it would inevitably spread to the free states; either all the states were going to be slave-free or all of the country would eventually be forced to permit slavery. This revelation finally woke some people to the biblical admonition, later quoted by President Lincoln, that a "house divided against itself will not stand" (Matthew 12:25). A determination had to be made one way or another. The result, of course, was the Civil War. See F.H. Hodder, "Some Phases of the Dred Scott Case," *The Mississippi Valley Historical Review,* Vol. 16, Issue 1, June, 1929, 3-22. Also see Don E. Fehrenbacher, "The Origins and Purpose of Lincoln's 'House Divided' Speech," *The Mississippi Valley Historical Review*, Vol. 46, Issue 4, March, 1960, 615-643. For more information on the effects of the Dred Scott Decision on the liberty of African Americans, see John Hope Franklin, Alfred A. Moss, Jr., *From Slavery to Freedom: A History of African-Americans* (New York: McGraw-Hill, 1994). An additional note on the Dred Scott Decision: Only a few weeks after the Supreme Court denied Dred Scott his freedom, Taylor Blow, one of the sons of Scott's first master, bought Scott as a slave and granted him his freedom. See Walter Ehrlich, "The Origins of the Dred Scott Case," *The Journal of Negro History*, Vol. 59, Issue 2, April, 1974, 139. As his source, Ehrlich cites the Permanent Records (No. 26, 1856-1857), 163, Circuit Court of St. Louis County, Missouri, Circuit Court, St. Louis; Daily Missouri Republican, St. Louis, May 27, 1857. A good source for understanding the Northerners' underlying economic motives — versus their "moral" reasons — for opposing slavery is *Free Soil, Free Labor, Free Men: The Ideology of the Republican Party Before the Civil War* by Edwin Burwinger (New York: Oxford University Press, 1970). Also, for an outstanding brief interpretive account of Northern and Southern White views about race throughout American history, see John Hope Franklin's *Racial Equality in America* (University Press: Chicago and London, 1976).

would have freed the slaves,[15] he was also tainted by the bigoted views of his time.

For example, although Jefferson knew that Southern laws prohibited white people from teaching slaves to read and that there had been no such laws in ancient Rome where slavery had also been practiced, he insisted the reason some slaves in ancient Rome were philosophers or scientists whereas African-American slaves were not was because these ancient slaves "were of the race of whites."[16]

> Hence his [Jefferson's] famous conclusion regarding African American slaves: "It is not their condition then, but nature, which has produced the distinction." Blacks could never be educated to the level of whites, not because they were slaves but because they were black.[17]

In *The Wolf by the Ears: Thomas Jefferson and Slavery*, John Chester Miller writes:

> Here Jefferson reflected the age-old belief that blackness was somehow a curse. As Henry Home, Lord Kames, an eighteenth-century Scottish philosopher whose writings influenced the development of Jefferson's philosophy, said, "The colour of the Negroes ... affords a strong

---

[15] Thomas Jefferson is credited with having written the Declaration of Independence, but Congress made numerous changes that resulted in reducing his original draft by approximately 25 percent. His clause condemning the enslavement of the inhabitants of Africa was struck out in deference to South Carolina and Georgia. See Frank Donovan, *Mr. Jefferson's Declaration: The Story Behind the Declaration of Independence* (New York: Dodd, Mead & Company, 1968), 93-96.

[16] James Oakes, "Why Slaves Can't Read: The Political Significance of Jefferson's Racism" in *Thomas Jefferson and the Education of a Citizen*, James Gilreath, ed. (Washington D.C.: Library of Congress, 1999), 180.

[17] James Oakes, 180.

presumption of their being a different species from the whites..."

Color — "the radical distinction which nature has made" — formed forever, in Jefferson's opinion, an insuperable barrier to the creation of a multiracial society.[18]

Miller goes on to say:

By expressing "suspicions" of the inferiority of blacks, Jefferson considerably weakened the impact of his appeal for freedom for the slaves. The alleged inferiority of blacks served as a justification for slavery; by raising doubts as to the slaves' capacity for freedom, it was possible to regard slavery as the proper condition of the non-Caucasian members of the human race. Slaveowners made it a point to inculcate in the slaves a sense of their unworthiness, their helplessness, and their complete dependence upon the mercy of their masters. By creating a slave mentality, they hoped to instill in the blacks a fear of freedom. Indeed, until the conviction of inferiority had been thoroughly implanted in the slaves, Southern slaveowners could not account themselves secure in either their person or their property. White superiority and black inferiority were psychological imperatives of the system.

In the nineteenth century, when slavery was acclaimed a "positive good" for both races, the biological inferiority of blacks was exalted into "an ordinance of Providence."[19]

---

[18] John Chester Miller, *The Wolf By the Ears: Thomas Jefferson and Slavery* (Charlottesville, Virginia: The Free Press, a division of MacMillan Publishing Company Inc., 1977), 47.

[19] Miller, 57-58. To read more about Jefferson's contradictory views of race and his unacknowledged relationship with his slave Sally Hemings, see the collection of articles and interviews on the Internet

The Necessity of Recognition

With centuries of this kind of thinking during the time of slavery, and the white society continuing to think of black people as inferior and treating us as inferior after slavery was abolished, it's been very difficult for the white church to accept black people as equals. And that's because the white church has been reacting as part of white society instead of acting on the Word of God. It identifies more with what the world in general has to say than with what God says in His Word. Without the Church as a whole standing up for the equality of black people, attitudes about black inferiority have been so thoroughly promulgated that many black people think they are inferior. Many have low self-esteem and inferiority complexes precisely because of the long tradition of racist thinking in our society.

Think about this: How long ago did Thomas Jefferson live? Thirty-five years ago? Forty years ago? We all know he died almost 200 years ago. But the opinions about black inferiority that he accepted and wrote about did not. They are as current as last week, last night or today. They have been passed on from minister to congregation, father to son, father to daughter, daughter to husband, husband to children. And this sick cycle goes on and on.

Of course, as we've seen, it wasn't just Thomas Jefferson who promulgated these racist beliefs. Miller tells us:

> Thomas Carlyle, the nineteenth-century English historian and publicist, asserted with the certitude of one privy

---

at PBS.org/Frontline, under the topic "Jefferson's Blood." This includes the latest DNA evidence that at least one of Hemings' children was fathered by a Jefferson, and interviews with renowned Jefferson experts, history professor Joseph Ellis and professor of law Annette Gordon-Reed. Suggested background reading: Fawn M. Brodie, *Thomas Jefferson: An Intimate History* (New York: W.W. Norton & Company, 1974); Joseph Ellis, *American Sphinx: The Character of Thomas Jefferson* (New York: Alfred A. Knopf, 1996); and Annette Gordon-Reed, *Thomas Jefferson and Sally Hemings: An American Controversy* (Charlottesville, Virginia: University of Virginia Press, 1997).

to the Divine Plan that blacks had been created inferior in order to serve the whites, and that their status was fixed by a decree of the Almighty for all time. "That," he told people of color, "you may depend on it, my obscure Black friends, is and always was the Law of the World for you and for all men."[20]

Miller explains:

To a degree which might have astonished Jefferson himself, the dogma of black inferiority proved to be one of the hardy perennials of American anthropological, sociological, and historical scholarship.

As late as 1925, the notion of the innate inferiority of blacks was accepted as axiomatic by most anthropologists and historians. Scripture, science, and history combined to relegate the American blacks to the status of poor, congenitally backward relatives — a relationship sometimes reluctantly acknowledged — of the White population....

Jefferson did not have to look far to find evidence that hatred of slavery was perfectly compatible with hatred of the blacks themselves. Arthur Lee, a Virginia patriot and slaveowner, although he detested slavery, considered blacks to be "a race the most detestable and vile that ever the earth produced" and therefore unfit to mix with the white race.[21]

Reconciliation? We've never been friends with the white society. Not with this kind of attitude. We've never been held in high esteem. We've never been respected. As for affection and for seeking our society and welfare, it doesn't show much affection to call black people "a race the most detestable and vile that ever the

---

[20] Miller, 58.
[21] Miller, 58, 61-62.

earth produced," nor does it show much desire for our society and concern for our welfare to say that we are "unfit to mix with the white race."

> Similarly, Landon Carter, a Virginia planter, held both the institution of slavery and the slaves themselves in abhorrence. "Slaves are devils," he said, "and to make them otherwise than slaves will be to set devils free." Carter's solution was to pack the "devils" off to Africa.[22]

It certainly must have been difficult for slave owners to deal with those "devils." Slaves who weren't totally convinced of their worthlessness and weren't totally dominated through fear of beatings or death at the hands of slave owners and overseers sometimes actually talked back. Some even begged to remain with their families instead of being torn from their husbands, or wives and children and sold separately, the common practice under Southern law, which did not recognize the existence of the slave family.[23] Some whose wills were not crushed were angry enough to rebel against being slaves, although the rebellions never succeeded in ending slavery.[24] Yes, it must have been a trial for white people to put up with those "devils" they owned.

---

[22] Miller, 62.

[23] See Miller, 107, for information about Southern law not recognizing slave families. It is also interesting to note that while slaves' lives were often treated as worthless by owners who maimed or killed them as punishment or allowed them to perish from disease because proper medical attention was thought too expensive, slave owners were able to get insurance on their slaves' lives. These insurance policies, some of which were sold by the company that later became Aetna Inc., paid slave owners back "for financial losses when their human chattel perished." See Los Angeles Times (Los Angeles: Times-Mirror Corporation, March 8, 2000), A-15.

[24] The three most famous slave revolts were led by Gabriel Prosser, Denmark Vesey and Nat Turner. Turner's revolt, which took place in 1831, was the most far-reaching and well-planned, as well as the most bloody. When it was over, 55 white people were murdered before Turner and his followers were suppressed by the militia. Turner was later hanged with 16 of his men. Not only were slave revolts

The influence of the Southern slaveholders' point of view about black people extended far beyond the South. Another fact that many people are unaware of is what the Constitution of the United States originally said about slaves. For almost 100 years, because of the power of slave owners and bigotry, Article I, Section 2, paragraph 3 of our Constitution stated:

> Representatives and direct taxes shall be apportioned among the several States which may be included within this Union, according to their respective Numbers, which shall be determined by adding to the whole Number of free Persons, including those bound to Service for a Term of years, and excluding Indians not taxed, three-fifths of all other Persons.

---

unsuccessful in freeing the slaves — in 1863, at the time of the Emancipation Proclamation, the number of slaves in the U.S. had grown to above 4 million — they made conditions worse for slaves. There were new regulations governing black people, both slave and free. According to F.H. Hodder, "Ever since the Vesey plot in Charleston in 1822, the South had felt that free Negroes were likely to foment slave insurrection and were, therefore, an element of danger." As a result, free Negroes were not permitted passage in the Southern states. See F.H. Hodder, 16. Slave revolts also led to most states outlawing Negro meetings that were not presided over by a white person. This resulted in Blacks having to attend the religious services of their masters. It was boasted that in the South, Negroes and Whites got along famously in worship; but the truth was that the slaves were usually seated together in a special section or in the gallery. They were not given the right to participate fully in the church service. And, in one extreme case, a white congregation erected a partition several feet high to separate the slaves from their masters. Thus, segregation began in the Church long before the end of the Civil War and the institution of Jim Crow laws. See *The Confessions of Nat Turner,* www.ups.edu/history/afamhis/longtxts/turner.htm. Also see Albert J. Raboteau, *Slave Religion: The "Invisible Institution" in the Antebellum South* (New York: Oxford University Press, 1978), 137-143.

In addition to black churches being closed down following the slave revolts, schools were also closed. Slave revolts were, of course, the exception rather than the rule. Indeed, in his 1905 review of

The "other" persons meant black slaves, and this article in the Constitution meant that slaves were considered three-fifths of a person.

The 14th Amendment, which was ratified in 1868, altered the Constitution so that it no longer reads that way. But despite the rights that the 14th Amendment gave to black Americans, it did not prove to be as liberating as some had hoped it would be. [25] The original view of the Constitution, that black slaves were less than full human beings, remained part of America's mind-set long after the 14th Amendment was passed.

We have seen what some statesmen, politicians and slave owners thought about slaves. I hope these examples make it even

---

Charles Carroll's *The Negro A Beast*, Edward Atkinson quotes one of his "valued correspondents, son of one of the great planters, of late holding judicial position in the South," as praising black people for virtuous qualities both before and after the Civil War. He notes Blacks' post-Civil War "eagerness for education" and calls attention to the non-vengefulness of black people during the Civil War as having greatly protected Southern Whites. It was because of Blacks' "freedom from vindictiveness and malice," Atkinson quotes his friend as saying, that "Southern women and children were saved from the horrors that might have occurred, had any other race than the Negro been in the position in which the Negroes were left on the scattered plantations of the South while nearly all the white men entered the Confederate armies." It is worth remembering that these slaves, who caused no harm to the white women and children with whom they were left during the years of Civil War, are the people whom Landon Carter refers to as "devils." See Atkinson (the pages of his book are unnumbered).

[25] The 14th Amendment declared that all persons born in the U.S. are citizens of the nation as well as of the state in which they live. It supposedly guaranteed equal protection under the law. The second section of this Amendment declared that if any state denied or abridged the right to vote to males 21 or older for any reason except for participation in rebellion or other crime, then the basis of representation in that state would be reduced in proportion to the number of those denied. Had this been enforced, the number of Southern members in

clearer why I say that reconciliation is not a valid concept at this time, and why the issue is recognition. First we must be recognized as the equals we are in God's creation along with every other so-called racial and ethnic group. Once we have been recognized as equals, if we have a falling out, we will have a valid basis for reconciliation.

---

the House of Representatives and their number of electoral votes would have been measurably reduced because of the Southern states' routine denial to black men of the right to vote. Another proof that the 14th Amendment was not enforced is the fact that black men were systematically excluded from serving on juries. See Rayford W. Logan, "The Progress of the Negro After a Century of Emancipation," *Journal of Negro Education*, Vol. 32, Issue 4, Autumn, 1963, 320-328. See Edward Atkinson. Also see Abraham L. Davis and Barbara Luck Graham, *The Supreme Court, Race, and Civil Rights* (Thousand Oaks: Sage Publications Inc., 1995), 60. Davis and Graham observed that "The Supreme Court's early restrictive interpretations of the Fourteenth Amendment ... proved to be the blacks' worst enemy from 1896 to the mid-1930s." For more information on the effects of the 14th Amendment on the liberty of African Americans, see John Hope Franklin and Alfred A. Moss, Jr., *From Slavery to Freedom, A History of African-Americans* (New York: McGraw-Hill, 1994).

12

"The Angels of Race Prejudice"?

The statements I'm about to quote are spiritually tragic, but they are also instructive about why our society and our world are so permeated by racism. They are part of *The Crucial Race Question, or Where and How Shall the Color Line Be Drawn?* published in 1907 by the Right Reverend William Montgomery Brown, Bishop of the Protestant Episcopal Church. Think about it: a *bishop* wrote a book asking *Where and How Shall the Color Line Be Drawn?* How can a human being draw a color line in the Church when God Almighty said in Galatians 3:28 that **There is neither Jew nor Greek, there is neither slave nor free, there is neither male nor female; for you are all one in Christ Jesus**? How can a man call himself a bishop of the Episcopal Church and ask, "Where and How Shall the Color Line Be Drawn?" The question itself screams that something is wrong. You'd have to be in a coma not to know that something is radically wrong.

We're talking about the Church of the Lord Jesus Christ! We're talking about people for whom Christ died! And someone in the Church is telling me that I should be divided from white Christians because I'm black. Someone in the Church is telling Jesus that He was a fool, that He died and was crucified and went to Hell and rose from the dead to redeem some inferior Blacks. Is anyone ready to stand before the Throne of God and tell Jesus that?

163

Apparently Bishop Brown was. In the preface to his book, Brown quotes a prominent journalist and lecturer of his day, John Temple Graves. Graves thought segregation was the only "solution" to what he saw as the race problem — not the problem of *racism*, but the race "problem."[1]

> "Separation is the logical, the inevitable, the only way. No other proposed solution will stand the test of logic and experiment.... Religion does not solve the problem, for the Christ Spirit will not be all-pervasive until the millennial dawn.... We have come in God's providence to the parting of the ways. In the name of history and of humanity; in the interest of both races, and in the fear of God, I call for a division.[2]

---

[1] Graves, a prominent White from Birmingham, Alabama, was born in 1856 and died in 1925. He served as editor-in-chief of William Randolph Hearst's newspaper *The New York American* from 1907 through 1915 and he sometimes spoke from the pulpit. His inflammatory style of journalism is said to have contributed to the slaughter of innocent Blacks during the Atlanta riot of 1906. While serving as editor of the *Atlanta Georgian*, his writings were often quoted by Southern Whites in defense of their stand for racial purity and hence the need for segregation of the races. His son, John Temple Graves II, wrote *The Fighting South*, which is considered to be a definitive source on the preservation of "the Good Old White South." See Horace Mann Bond, "The Influence of Personalities on the Public Education of Negroes in Alabama I," *Journal of Negro Education*, Vol. 6, Issue 1, January 1937, 24 and Louis R. Harlan, "Booker T. Washington and the Voice of the Negro, 1904-1907, *The Journal of Southern History*, Vol. 45, Issue 1, February 1979, 56.

[2] The Rt. Rev. William Montgomery Brown, *The Crucial Race Question, or Where and How Shall the Color Line Be Drawn?* (Arkansas: The Arkansas Churchman's Publishing Company, c. 1907), x. Brown, who was born in 1855 and died in 1937, was a missionary and archdeacon of Ohio before he became a special lecturer in the Theological Seminary of Bexley Hall in Gambier, Ohio. He was the

Here is Graves, a white Christian man, quoted by nothing less than a bishop in the Episcopal Church, saying "religion does not solve the problem, for the Christ Spirit will not be all-pervasive until the millennial dawn." Does this mean he and the bishop believed Christ was not working at the time? That He wouldn't be working until the new millennium?

And then Graves has the nerve to say:

> We have come in God's providence to the parting of the ways. In the name of history and of humanity; in the interest of both races, and in the fear of God, I call for a division.

Did people actually believe this in the face of what the Bible says? At the time Bishop Brown wrote his book, there were fewer than 100 bishops in all of the United States,[3] and yet he, a leader of the Church, quoted and spread this garbage. That's the reason I'm so hard on Church leaders, because the mess the Church is in today is the fault of religious leaders; it's not the sheep who have caused this mess, it's the so-called shepherds!

Bishop of Arkansas from 1898 until 1912 and published his book *The Crucial Racial Question* in 1907. Shortly after he was ordained as Bishop of Arkansas he began publicly advocating the dividing of the Protestant Episcopal Church with a color line. See *Who Was Who, 1929-1940: A Companion to Who's Who...* (London: Adam & Charles Black, 1941, c. 1967), 174. See also J. Gordon Melton, *Religious Leaders of America*, s.v. "Brown, William Montgomery" (Detroit: Gale Research Inc., 1991), 70.

[3] In 1905, there were approximately 89 bishops in the United States. See *The American Church Clergy and Parish Directory for 1905* (Uniontown, Pennsylvania: Frederic E.J. Lloyd, 1905), 41-42. In 1910, there were approximately 93 bishops in the United States. See *Lloyd's Clerical Directory: A Treasury of Information for the Clergy and Laity of the Protestant Episcopal Church in the United States, and the Church of*

Let's read that again:

In the name of history and of humanity; in the interest of
both races, and in the fear of God, I call for a division.

How does a Christian leader reconcile that statement with
the Bible, the living Word of God?

In 1 Corinthians 1:10, Paul the Apostle says:

**Now I plead with you, brethren, by the name of our
Lord Jesus Christ, that you all speak the same thing,
and that there be no divisions among you, but that you
be perfectly joined together in the same mind and in
the same judgment.**

Paul begs for **no divisions among you**; yet Graves and Bishop
Brown "call for a division," and they do it "in the fear of God"!

Graves continues:

We can make it peaceably now. We may be forced to
accomplish it in blood hereafter.

Is that awesome? A bishop quoting — and obviously agreeing
with — a man who is calling for segregation with the threat of
violence if it doesn't come about soon!

Brown goes on to say:

This book is written partly for the purpose of commend-
ing as strongly and as widely as possible the Memorial
or Petition provided for in these resolutions but the chief
end in view is the recommendation to the general public of the author's solution of the whole Great American
Race Problem by the drawing of the Color-Line.[4]

England in Canada and Newfoundland (Chicago: American Church
Publishing Company, 1910), 43-44.

[4] Brown, xi, xii.

In the above passage, Brown calls for the drawing of the Color-Line. As if that weren't bad enough, next he states:

> I am among those who do not regard the General Convention of the Protestant Episcopal Church in the United States of America as being of Divine institution or as absolutely necessary to the existence of our American branch of the Catholic and Apostolic Church of the Anglo-Saxon race.[5]

I hope that you see the enormity of this statement. No wonder some black people say that Christianity is the white man's religion!

The bishop's attitude about the Church has been shared by many before and after him. Black people have been tolerated. Other ethnic groups have been tolerated. But way down deep — and for Brown and some others it hasn't even been way down deep — the Christian Church belongs to "the Anglo-Saxon race." Many Whites have said for years, "This is ours," and here an ordained bishop is saying it! He actually calls the Church of the Lord Jesus Christ "…the Church of the Anglo-Saxon race"!

White Anglo-Saxon Protestant — or *WASP* — is a common term in our culture. It refers to Caucasian Protestants whose ancestors came to America from England. Historically, they have been the people with money and power. But white Anglo-Saxon Protestants make up only a portion of the Church's membership. The reason we have a problem with racism in the Church today is that some people still share the bishop's attitude that it is the "church of the Anglo-Saxon race." This is totally un-Christian, yet it's the kind of

---

[5] Brown, xiv. Please note that when Brown uses the term "branch of the Catholic and Apostolic Church," he does not limit it to mean *Catholic* in the sense of the Roman Catholic Church. He is referring to the overall Church of the Lord Jesus Christ.

pollution some Christian leaders have been spewing from their pulpits and communicating in overt and covert ways since our country was founded.

Church leaders are supposed to be representing God, they are supposed to be speaking on behalf of God. They're supposed to say, "Thus saith the Lord," not "Thus saith my own racially, ethnically, color-prejudiced racist attitude." But that's what they've done. Then they have tried to embellish their personal thinking with a little Scripture to give it authenticity.

We trust our leaders. That's the awesome thing about being a leader: People are going to believe that what you say is true whether it's good or bad, right or wrong. That's dangerous, especially if you're not a person of high integrity. Having people believe what you say about God is an enormous responsibility.

I don't know about other ministers, but I am scared to mess with God. People don't scare me, God does! What I mean when I say God scares me is not that I am motivated by the spirit of fear; I mean that I do not play with God. Why? Because Judgment Day is coming. Everything is being recorded in the books, and the Bible says the books will be opened (Revelation 20:11-15). I think some of these preachers and ministers don't really believe in God. They have to be merely religious; they can't be born again. You can't have the Spirit of God in you and quote John Temple Graves saying, "I call for a division" in the face of the Scripture pleading **that there be no divisions among you**. You can't have the Spirit of God in you and say the "church of the Anglo-Saxon race." How presumptuous! If it were "the church of the Anglo-Saxon race," we ought to be able to find a statement about that in the Bible. But in Matthew 16:18, Jesus Christ does not say, "And I also say to you that you are Peter, and on this rock I will build the church of the Anglo-Saxon race," Jesus says:

> **"And I also say to you that you are Peter, and on this rock I will build My church, and the gates of Hades shall not prevail against it."**

It is Jesus's church, not the church of any one racial or ethnic group, nor the church of one denomination or another. It is the Church of the Lord Jesus Christ. Our problems have come from people not realizing this. The worst thing that has happened to the Church was denominations. Denominations mean more to people than the Church of the Lord Jesus Christ. People get ugly when you start talking about their denomination. You can talk about their family and they won't get as angry as they would if you talk about their church. If you talk about their church, they're immediately ready to go on the attack. They forget that Jesus said **"on this rock I will build *My* church."** The Church belongs to Jesus! Not to the Anglo-Saxons, not to black people, not to red people, not to yellow people, or brown people — it belongs to Christ. He's the One who died. He is the One who said **"on this rock I will build My church."** And yet Bishop Brown talks about the "church of the Anglo-Saxon race."

That's the problem with denominations. They siphon off people's attention away from Jesus. All of this could have been settled a long time ago if people hadn't divided the Church into denominations but had just let the Church be what it is in God's Word: the Church of the Lord Jesus Christ.

Let's look at Colossians 1:24, in which Paul says:

I now rejoice in my sufferings for you, and fill up in my flesh what is lacking in the afflictions of Christ, for the sake of His body, which is the church.

I don't see the words *Anglo-Saxon church* in this passage; I don't see the words *black church* or *red, yellow* or *brown church*; I don't see the names of any denominations; it is the Church of the Lord Jesus Christ.

Let's see what Hebrews has to say about the issue of the "church of the Anglo-Saxon race." In Hebrews 12:23, it says:

to the general assembly and church of the firstborn who are registered in heaven, to God the Judge of all, to the spirits of just men made perfect.

169

The phrase **church of the firstborn** refers to Jesus Christ; He is the firstborn from the dead. It's His Church. All of our problems have come from not recognizing this basic truth.

What Brown wrote next must break the heart of Jesus! Let's read it in the context of what we've just read:

> I am among those who do not regard the General Convention of the Protestant Episcopal Church in the United States of America as being of Divine institution or as absolutely necessary to the existence of our American branch of the Catholic and Apostolic Church of the Anglo-Saxon race. Nevertheless, I think that the General Convention is a good thing, and that it will be an *evil day for the Church when its doors are opened to any considerable number of Negro Bishops and delegations* [italics mine]...[6]

This is shocking: an ordained bishop stating that "it will be an evil day for the Church when its doors are open to any considerable number of Negro bishops and delegations." Yet this is fact, and it is part of the past that has produced the present. It is in the warp and woof of the fabric of this society. It is in the white psyche; it's in the white church.

Again, if you're a white reader of this book, I'm not attacking you. I'm attempting to get to the bottom of the race issue in America and in the Church so that we can root out racism once and for all. So much of it has been subliminally planted that it can be an automatic reaction. If you ever find yourself uncomfortable when you're with black people, look deep inside and ask, "Why do I get upset when I see a black person getting too close to me? Why do I suddenly start feeling uneasy?" You don't even know the person, he or she has never done a thing to you in your life, and yet you may feel uncomfortable just because that person is black.

---

[6] Brown, xiv.

Perhaps the tendency to react this way was planted in you when you were a little child. Your parents may not have been overt racists. They may have passed on to you their attitudes toward black people, not with words but with looks or body language. You may have been programmed to be fearful, to think of black people as different, inferior, even dangerous. Now when a black person is present, you respond automatically.

We can see a justification for these responses to black people in Bishop Brown's writing. He goes even further than saying "it will be an evil day for the Church when its doors are open to any considerable number of Negro Bishops and delegations." In talking about racial prejudice, he says:

> Race prejudice being a deep-rooted, God-implanted instinct, it is inevitable that either the white or the black race will ultimately occupy the political field of this country to the practical exclusion of the other.[7]

The implications of this are astounding. Brown is letting the Ku Klux Klan off the hook; he's letting all white people in America with any leanings towards racism off the hook, because he is saying racial prejudice is a "God-implanted instinct."

Reconciliation? No. This man and others like him are the forebears of those living today; their attitudes gave birth to the racist attitudes of today. Notice how cleverly his statement weaves in the mention of God. This man could not have been saved. There is no way that he could have known Jesus and written that racial prejudice is a "God-implanted instinct." How could it be "God-implanted" when there is neither slave nor free, Jew nor Greek, male nor female, when we are all one in Christ Jesus?

Racial prejudice is a "God-implanted instinct," according to Bishop Brown of the Protestant Episcopal Church — not the Church of the Lord Jesus Christ, thank God!

---

[7] Brown, 118.

Let's look further at the bishop's statement about racial prejudice in the light of what Almighty God teaches us. Webster's dictionary defines *prejudice* as:

> preconceived judgment or opinion ... an irrational attitude of hostility directed against an individual, a group, a race, or their supposed characteristics.[8]

What does the Bible say about this propensity for a person or group to prejudge another?

Romans 14:10-11 tells us:

But why do you judge your brother? Or why do you show contempt for your brother? For we shall all stand before the judgment seat of Christ.

For it is written:

"As I live, says the Lord,
Every knee shall bow to Me,
And every tongue shall confess to God."

Let's read that again: **But why do you judge your brother?** Perhaps white society has thought it could get away with judging black people because it has never accepted us as brothers. You don't Jim-Crow your brother. You don't make your brother ride in the back of the bus, drink out of a separate water fountain, and you surely don't put your brother in chains.

I know it hurts to read this, it even hurts me to write it, but it must be said, because we can't bury these truths anymore and just pretend that everything's okay or that all we have to do is reconcile. Instead we must have recognition — not only recognition that we are brothers, but

---

[8] *Webster's Seventh New Collegiate Dictionary* (Springfield, Massachusetts: G. and C. Merriam-Webster Company, 1976), 670.

recognition of all that has kept us from being accepted and treated as brothers for so long. Part of recognizing us as brothers is recognizing that we have *always* been brothers; we have not changed, it's just that many of our white brothers have been slow to recognize our brotherhood.

Again, Verse 10 says:

… Or why do you show contempt for your brother? For we shall all stand before the judgment seat of Christ.

The Bible plainly states that **we shall all stand before the judgment seat of Christ.** White society has apparently felt that this doesn't apply to black people, because black people are not brothers. We're animals — that's what Carroll wrote in *The Tempter of Eve*, isn't it? We're apes, at the top of the ape chain, but still apes, not brothers. This is what the present white generation's ancestors burdened us with.

Verse 11 says:

For it is written:
"As I live, says the Lord,
Every knee shall bow to Me…."

This means the ape's knee is going to bow, too. It takes it out of the realm of brotherhood; if you have a knee, it's going to bow to God. Even the bishop's knee is going to bow.

Based on what we have learned in verses 10 and 11, verse 12 tells us:

So then each of us shall give account of himself to God.

And Verse 13 says:

Therefore let us not judge one another anymore, but rather resolve this, not to put a stumbling block or a cause to fall in our brother's way.

Whether everybody believes it or not or likes it or not, black people are white people's brothers, red people's brothers, yellow people's brothers, and brown people's brothers. As we've seen, the Bible tells us that we are all of one blood and of one kind of flesh, and when you are of one blood and one kind of flesh, you are brothers. Romans 14:12-13 tells us how we must act towards our brothers, and it tells us that in this as in everything we do, we are accountable to God for our actions.

Let's look again at what Romans 14:13 says:

Therefore let us not judge one another anymore....

The word *anymore* is a time constraint; when Paul asked us not to judge each other **anymore**, it was 2,000 years ago. So the bishop and the Klan and other people expressing racially prejudiced views don't have any business talking the talk they've been talking or printing the garbage they've been printing. We are not supposed to judge each other, and prejudice isn't just judgment, it's *pre*-judgment, judgment based on no evidence. Remember *Webster's* definition:

> Preconceived judgment or opinion ... an irrational atti-
> tude of hostility directed against an individual, a group,
> a race, or their supposed characteristics.

A characteristic of black people is our black color. That is all it is: a physical characteristic. It has nothing to do with personality, character or integrity. It has nothing to do with ability, talent or education. Prejudice is all about the color of my skin. And the Bible tells us it is wrong.

Brown goes on to reveal his own prejudices when he makes this remarkable statement:

> Science and philosophy are agreed that the God of na-
> ture and of the universe is a God that changeth not. The
> light of reason as well as that of revelation shows the

Divine Being to be the same yesterday, today and forever. Therefore, since he saw fit to differentiate mankind into separate races at the beginning, we must conclude it to be his will that racial differentiations should be preserved and continued in their integrity to the end, and that the amalgamation of races involves the disregard of God's will by every individual who has any part in bringing it about. The proof positive that this reasoning is correct and that amalgamation is a ruinous crime is found in the curse of inferiority which rests upon all hybrid races.[9]

These are powerful words, indeed. But if what the bishop says is true, that God did not intend for anyone ever to mix, then I don't understand the meaning of Galatians 3:28, which eloquently states,

"There is neither Jew nor Greek, there is neither slave nor free, there is neither male nor female; for you are all one in Christ Jesus."

The bishop continues:

I need not further argue in favor of the contention that any disregard of the Color-Line which tends to the amalgamation of the Anglo-American and Afro-American races...[10]

I want to interrupt Bishop Brown midstatement to point out that once again the issue is black people and white people. In the three years of research I did to write this book, most of the American history about racial issues centered on black and white, and in all the so-called Christian literature, it is always black and white. Doesn't

---

[9] Brown, 133, 134.
[10] Brown, 135.

that tell us that something is wrong? Why is it one race? Why is it the black race?

In its entirety, Brown's statement reads:

> I need not further argue in favor of the contention that any disregard of the Color-Line which tends to the amalgamation of the Anglo-American and Afro-American races is a sin of the blackest dye.

Thus, according to the bishop, interracial marriage between black people and white people is "a sin of the blackest dye." How many bishops think that way today? How many bishops' children and bishops' wives and bishops' relatives and friends think that way today?

He goes on to say:

> How fortunate, therefore, it is that the angels of race prejudice stand at the Civil and Ecclesiastical gates with their flaming turning swords to guard the way to the Tree of Life. The sum of the whole matter is this: One race cannot admit another race to political and ecclesiastical equality because, to do so is to open the way to social equality.[11]

Now the bishop has the angels involved! I've heard of Michael the Archangel, I've heard of Gabriel, but I have never heard of race angels! Even though God gave Miriam leprosy for her prejudice regarding Moses' Ethiopian wife, Bishop Brown actually says there are special angels helping people to be prejudiced. To place angels on the same side as racial prejudice is a contradiction in terms. For a bishop to assert that angels are on the side of racial prejudice is a sin.

---

[11] Brown, 135.

13

To Whom Does the Church Belong?

 Let's review the last passage I quoted from Bishop Brown and look beyond his race angels to the real heart of the matter.

How fortunate, therefore, it is that the angels of race prejudice stand at the Civil and Ecclesiastical gates with their flaming turning swords to guard the way to the Tree of Life. The sum of the whole matter is this: One race cannot admit another race to political and ecclesiastical equality because, to do so is to open the way to social equality.

The bishop couldn't be clearer: As far as he is concerned, there should never be social equality between white people and black people. He also says black people cannot have equality in politics or in the Church, but that's just a side issue to his main point, that we should not have social equality. And because of poisonous statements like this made by so-called Christian leaders in print, in church, at the dinner table — statements that have been passed on from generation to generation — people still have the same beliefs today. I've said this before, but it's a concept that's really important to fully understand and acknowledge: The racism of the past is not dead; if Bishop Brown's thoughts and statements had died with him, we would not be dealing with them now.

The bishop continues:

> The libertine who crosses the Color-Line in quest of his prey is the most execrable of all criminals; especially is this true here in the United States where two such dissimilar races are living in the closest proximity and where consequently the danger of the weakening and extinction of the inferior race and the degradation of the superior is so perilously eminent.[1]

Here we see again those familiar words *inferior* and *superior* appearing in religious writing. Society and the Church are permeated with this kind of thinking about black people and white people. That's why we must deal with it once and for all, and the only way to do it is out in the open. Jesus says it this way in Luke 12:3:

> **"Therefore whatever you have spoken in the dark will be heard in the light, and what you have spoken in the ear in inner rooms will be proclaimed on the housetops."**

The Bible tells us that everything hidden or covered is coming into the light. How can a man who is supposed to be a Christian talk about "the inferior race" and "the superior race" in the light of the Scriptures?

Bishop Brown's view of the proper relationship between black and white people is evident in the title of his book, *The Crucial Race Question, or Where and How Shall the Color Line Be Drawn?* Notice that the title is not *Shall We Have a Color Line? Do We Need a Color Line? Has God Ordained a Color Line?* or *Does Jesus Approve of a Color Line?* The bishop is telling us there is no need to debate whether a color line is right; he assumes we are going to have one, we just have to figure out how we're going to draw it!

---

[1] Brown, 134

To Whom Does the Church Belong?

Bishop Brown says later:

> There is a political side to the Church as well as to the
> State, and it will not do for the Colored man to touch
> either the religious or civil politics of the White man.[2]

Think about it: This is a bishop of the Protestant Episcopal Church saying that black people should not be involved in the "religious or civil politics of the white man." This isn't the Grand Wizard of the KKK; it's not a deacon, an elder, or a Sunday school teacher; it is a bishop. That's almost the highest level to which a minister can rise in the Protestant Church. When you get to be a bishop, you're supposed to know what you're talking about. And what does Bishop Brown talk about?

> There is a political side to the Church as well as to the
> State, and it will not do for the Colored man to touch
> either the religious or civil politics of the White man.

This is the reason so many black people have left so-called Christianity and Christian churches, because of statements like this, which, in essence, say that Christianity is the white man's religion. The bishop continues:

> Therefore Afro-American Churchmen should not seek
> representation in the Parochial Vestries, Diocesan Coun-
> cils, or General Conventions of the Anglo-American
> Churchmen. The "peace and good will among men" of
> different races upon which so much depends, especially
> for the weaker race, render it absolutely necessary that
> Colored men should not claim and exercise the rights of
> citizenship in this White man's country, or of member-
> ship in our Anglo-American Churches.[3]

[2,3] Brown, 140

Here the bishop says "weaker" instead of "inferior," but they're both the same; they're both part of the mentality of white superiority, the mentality that makes it hard for some white people to accept black people as equals. If we ever wonder why race relations are in such a mess, all we have to do is think about Bishop Brown telling this to people of his day who passed the information along in one form or another until it was absorbed by people of our day.

> The "peace and good will among men" of different races upon which so much depends, especially for the weaker race, render it absolutely necessary that colored men should not claim and exercise the rights of citizenship in this White man's country, or of membership in our Anglo-American Churches.

I wouldn't be shocked if I had read this in a book by a leader of the white-supremacist group the Aryan Nation; I would expect it. But if you're a bishop of the Protestant Episcopal Church, if you've reached the highest echelon of the denomination of which you're a part, you can't spew garbage like this and not have the denomination know about it and accept it. If you say things that are contrary to the beliefs and the protocol of your denomination, other leaders of your denomination will call you on the carpet for it. Undoubtedly, Bishop Brown expressed these views verbally before he ever wrote his book. Once you write something down, it goes on forever. If the Protestant Episcopal Church had censored Bishop Brown, his book would never have been released. So in writing and publishing the book, Bishop Brown incriminates his whole denomination.

> Colored men should not claim and exercise the rights of citizenship in this White man's country, or of membership in our Anglo-American Churches.

This is another example of why many black people have accused Christianity of being the white man's religion. It's also an example of why many white people have felt that Christianity is the white man's religion and that America is "the White man's country" — and why so many still feel that way more than 90 years since the publication of the bishop's book.

In the same racist vein, Bishop Brown writes:

> I often am asked, "Why do you advocate so strenuously the exclusion of the Negro from civil governmental affairs, and at the same time, are willing to entrust the weighty interests of the Church to him?" To this inquiry I make one all-sufficient reply: "Because (1) this is an Aryan White man's country and he will not allow the Negro or any other race to share the government with him...."[4]

Here, the bishop clarifies that it's not only black people whom he "will not allow" to "share the government" with white people in this "Aryan White man's country," it's "any other race." So if you're Hispanic, Asian, Arab or Native American, for example, you may be tolerated because your skin is lighter and more pleasing to the aesthetics of the white man's eye, but ultimately you fall into the same category that we do. Black people may head the list of the "other" races, but you are right behind.

Let's look again at one of the things the bishop says:

> ... this is an Aryan White man's country and he will not allow the Negro or any other race to share the government with him.

How can America be called an "Aryan White man's country" when it was stolen from its original inhabitants, the Native Americans? This is a fact, and we all know it. The Europeans who came over here were thieves of the highest order. They stole the land from the Native Americans and stole the black people from Africa, their native homeland.

---

[4] Brown, 157

The bishop paints a truly shameful picture of the Church, and of his own heart, in the following statements:

> There is no use of trying in any way by any means to disguise the simple palpable fact that practically all white Churchmen in the South and many in the North feel it to be necessary to rid our Parochial and Diocesan organizations of their colored constituency, and by one means or another they are saying to it: "We do not want you to come in too great numbers, or in small numbers too frequently, to our Services for Divine worship; we do not want you to send your children to our Sunday schools, and above all we do not want you in any capacity as officers and representatives in the Church."[5]

This is the reason why to this day in most white-dominated churches, even in those with a large black constituency that gives substantial offerings, black people don't get many positions of real leadership. Blacks are tolerated in some positions, because it gives the appearance of a church being an "equal-opportunity employer," but black people are not allowed to make major decisions. The attitude is much the same as Bishop Brown's: Those in power don't want to have an "inferior" decision-maker in their ranks!

Bishop Brown ends the passage I just quoted by saying:

> "Still, we realize your need of our [italics mine] Church and we are ready to give it to you as far as this can be done without disregard of the Color-Line and without creating a schism in the Body of Christ, the Church."

Before we analyze this, let's put it in the context of Bishop Brown's other statements.

> ... we do not want you in any capacity as officers and representatives in the Church....

---

[5] Brown, 165

To Whom Does the Church Belong?

> ... we realize your need of our Church....

> ... we are ready to give it to you ... without disregard of
> the Color-Line and without creating a schism in the Body
> of Christ, the Church.

"Without creating a schism"? Bishop Brown and those like him have invented the schism! They ought to get a patent issued on it; they ought to copyright and trademark it! How could he say, "We do not want you in any capacity as officers and representatives of the church," "we realize your need of our church," "We are ready to give it to you ... without disregard of the Color-Line," and then add "and without creating a schism in the Body of Christ, the Church"? What world is he living in?

The answer is that Bishop Brown is living in a white-dominated world that he believes will, and should, always be white dominated. He considers that dividing black people (and others of color) from white people in the Church isn't a schism; in his mind, a schism could only take place in the Church that counts — the white church. Bishop Brown's solution to preserving the purity of the "Anglo-American churches" and to sharing what he sees as "our [white people's] church" with those of the "weaker," "inferior" black race is to give black people a black church.[6]

It is interesting to note the bishop's use of the words "our church" and "the Body of Christ, the Church," and his saying, "We are ready to give it to you" as if the Church belonged to the white race. I recognize that there is a white religious social organization that runs under the "church," but it really isn't *the* Church. *The* Church couldn't be "our church," because as we know, *the* Church is the Church of the Lord Jesus Christ. If by "our church" Bishop Brown

---

[6] Indeed, Brown's plan was to create separate Protestant Episcopal churches for Whites and Blacks, a move that he thought would increase black membership as well as keep white membership happily separate. See J. Gordon Melton, 70.

means the religious social club for Whites only, I have to bow to that. Then he's just referring to a club like many other clubs Blacks still can't get into, like some country clubs that no longer post signs they know would be illegal but have figured out other ways of keeping black people out. The problem is that Bishop Brown keeps confusing "our church" with *the* Church. Apparently, he doesn't realize that Jesus Christ not only never authorized a Whites-only "church," He wouldn't have even been allowed to join it, because as we saw in Chapter 2, Jesus had at least one black ancestor Himself and possibly more.

Again, we're exposing the root system of why people think the way they do today — why not long ago, for example, executives at Texaco were found to have been making prejudiced remarks about their black employees behind closed doors.[7] This and similar

---

[7] On November 4, 1996, *The New York Times* made public a conversation taped in 1994 in which two top Texaco Company officers referred to African-American employees as "niggers" and "black jellybeans." Their discussion centered around plans to destroy documents that were wanted as evidence in a lawsuit filed by Bari-Ellen Roberts, an African American (and one of the company's senior financial analysts) claiming discrimination. Within days, Texaco's Chairman and CEO, Peter I. Bijur, issued a statement saying that a settlement in the case had been reached, part of which included extensive changes to be made in the company's management staff and style in order to effectively change the cultural climate of Texaco. This case and a number of other discrimination cases that soon followed proved to America that, according to Diane Weathers, of *Essence Magazine*, "the civil rights struggle isn't over — it has simply changed the front lines." See "Texaco Chairman on Alleged Racial Slurs by Executives," *Historic Documents of 1996* (Washington, D.C.: Congressional Quarterly Inc., 1997), 764-769. Also see Diane Weathers, "Corporate Race Wars," *Essence*, Vol. 28, No. 6, October, 1997, 80-88.

incidents that happen every day and go unreported are the legacy of hundreds of years of people like Bishop Brown thinking that America is "the white man's country," that black people and "any other race" besides white are "inferior," and that "our church" is *the* Church.

Given Bishop Brown's assumptions about "our church," what would he say about Scriptures such as Romans 12:4-5?

> **For as we have many members in one body, but all the members do not have the same function,**
>
> **so we, being many, are one body in Christ, and individually members of one another.**

If you're in the Church of the Lord Jesus Christ, there is only one way in — only one way for black people, white people, red people, yellow people, brown people, males, females, children, senior citizens, blind, lame, bald-headed, long-haired, short-haired, big-nosed, small-nosed, big-earred, big-footed, whatever. If you are in it, you had to be adopted into the family. No one white, black, red, yellow, or brown is automatically a child of God; all are creations of God, but so are rocks — however, they are not His children. The only way we get into the family of God is by adoption, and Jesus Christ is the Head of the adoption agency.

In John 14:6, Jesus says:

> **"... No one comes to the Father except through Me."**

He doesn't say no white man, no black man, no red man, no yellow man, no brown man, He says **"No one comes to the Father except through Me."** So if you are in God the Father, you had to come through Jesus. If you've been adopted through Jesus and you are white, and I came in through Jesus and I am black, and you are in the family and I am in the family, then I am your brother.

Romans 12:5 says it all:

> **so we, being many, are one body in Christ, and individually members of one another.**

This is the Bible, not Bishop Brown. The bishop calls it "our church"; he says, "We are ready to give it to you." He has forgotten that you cannot give something unless it belongs to you. Do you have the ownership papers? Do you have the title deed? If so, show it to me!

Let's look at what 1 Corinthians 12:12-13 has to say about it:

For as the body is one and has many members, but all the members of that one body, being many, are one body, so also is Christ.

For by one Spirit we were all baptized into one body — whether Jews or Greeks, whether slaves or free....

I want you to notice what Verse 13 does *not* say: It does not say "for by one Spirit were all white people baptized into one body; by one Spirit were all black people baptized into one body; by one Spirit were all red people baptized into one body; by one Spirit were all yellow people baptized into one body; by one Spirit were all brown people baptized into one body." No, it says:

For by one Spirit we were all baptized into one body — whether Jews or Greeks, whether slaves or free....

The Bible says **all**, meaning everybody of every race. It says **Jews or Greeks**, meaning everybody of every ethnic group. It says **slaves or free**, meaning that even slaves could get into the Church of the Lord, Jesus Christ.

This Scripture concludes:

... and have all been made to drink into one Spirit. For in fact the body is not one member but many.

The bishop says, "We are ready to give it to you." What is he ready to give — the Church? It looks to me as if the Bible tells us pretty plainly that the Church doesn't belong to the bishop. But that's what happens with thieves; they always try to make you think they own something when they really don't.

Colossians 3:11 has something interesting to say about this issue:

> **Where there is neither Greek nor Jew, circumcised nor uncircumcised, barbarian, Scythian, slave nor free, but Christ is all and in all.**

Thank God the Church belongs to Jesus, because we black people would be up the creek in a boat with no oars if it belonged to people like the bishop. Look what people like the bishop have done with it, even though it belongs to Jesus!

Galatians 3:26-28 sheds further light on the matter:

> **For you are all sons of God through faith in Christ Jesus.**

> **For as many of you as were baptized into Christ have put on Christ.**

> **There is neither Jew nor Greek, there is neither slave nor free, there is neither male nor female; for you are all one in Christ Jesus.**

God's view cannot be stated any more clearly than that: **You are all one in Christ Jesus.** Any other view is not just sinful; it is heresy.

It's interesting to note what happened to Bishop Brown, because it's a perfect illustration of how the Church has tolerated prejudice against black people. While some in the Church did criticize the bishop for his proposal to segregate black members, as mentioned, he was not stopped from publishing his book and, despite his segregationist views, he continued to enjoy his office as a bishop for six years after his book's publication, resigning in 1912. In 1925, he was forced to leave the ministry, not for being a segregationist, but for becoming a Communist.[8] Apparently, it was acceptable to most of his colleagues when he ignored the Bible and spoke about dividing black people from white people in the Church, but advocating a form of government that didn't believe in God was going too far. What the supposedly Christian leaders around him didn't realize was that not believing in God's Word is the same as not believing in God. It is impossible to be a racist and to truly believe in God.

---

[8]   See J. Gordon Melton, 70.

14

The Myth of the Curse of Ham

 Summarizing his view of "the American Negro" as a "race," Bishop Brown writes:

> ... the Gentiles were the equals of the Jews in many respects, though not in religious aspects, while the American Negro is of inferior race.... A great deal is said about the inferiority of the Negro ... and, as compared with the Caucasian, there is no doubt in my mind that his race is among the inferior ones.[1]

Over and over we have been subjected to the idea of the inferiority of black people. Over and over we have read the work of Church leaders who have said or appeared to imply this. Over and over we have observed that the Church did not stop these leaders who were racist or, at the very least, who appeared to be racist, from publishing their views. Why? I believe that the explanation can be found in a book I quoted from earlier, *The Wolf by the Ears: Thomas Jefferson and Slavery*. In describing Jefferson's views about the inferiority of African slaves, you'll recall that Miller states:

---

[1] Brown, 192.

> ... Jefferson reflected the age-old belief that blackness was somehow a curse....[2]

For centuries, we have let people tell us about this so-called curse of Ham. I mentioned it briefly in reference to the *Scofield Bible*, but we will look at it here in greater detail, because it is so fundamental to the culture of racism.

Ham was one of Noah's sons, and the black populations of the earth after the flood were descended from him.[3] One morning, when Noah was waking up from a drunken stupor, Ham walked in on him and saw him naked. Supposedly, Ham was cursed for this. And supposedly, the curse was blackness. Many black people heard about this ostensible curse so often while growing up that we believed it, and it contributed to the development of a low self-image.[4]

What does the Bible actually say about "the curse of Ham"? Let's begin with Genesis 9:1:

So God blessed Noah and his sons....

Since Ham was one of Noah's sons, Ham was blessed by God. In my Bible, the word *blessed* is not spelled *c-u-r-s-e-d*. So the first thing the Bible tells us is that Ham was blessed, not cursed. We must ask ourselves, then, if God blessed Ham, how could He curse Ham? If God did this, He would be double-minded, and we wouldn't be able to count on Him. If God were double-minded, one minute

---

[2] Miller, 47.

[3] See *Race, Religion & Racism*, Vol. 1, 122.

[4] According to Robert E. Hood, professor of religious studies and director of the Center of African-American Studies at Adelphi University, the myth of the curse of Ham has caused internalized oppression among some Blacks who have believed the myth. See Robert E. Hood, *Begrimed and Black: Christian Traditions on Blacks and Blackness* (Minneapolis: Fortress Press, 1994), 115-131.

He would be blessing, the next He would be cursing the same people He blessed. And that's not God.

Let's return to Genesis to read the entire passage that so many Bible commentators have used as a source for the so-called curse of Ham. We'll begin with Chapter 9, Verse 18:

Now the sons of Noah who went out of the ark were Shem, Ham, and Japheth. And Ham was the father of Canaan.

These three were the sons of Noah, and from these the whole earth was populated.

And Noah began to be a farmer, and he planted a vineyard.

Then he drank of the wine and was drunk, and became uncovered in his tent.

And Ham, the father of Canaan, saw the nakedness of his father, and told his two brothers outside.

But Shem and Japheth took a garment, laid it on both their shoulders, and went backward and covered the nakedness of their father.

Their faces were turned away, and they did not see their father's nakedness.

So Noah awoke from his wine, and knew what his younger son had done to him.

Then he said:

**"Cursed be Canaan;
A servant of servants
He shall be to his brethren."**

And he said:

"Blessed be the Lord, the God of Shem,
And may Canaan be his servant.
May God enlarge Japheth,
And may he dwell in the tents of Shem;
And may Canaan be his servant."

As I pointed out in Chapter 9, notice what is conspicuously absent from this account: Nowhere in it does God curse Ham. In fact, not only does God not curse Ham, Noah doesn't curse Ham either! Because, as drunk as he was, Noah realized he could not overturn the word of the Almighty God. Remember, Verse 1 tells us: **So God blessed Noah and his sons....** God did not bless Noah's grandsons; He blessed his sons. God did not bless Noah and all his posterity; He blessed Noah's sons. And Noah, waking up while he was still coming off his wine, had enough sense to know, "I cannot overturn the judgment of the Almighty."

My question is, how can anyone overturn what God has done? How dare any person, be he or she a preacher, minister, bishop or teacher, say that Ham was cursed when there is *nothing* in the Book stating that Ham was cursed?

Indeed, as we have seen, God did not even curse Ham's son Canaan. Noah did the cursing, and Noah was a man just like every other man, in this case a man with a hangover. It is remarkable and tragic that so many people up to the present day could be so deceived, so ignorant, so foolish as to think that God would honor the word of a drunk. There is no indication in the Scripture that Noah, having awakened from his wine, pronounced the curse on Canaan at the behest of God. It doesn't say, "God said to Noah, 'Noah, curse Canaan.' " Thus, the Bible tells us that Noah's reaction to the situation is his own, not on behalf of God.

Notice exactly what Noah's curse was: He said Canaan shall be **"A servant of servants ... to his brethren"**; he did *not* say that Canaan shall be **"A servant of servants"** to the white race, the red, yellow, brown or black races. Also, Noah does not say, "Cursed be Canaan *and his posterity forever*"; he says, **"Cursed be Canaan."** The Bible does not say that Noah's curse extended beyond Canaan himself.

We will now look at Numbers 23 so that we can see exactly why from a scriptural point of view Noah could not have cursed Ham. I'm making an issue out of this because in the next few pages we're going to look at some material that I'm certain most people have never come across, and as we read it it's important to bear in mind what we learn in Numbers 23.

The context for this Scripture is that the Hebrews were on their way from Egypt to the Promised Land. They came to a place that was ruled by a king named Balak, who tried to hire a supposed prophet or soothsayer, Balaam, to curse Israel. In Numbers 23:8, Balaam asks:

> **"How shall I curse**
> **whom God has not cursed?**
>
> **And how shall I denounce whom the Lord has not de-**
> **nounced?"**

Again, this is why Noah didn't place a curse on Ham: because God blessed Ham.

We can see a further development of the biblical principle behind this in Numbers 23:16-20:

> **Then the Lord met Balaam, and put a word in his**
> **mouth, and said, "Go back to Balak, and thus you**
> **shall speak."**
>
> **So he came to him, and there he was, standing by his**
> **burnt offering, and the princes of Moab were with him.**
> **And Balak said to him, "What has the Lord spoken?"**
>
> **Then he took up his oracle and said:**

"Rise up, Balak, and hear!
Listen to me, son of Zippor!
"God is not a man, that He should lie,
Nor a son of man, that He should repent.
Has He said, and will He not do?
Or has He spoken, and will He not make it good?
Behold, I have received a command to bless;
He has blessed, and I cannot reverse it."

Balaam is instructed by God to state that what God has blessed, Balaam cannot reverse. God blessed Ham. Therefore, neither Noah nor anyone else could reverse that blessing. Again, I want to stress this critical point: There is no evidence that God wanted Canaan cursed; it was strictly Noah's doing.

There is another critical point. The Scriptures do not say that Noah's curse on Canaan was blackness. Only racists say that. I challenge every racist promulgator of white supremacy to show me the Scripture that says that Noah's curse on Canaan was black skin!

So those who spread the idea that God cursed Ham and that the curse was blackness in order to justify the enslavement of black Africans were putting forth something totally untenable. The slave owners' old defense, "We have a right to enslave them, misuse them and do whatever we want to them because they're cursed," was wrong. Any argument that anyone has used to justify the mistreatment of black people on the basis of our being cursed is wrong. Regardless of what some people believe, blackness is not a curse of God.

We're going to look at some other historical material on Ham and the so-called curse of blackness, because I want you to see how deeply rooted it is in this society and in the Church. As you read the following interpretation of the Scriptures and what it has to say about black people, look into yourself to see if it resonates with anything that you believe or have believed.

I'm not talking only about things we know we've been taught; I'm talking about the subtle things we've learned that we don't even remember consciously being told. We need to go inside and make sure that we don't harbor anything in our hearts that causes us to support racial prejudice or to be victims of racial prejudice. If we find something there, we have to expose it for the lie it is, and root it out of us once and for all. Otherwise, we'll just continue to pass down our feelings to our children and to the coming generations. In other words, "the beat goes on." And I'm telling you that the beat must stop now!

In the *Encyclopedia Judaica*, under the section on Ham, we find an interesting account in a subsection entitled "In the Aggadah." The Aggadah is part of the Oral Law, which was first recorded between the 2nd and 5th Centuries. It is a compilation of commentary by rabbis on narrative, historical and ethical parts of the Bible, as well as folklore, legends and conjecture about the meaning of Scriptures relative to other subjects.[5]

Before giving the Aggadah's commentary on Ham, the *Encyclopedia Judaica* states that "the Bible does not specify the nature of Ham's sin. Rabbinic exegesis attributes great sinfulness to him in order to explain the severity of the punishment."[6]

Here's the commentary on Ham and on the nature of his "sinfulness" and "the punishment":

> Ham's descendant (Cush) is black-skinned as a punishment for Ham's having had sexual intercourse in the ark (Sanh. 108b). When Ham saw his drunken father exposed, he emasculated him, saying, "Adam had but

---

[5] *Encyclopedia Judaica* (Jerusalem: Keter Publishing House Limited, 1971), 1216. The commentary in the Aggadah was not considered binding to all Jewish scholars. One of the most famous books in Jewish scholarship, *The Debate at Barcelona* by Rabbi Mosheh ben Nachman, makes this point strongly.

[6] The *Encyclopedia Judaica*, 1216. The *Encyclopedia Judaica* also explains that Ugaritic epic poetry of the day reveals "that the disgrace of a drunken father was considered by Canaanites to be a crime of the utmost gravity."

two sons, and one slew the other; this man Noah has three sons, yet he desires to beget a fourth" (Gen. R. 36:5). Noah therefore cursed Canaan (Genesis 9:25), Ham's fourth son, since through this act he was deprived of a fourth son (Gen. R. 36:7). According to another opinion, Ham committed sodomy with his father (Sanh. 70A) and Noah cursed Canaan because Ham, together with his father and two brothers, had previously been blessed by God (Gen. R. Loc. Cit.). Another tradition attributes the curse to the fact that it was Canaan who castrated Noah. Ham was nevertheless to blame because he informed his brothers of their father's nakedness (PdRe 23). Canaan was so wicked that his last will and testament to his children was: "Love one another, love robbery, love lewdness, hate your masters, and do not speak the truth" (Pes.113b). Ham was also punished in that his descendants, the Egyptians and Ethiopians, were taken captive and led into exile with their buttocks uncovered (Isa. 20:4; Gen. R. 36.6). Ham was responsible for the ultimate transfer to Nimrod of the garments which God had made for Adam and Eve before their expulsion from the Garden of Eden. From Adam and Eve these garments went to Enoch, and from Him to Methuselah, and finally to Noah, who took them into the ark with him. When the inmates of the ark were about to leave their refuge, Ham stole the garments and kept them concealed for many years. Finally, he passed them on to his firstborn son, Cush, who eventually gave them to his son, Nimrod, when he reached his 20th year. (PdRe 24; Sefer ha-Yashar, Noah, 22)."[7]

---

[7] *Encyclopedia Judaica,*1216. Note that in the passage quoted, abbreviations are given after each piece of commentary. For example, "Sanh.108b" refers to the tract or volume name of the section of the Talmud known as Sanhedrin; 108b is the page number.

The Myth of the Curse of Ham

It is interesting indeed how many aspects there are to this account of Ham. But there are even more. Let's look at *Legends of the Jews* by Louis Ginzberg. In it we find these words:

> After the sacrifice [Noah's sacrifice to God of an ox, a sheep, a goat, two turtledoves, and two young pigeons] was completed, God blessed Noah and his sons. He made them to be rulers of the world....[8]

This alone tells me that there's an inconsistency in the thinking of those who believe in the supposed curse of Ham. If God blessed Noah and his sons, which we've already noted, and "He made them to be rulers of the world," that means that Ham was a ruler!

> ... He made them to be rulers of the world as Adam had been, and He gave them a command, saying, "Be fruitful and multiply upon the earth," for during their sojourn in the ark, the two sexes, of men and animals alike, had lived apart from each other, because while a public calamity rages continence is becoming even to those who are left unscathed. This law of conduct had been violated by none in the ark except by Ham, by the dog, and by the raven. They all received a punishment. Ham's was that his descendants were men of dark-hued skin.[9]

Have you ever heard of anything so ridiculous? Well, believe it or not, it gets even more ridiculous. Later, in the entry under Noah, we learn about other aspects of the legend:

> In his drunken condition Noah betook himself to the tent of his wife. His son Ham saw him there, and he told his brothers what he had noticed, and said: "The first

---

[8] Louis Ginzberg, *The Legends of the Jews, Vol. 1* (Philadelphia: Jewish Publication Society of America, 1909-1938), 166.

[9] Ginzberg, 168-169.

man had but two sons [referring to Adam, whose sons were Cain and Abel], and one slew the other [referring to Cain killing Abel]; this man Noah has three sons, yet he desires to beget a fourth besides." Nor did Ham rest satisfied with these disrespectful words against his father. He added to this sin of irreverence the still greater outrage of attempting to perform an operation upon his father designed to prevent procreation.

When Noah awoke from his wine and became sober, he pronounced a curse upon Ham in the person of his youngest son Canaan. To Ham himself he could do no harm, for God had conferred a blessing upon Noah and his three sons as they departed from the ark. Therefore he put the curse upon the last-born son of the son that had prevented him from begetting a younger son than the three he had. The descendants of Ham through Canaan therefore have red eyes, because Ham looked upon the nakedness of his father; they have misshapen lips, because Ham spoke with his lips to his brothers about the unseemly condition of his father; they have twisted curly hair because Ham turned and twisted his head round to see the nakedness of his father; and they go about naked, because Ham did not cover the nakedness of his father."[10]

As foolish as this is, some people have believed it. Some people have actually believed our curly hair is the result of Ham having turned around to see the nakedness of his father!

---

[10] Ginzberg, 168-169. It is interesting to note that while other legends in Ginzberg's book indicate where they come from in the oral tradition, this particular passage gives no source at all. It is therefore impossible to trace its source or to determine how widespread it was.

The Myth of the Curse of Ham

In his book *Sex and Race*, historian J.A. Rogers, looking at the ancient people's conception of how black people became black, summarizes what we have observed in *The Encyclopedia Judaica* and *Legends of the Jews*:

> The beliefs that the descendants of Ham, that is, the Egyptians and Ethiopians, became black because Ham was cursed by Noah, originates in the Talmud, Midrash, and other rabbinical writings from the second to the fifth centuries A.D.[11]

The reason I'm focusing on this isn't only to point out what some people have believed in the ancient past, but to look at it in terms of the present. How many people of all religions and denominations have inherited this attitude? According to racists, the white race is supposed to be of superior intelligence. But it is unintelligent to judge anyone without having any personal contact with him or her. You can't even make an intelligent judgment about someone on the spot; you have to evaluate people over time. You have to see people in good times and bad before you can draw conclusions about them. That's what intelligent people do. The reason these false beliefs are still in the Church is that nobody wants to acknowledge them and deal with them intelligently.

Rogers goes on to say:

> The chief one [version of this legend] is that Noah forbade all the persons and the animals in the ark to have ... intercourse. Ham disobeyed the order; the dog followed his bad example; and then the raven. As a result all three were cursed: Ham was made black; the dog was attached to the body of the female after intercourse;

---

[11] J.A. Rogers, *Sex and Race: Why White and Black Mix in Spite of Opposition*, Vol. III, 5th ed. (St. Petersburg, Florida: Helga M. Rogers, 1944; reprint, 1972), 316.

and the raven which had incited the other animals to have intercourse was punished by being made "to copulate through his mouth." (Sanhedrin 108b).[12]

Rogers points out that all three versions of the legend are about sexual relations. So much of the hatred that white racists have expressed towards black people has been in regard to sex. In fact, as we've noted, from slave times until today, the idea of interracial marriage has been a major focus of racist propaganda.

Rogers now comments on another section of *Legends of the Jews*:

> Louis Ginzberg (*The Legends of the Jews*, Vol. 5, p. 56. 1925) says, "The older sources (Sanhedrin 108b; Br. 36:7. Yerushalmi Ta'anit I, 64d; Tan.Noah 12) state that three were punished because they did not observe the law of abstinence while in the ark. Ham, the dog, and the raven. Ham became the ancestor of the black (colored) race." (See also Vol. 1, p. 166 of this work)....

> The Midrash Rabbah, Genesis, Noah, chap. 37, gives a different version. It says that in the quarrel between Noah and Ham, the former said, "You have prevented me from doing something in the dark (sc. cohabitation) therefore your seed will be ugly and dark-skinned. Rabbi Huja said: Ham and the dog copulated in the Ark therefore Ham came forth black-skinned while the dog publicly exposes its copulation." (Page 293, 1939, I. Epstein, Editor).

> Ham, one part of the legend goes, prevented Noah from having sex relations by castrating Noah while the latter

---

was in the ark. Another part of the legend says that it was not Ham, but a lion, that struck Noah in his privates, mutilating him, as Noah was leaving the ark. When Noah got drunk, as the fable goes, and started to cohabit, he forgot his injury, with the result that his semen was scattered over the ground. In this humiliating state Ham laughed at him. (See also HAM in Jewish Encyclopedia.)

In other words, this twisted legend, which has no more scientific foundation than the Uncle Remus stories of Br'er Rabbit, was firmly believed in for centuries by supposedly intelligent white Americans and is still accepted by millions of them. Moreover, as I showed (Sex and Race, Vol. I), Noah's alleged curse actually worked in reverse because the sons of ... Shem became slaves to ... Ham for more than four hundred years in Egypt.

This rabbinical concept of how Negroes became black was written long after the Jews had left Egypt and were in Europe, at which time the Jews, who were very likely a black people originally, had become fairer through mixing with lighter-skinned Asiatics and Europeans. The whole story evidently had its basis in the rivalry over the land of Canaan, which the Jews claimed that God had given them as an inheritance forever, or more likely because the Egyptians had made concubines of the Jewish women.[13]

So Rogers is saying two things. First, he says that the theory that blackness was a curse emerged after the Hebrews, through mixing with Europeans and Asiatics, had become lighter-skinned than they

---

[13] Rogers, 316-317.

had been when they gained their freedom after 430 years of slavery in Egypt. Second, he says that most likely the commentary was founded on Hebrew animosity towards the Canaanites, their pagan enemies who occupied the Promised Land, or on the fact that the black Egyptians had made Hebrew women concubines during the Hebrews' enslavement in Egypt.[14]

Rogers comments:

> Placing a curse on a people is still used as a justification for taking what they have and otherwise exploiting them. This myth becomes all the more contradictory and ridiculous when one recalls that the thing held most sacred by the Jews, the holy fire in which Jehovah used to make Himself manifest, as in the burning bush of Moses, was black (Ginzberg, Vol. 2, p. 303). Add to this that in Daniel (VII, 9) Jehovah, "the Ancient of Days" is pictured as having "the hair of His head like the pure wool."

---

[14] This is what had made the Hebrews darker skinned when they first emerged from Egypt. The black Egyptian slave masters took the Hebrew women as concubines, just as the white slave masters of the South took our black forebears and made them concubines. That's why today we have the great variety of black-skinned people that we do, from very white to very black and every shade in between.

   In connection with the mixing of races in America that began during the time of slavery, Atkinson makes a fascinating comment in his 1905 review of *The Negro A Beast*. He writes: "The effort to prove that the Negro is a beast, not a descendant from the same parents as white persons, would simply prove that a very large portion of the white citizens of Virginia and other border States were also beasts. It is now declared that not twenty percent of the colored people of the South are of pure Negro origin, and that the race is pervaded by the 'best white blood' of the States in which they were born. Man and beast do not propagate; were the generators of the best blood of Virginia beasts?" See Atkinson (the pages of his book are unnumbered).

That is, according to Jewish legends he was both black and wooly-haired.[15]

Rogers' point is so important that I want to make sure it sinks in. The idea of blackness being a curse in legends surrounding the Old Testament makes no sense at all, since, according to legend, the holy fire God used to make Himself manifest in the burning bush was black, and the Old Testament tells us that in the vision of the prophet Daniel, God Himself (the Ancient of Days) has hair like pure wool (Daniel 7:9). If blackness and a physical feature of black people are associated with God, how can blackness be a curse?

It amazes me that some people never recognized that we got our color from the same place they got theirs. Yet, our color has to be a curse; their color came from God.

It is interesting to note that virtually every white commentator whose work I've read has used the expression "the curse of Ham," although, as we've seen, Ham was not cursed. Only one reference called it the "curse of Canaan."[16] Whatever it's called, God did not curse Canaan, Noah did, and the curse was not blackness.

In order to be thorough in my exposure of the myth of "the curse of Ham," I'd like to examine another point. We've seen that Noah's curse on Canaan was that Canaan would be a servant to his brothers; this is how the passage is usually translated. But since the passage about Noah, Ham and Canaan has been used to justify slavery, we have to ask, Can the same Hebrew word that has been translated as servant also mean slave? The answer is that the Hebrew word *eved* has three meanings. Its first meaning is *servant*, but it may also mean *slave* or it may mean *worshiper of God*.[17] *Eved* was used to mean all these things in the Old Testament.

---

[15] Rogers, 317.

[16] *Encyclopedia Judaica*, 1216.

[17] Charles A. Briggs, Francis Brown, S.R. Driver, *A Hebrew and English Lexicon of the Old Testament* (Oxford, England: Clarendon Press, 1951), 713-714.

For argument's sake, let's say Noah's curse on Canaan was that he should be a slave to his brothers. Even then, there is no scriptural validity for the so-called curse of Ham as a justification for the enslavement or any other kind of subordination of black people. Whether *eved* is translated to mean slave or servant, the Scripture still does not say God cursed Canaan. It still says Noah did. It still does not say that the curse had anything to do with blackness. And it still does not say Canaan's descendants shall be "slaves to white men forever," or that Canaan's descendants shall be "in a servile position to white men forever." As we've seen, there is no mention of Canaan's descendants; there is no mention of "forever."

While doing my research I found an interesting fact. There are approximately 203 verses where the words *curse, cursed, cursedst, curses, cursest, curseth* and *cursing* appear, and in all of these verses, there is not one reference to a man, men, group or nation where the curse is eternal, leaving no possibility of ever being lifted. Not one! So Noah's curse on Canaan not being "forever" is in line with all the other biblical precedents.

It is also significant that Noah's curse on Canaan is found in the Book of Genesis. This is the first book of the Bible, better known as the first book of the law, meaning God's law. This is important because if a curse was pronounced upon a man or men in the Book of Genesis that could not be lifted or circumvented, then God's Word would be compromised. Why is this so? Simply because God knew in eternity past that He was going to send Jesus Christ to redeem mankind, and included in that redemption is redemption from the curse of the law.

Galatians 3:13 says:

Christ has redeemed us from the curse of the law, having become a curse for us (for it is written, "Cursed is everyone who hangs on a tree").

Any curse pronounced during the time of the law is lifted in Jesus Christ. So the racist segment of the Church cannot use its justifications anymore.

If we are redeemed from the curse of the law, we are redeemed from all curses of the law. This means that even if all of Canaan's descendants had been cursed — and we have seen they were not — that curse would have been lifted with the coming of Christ. If slavery was a curse of the law, and now through Christ I am redeemed from the curse of the law, then I am redeemed from slavery. So I don't have to be a slave anymore. If blackness was a curse of the law, then I'm redeemed from blackness. So I don't have to be black anymore. Now the question is, before I was cursed black, what color was I? If I was black already, how could I be cursed black? If I wasn't black, was I white, red, yellow or brown? If so, should I be that color again now? Interesting question, isn't it?

At this point I feel safe in saying we can see that all of the mythology connected to the so-called curse of Ham, all the lies about blackness being a curse of God and about the enslavement of black people being a curse of God, is a destructive, hateful sham. Blackness is not a curse, just as being red, yellow, brown or white is not a curse; it is the way God made humanity from the beginning.

As John 3:16 says:

"For God so loved the world..."

The Bible doesn't say "the black world, the white world, the red world, the yellow world and the brown world," because God does not divide the world; the Bible says, **"For God so loved the world...."**

It seems to me that black people must be something special indeed. To my knowledge, the black race is the only race that everyone in human history, at one time or another, has commented on negatively or oppressed. And everything people have done to or said about us relates in some way to the color of our skin. God must have a purpose for us, otherwise why would Satan have fired his artillery at us for all these years?

I firmly believe that we have come to the Kingdom for such a time as this!

15

More Racist Myths

 Let's examine historical documentation of others' opinions about why black people are black and why we should be mistreated and looked down upon. You may not have been aware of it, but in the past even the Mormons have been against us. Now all of a sudden they're trying to proselytize among us. I guess they've had a change of heart, but it's not something that they are making a public declaration about. They're not saying in newspapers, magazines, books or on the six o'clock evening news that they were wrong, that they had said certain things about black people that were harmful, and now they see the error of their ways. Instead, they're just going on as if what had occurred for years had never happened.

In *Mormonism and the American Experience*, Klaus J. Hansen says:

"Just exactly when, how, and why Mormon prejudice against Negroes developed into discriminatory policy is a matter of considerable controversy, though its existence is an incontrovertible fact. For more than a century and a quarter the Mormon church denied the priesthood to blacks, a policy publicized by Brigham Young in 1852 after the arrival of the pioneers in Utah. Because there is no evidence that Joseph Smith made an unequivocal, authoritative statement regarding black ineligibility for the priesthood, some scholars believe that the policy was in fact initiated by Brigham Young, while others insist that, because Young based virtually all of his teaching on the authority of Joseph, this would be particularly true of a doctrine as controversial and far-reaching as priesthood denial to blacks."[1]

Hansen goes on to state:

It is perhaps not surprising, then, that when the Saints, like a modern Israel, sojourned to their own promised land they were mindful of the racial injunctions their God had issued to their predecessors. Though there were no Canaanites to rout, Brigham Young wanted to make sure that the time would not come when he might have to.

This may explain the hardening of racial attitudes after the Saints had removed themselves from the world of the Gentiles, with only a handful of blacks (servants) in their midst. Certainly, Brigham Young's opinion regarding miscegenation appears extreme.[2]

Hansen says Brigham Young's opinion about the mixing of races "appears extreme." This is an understatement. As you read what Brigham Young said, remember that Young was one of the founding fathers of Mormonism, and that these are his exact words. Note, too, that like so many others whose commentary we have read, Young doesn't say he's giving his own opinion about black people and about the mixing of black and white, Young attributes his opinion to God. He says:

---

[1] Klaus J. Hansen, *Mormonism and the American Experience* (Chicago: University of Chicago Press, 1981), 184-185.

[2] Hansen, 195-196.

"Shall I tell you the law of God in regard to the African race? If the White man who belongs to the chosen seed mixes his blood with the seed of Cain, the penalty, under the law of God, is death on the spot. This will always be so."[3]

Why don't so-called Christian leaders take credit for their own racism instead of trying to blame God? Because there's nothing in the Bible to support it; it's all in their prejudiced minds.

Let's look again at the last part of Young's statement:

This will always be so.

If this is God's law and it will always be so, how can anyone change it? We know the Bible says that God doesn't change. So if that was ever God's law, it has to be God's law now. Keep this in mind.

In regard to Young's practice regarding Blacks at the time, Hansen comments:

There's no record that Young ever applied this "law." In any case, it is doubtful that he had much reason to do so, since Mormon missionaries were instructed not to proselytize among Blacks.[4]

How about now? Now apparently God *has* changed His mind, because today, according to Hansen:

Mormon missionaries are running to and fro, even to Africa, to win converts.[5]

This is in total contrast to the past, when Hansen tells us Mormons actually tried to discourage black people — whom Young calls "the seed of Cain" — from wanting to become Mormons.

---

[3] Hansen, 195, 196.
[4] Hansen, 195, 196.
[5] Hansen, 195, 196.

One of the most effective ways of discouraging blacks from becoming Mormons was to deny them the priesthood. This, of course, was a male prerogative, whose "blessings" were extended to women through marriage. Only those who held the priesthood could enter into the "new and everlasting covenant," to be sealed in the temple for "time and eternity." Thus, when Brigham Young declared in 1852 that "any man having one drop of the seed of [Cain] ... in him cannot hold the priesthood," he brought into the open a doctrine that made it very unlikely that he would ever be called upon to administer "death on the spot."[6]

With my limited intelligence, the absence of gray matter in my cranial cavity, and my inferior black skin, I just have one simple question to ask: How in the world can anyone determine that someone has "one drop" of black blood in him? The impossibility of it makes the statement pitiful. And it is pitiful that anyone would believe that one drop of blood would determine whether you will accept or reject a person. It is absurd. It is sick. It is straight out of the pit of hell.

As Hansen explains, Brigham Young promulgated a doctrine that made it very unlikely that he would ever be called upon to administer "death on the spot" for mixing the races. How could white Mormons and black Mormons mix if there were no black Mormons? Young prohibited all black men from entering the priesthood, thereby discouraging them, as well as their wives, from becoming Mormons. Isn't it amazing that at that time even one drop of black blood was considered so powerful that it would disqualify a man from entering the priesthood? I'm telling you, we black people must really be something!

Hansen explains:

---

[6] Hansen, 195-196.

The reference to the "seed of Cain," while not inconsistent with the traditional justification for slavery, represents a shift in emphasis from the stock biblical genealogy through the "curse of Ham" as passed on to Canaan. When asked what "chance of redemption there was for the Africans," Young answered that "the curse remained upon them because Cain cut off the lives of Abel ... and the Lord had cursed Cain's seed with blackness and prohibited them the Priesthood."

Noah's curse on Ham's posterity, in fact, may have been a kind of added insult to an injury incurred because of Ham's marriage to a "Canaanite" through whom his descendants would have inherited Cain's curse in any case.[7]

I think it will be profitable for us to look at the curse of Cain. In Young's interpretation, God cursed Cain and his curse was blackness. That's why Young said that just one drop of black blood would disqualify a man from the priesthood. What does the Bible say?

In Genesis 4:9-15, it says:

Then the Lord said to Cain, "Where is Abel your brother?" He said, "I do not know. Am I my brother's keeper?"

And He said, "What have you done? The voice of your brother's blood cries out to Me from the ground.

"So now you are cursed from the earth, which has opened its mouth to receive your brother's blood from your hand.

"When you till the ground, it shall no longer yield its strength to you. A fugitive and a vagabond you shall be on the earth."

---

[7] Hansen, 196.

And Cain said to the Lord, "My punishment is greater than I can bear!

"Surely You have driven me out this day from the face of the ground; I shall be hidden from Your face; I shall be a fugitive and a vagabond on the earth, and it will happen that anyone who finds me will kill me."

And the Lord said to him, "Therefore, whoever kills Cain, vengeance shall be taken on him sevenfold." And the Lord set a mark on Cain, lest anyone finding him should kill him.

This last verse is where Young got his idea: When God set a mark upon Cain, the mark obviously must have been black skin! It couldn't have been anything else but black skin, could it? That was the curse. Now, to show you how slick and tricky people can be, how they can talk out of both sides of their mouths, and why Native Americans used to say that white men spoke with a "forked tongue," I want to go back to the Scripture so you can see the huge inconsistency in the way white people treated the black people who supposedly bore "the curse of Cain." Let's look at Verse 15 again:

And the Lord said to him, "Therefore, whoever kills Cain, vengeance shall be taken on him sevenfold." And the Lord set a mark on Cain, lest anyone finding him should kill him.

If Cain and all his posterity were cursed with blackness and the purpose of the curse was so that no one would kill them, why have so many white people been lynching and burning black people all these years? It's ridiculous — white bigots haven't even believed their own interpretation. First, they say we're marked with the curse of Cain, then they forget why a mark — which the Bible never says was blackness — was put on Cain to begin with. And the Church! The Church has fostered and perpetuated this garbage.[8]

In practically all of the interpretations and commentary we've looked at we've been told that the "curse of blackness" was the will of God, thereby making God Himself responsible for initiating the curse. Then, of all things, according to these Mormons, God changed His mind, although in reality that would be contrary to the Bible, which we know says in Malachi 3:6:

"For I am the Lord, I do not change...."

But Hansen tells us:

"... On June 8, 1978, the First Presidency of the Mormon Church, in an historic letter, made the unexpected and dramatic announcement that "all worthy male members of the Church may be ordained to the priesthood without regard for race or color."[9]

God changed! That's religion for you. The worst thing that ever happened to mankind is religion. I didn't say Jesus; I said religion. It's amazing to me how all these people suddenly get revelations that God has changed. What's so sad is that they never

---

[8] In reference to Cain, J. A. Rogers makes an important point. He says that according to *Legends of the Jews*, the rabbis also taught that "Cain's face turned black." (In *Sex and Race*, Vol. III, 5th ed., Rogers cites Ginzberg's *Legends of the Jews*, Vol. 1, 108, and Vol. 5, 137), 317. Rogers also states, "But it happens that West Africans who had, it appears, an ancient Egyptian connection, teach the opposite, namely, that Cain was originally black but that when he killed Abel and God shouted at him in the garden he turned white from fright and his features shrank up," 317. What you want to believe depends upon which culture you're in, because the Scripture does not tell either story. The prejudices that go into these interpretations are cultural, not biblical!

[9] Hansen, 198.

admit that they were wrong. You would think they would say, "Well, you know what? We have to repent; we have been wrong." Oh no! They just announce a change, and the implication is that the Lord has changed His mind.[10]

Hansen goes on to say something very illuminating that I doubt most people are aware of:

> ... Those dissident Mormons who had rejected "corporate" Mormonism as it manifested itself in plural marriage and the political kingdom, who had refused to follow Young to the Rocky Mountains, and who had started the Reorganized Church with headquarters in Independence, Missouri, never felt it necessary to invent a Negro doctrine. Unlike the Utah Mormons, they refused to canonize the Book of Abraham, regarding it as one of Smith's more adventurous and unreliable excursions into "revelation." The Reorganized Church has always admitted Negroes to full membership, including the privileges of the priesthood.[11]

---

[10] Another example of this happened in the Catholic Church. For years it was a sin in the Catholic Church to eat meat on Friday. Then apparently God changed: Suddenly it became all right to eat meat on Friday. Church leaders never admitted that they were wrong. They just changed the rule, and what had been a sin was now no longer a sin. This is the reason I say you had better stay with the Book. There is no Scripture in the New Testament that tells Christians not to eat meat on Friday. But because people don't read and study their Bibles, they become victims of religious systems. In certain churches, parishioners are not even encouraged to read or study the Bible. In such churches, people are supposed to accept what the priest says. I don't think you should accept what anyone says — not even me — *unless you can validate it in the Book.* That's why I'm giving you scriptural references. Don't take my word for what God says. I am telling you the truth, but you need to check things out for yourself before you believe anyone.

[11] Hansen, 200.

So which is the true, "God of Heaven, New Testament, Holy Spirit, Body of Christ, inspired Mormon Church"? Before I started my research for *Race, Religion & Racism*, I never knew there was more than one Mormon Church. Even now it's a difficult thing to comprehend: How can they both be Mormon churches and believe two entirely different things about black people?

The Broadman Bible Commentary presents an overview of how the "curse of Ham" has been used to oppress black people in America. Commenting on Genesis 9, verses 18 to 29, the Broadman says:

> There is hardly an Old Testament passage more difficult to interpret. This Scripture was the favorite text of Southern preachers during the Civil War as they asserted the right of white men to enslave the Negro. Often used in recent times to defend segregation, the passage is the unrecognized source of the common saying, "A Negro is all right in his place," by which is meant that his proper position is secondary to that of the white man.[12]

Explaining this attitude toward black people, Broadman says that some expositors of the Bible insist that "Noah's curse must have fallen on Ham's descendants." Their reasoning, Broadman states, is that "Canaan was singled out by Noah; but obviously, they say, Ham himself must have been cursed if his son had such a blow, else God was not just. Therefore, they say, the Negro as Ham's descendant must still bear the curse!"[13]

Remember, Broadman isn't just talking about lay people believing and propagating this; all of these ideas about Ham, black people and blackness being a curse have been perpetuated by religious people. Indeed, Johnny Lee Clary, the former Imperial Wizard

---

[12] *The Broadman Bible Commentary,* Vol. 1, Revised (Broadman Press: 1969) 147.

[13] Broadman, 148.

of the KKK who has come over to Christ, makes the following observation about racism in America:

> ... Motivated by a white-supremacist-oriented society,
> some white Christians developed an erroneous and un-
> founded theory that implied the blackness of skin tone
> in Africans resulted from the curse that Noah imposed
> upon his grandson Canaan. Some white clergy and
> Christians alike used this particular biblical passage,
> emphasizing the issue of servitude, to validate and sanc-
> tion slavery, racism, exploitation, oppression, terrorism,
> and every other cruel and evil deed and inconceivable
> wicked act against blacks....
>
> The sad commentary to all of this was the fact that the
> "Curse Theory" was started by white Bible-believing
> Christians, who in turn introduced this theory to the rest
> of society.[14]

These are sobering words. And bear in mind that they are not
coming from angry black people accusing white people of racism,
they are coming from white people who are honest enough and brave
enough to look at their past and acknowledge how it has helped to
create the racism of the present.

---

[14] Clary, 169-170. I am impressed with the openness of the Broadman
Bible Commentary and Clary on the subject of "the curse of Ham."
But for the sake of completeness, I want to note that some of their
comments that I have not quoted here differ from the conclusions I
have drawn from my research. Broadman states the belief that
although the Canaanites were the descendants of Ham "ethnically or
politically or both," they "were not Negroes," and Clary his belief that
Ham was not the father of the black race. But many historians and
Bible scholars alike agree that the Canaanites were black and that
Ham was the father of the black race, and I agree. See *Race, Religion
& Racism*, Vol. 1, 122. Also see the works of historian J. A. Rogers.

16

What the Church Must Do

 In his book *Two Nations, Black and White, Separate, Hostile, Unequal*, political scientist Andrew Hacker, writes:

> From slavery through the present, the nation has never opened its doors sufficiently to give black Americans a chance to become full citizens. White Americans often respond that it rests with blacks to put aside enough of their own culture so they can be absorbed into the dominant stream. Blacks can only shake their heads and reply that they have been doing just that for several centuries, with very little to show for it.[1]

Hacker comments that black people's pride in our heritage as African Americans has helped us survive slavery and the discrimination that has lasted to this day. He also points to the benefits that America has gotten from the culture that our ancestors brought with them. Then Hacker adds these grave words:

> However, most white Americans interpret the African emphasis in another way. For them, it frequently leads to

---

[1] Andrew Hacker, *Two Nations, Black and White, Separate, Hostile, Unequal* (New York: Charles Scribner Sons, 1992), 26.

a more insidious application of racism. As has been reiterated, there persists the belief that members of the black race represent an inferior strain of the human species. In this view, Africans — and Americans who trace their origin to that continent — are seen as languishing at a lower evolutionary level than members of other races.

Of course, this belief is seldom voiced in public. Still, the unhappy fact remains that most white people believe that compared with other races, persons of African ancestry are more likely to carry primitive traits in their genes. Given this premise — and prejudice — the presumption follows that most individuals of African heritage will lack the intellectual and organizational capacities the modern world requires.

Most whites who call themselves conservatives hold this view and proclaim it when they are sure of their company. Most liberals and those further to the left deny that present racial disparities are based on genetic inheritance. If they harbor doubts, they keep them to themselves.[2]

This statement is devastating, especially coming as it does from a white political scientist. Over and over we have been confronted with the idea of the inferiority of black people. Over and over we have been confronted with the idea that blackness and the domination of black people by white people are the consequences of the "curse of Ham." It seems that from the points of view of Christians and non-Christians alike black people should have been treated the way we were treated and should now be treated the way we are treated just because we are black.

In his conclusion, Hacker discusses the observations of Alexis de Tocqueville, a French lawyer and sociologist who traveled to

---

[2] Hacker, 26-27.

America in 1831 to study the American prison system, and ended up writing *Democracy in America,* a definitive book about the American continent and character.[3] Hacker's discussion of Tocqueville touches on many of the subjects we've looked at in this book, including the connection between slavery and the point of view held by the dominant white society that black people were inherently inferior, a point of view that has not yet disappeared.

> White Americans, Tocqueville noted, could countenance slavery only by persuading themselves that human beings of African origin were inherently "inferior to the other races of mankind" and hence suited for bondage. This view, so firmly entrenched, would persist after emancipation. "You may set the Negro free," he told his American readers, "but you cannot make him otherwise than an alien to those of European origin." So citizenship for black Americans would always be shadowed by their past; they would ever remain aliens among the nation's native-born inhabitants."[4]

Writing 170 years ago, Tocqueville saw that eventually black Americans would "revolt at being deprived of their civil rights," including their social and economic rights, and he predicted that their future held "the danger of conflict."[5] Even then, Tocqueville could see how our country's past was going to determine its future.

---

[3] Tocqueville's *Democracy in America* has been heralded as one of the greatest commentaries ever written on the American government and society. Tocqueville expressed grave concerns about the relations between white and black people in the young republic. Suggested reading: *Democracy in America,* Vols. I and II *(New York: Alfred A. Knopf, 1989),* the Henry Reeve text as revised by Francis Bowen, and further corrected and edited with introduction, editorial notes and bibliographies by Phillips Bradley.

[4] Hacker, 215.

[5] Hacker, 215.

Alexis de Tocqueville knew that relations between the races — or their lack — are not formed in isolation. If race figures centrally in the life of the United States, it has much to do with the kind of country America is and has been from its start. A combination of forces has served to heighten racial awareness and exacerbate tensions.[6]

Hacker points out that while America isn't the only country to perpetuate racial and ethnic prejudice, we consider ourselves to be more socially advanced as a country than Lebanon or Ceylon, for example, with higher standards for the value of human life and racial harmony. But unfortunately we don't meet these standards. Hacker says that perhaps the primary explanation for this is that facing the pressures of extreme competitiveness, white Americans have looked for ways to feel superior to someone — and that "someone" is black people.

Hence the weight Americans have chosen to give to race, in particular to the artifact of "whiteness," which sets a floor on how far people of that complexion can fall. No matter how degraded their lives, white people are still allowed to believe that they possess the blood, the genes, the patrimony of superiority. No matter what happens, they can never become "black." White Americans of all classes have found it comforting to preserve blacks as a subordinate caste: a presence, which despite all pain and problems, still provides whites with some solace in a stressful world.[7]

It's been a lose-lose situation for Blacks; pre-slavery and post-slavery, white society has had something to gain from casting us in the role of inferiors, and that's exactly what it's done.

---

[6] Hacker, 216-217.

[7] Hacker, 217.

In talking about the tragic problems that plague our black inner-city neighborhoods, especially the extremely high murder rate among black young men,[8] Hacker comments:

> In allocating responsibility the response should be clear. It is white America that has made being black so disconsolate an estate. Legal slavery may be in the past, but segregation and subordination have been allowed to persist. Even today, America imposes a stigma on every black child at birth....
>
> A huge racial chasm remains, and there are few signs that the coming century will see it closed. A century and a quarter after slavery, white America continues to ask of its black citizens an extra patience and perseverance that whites have never required of themselves. So the question for white Americans is essentially moral: is it right to impose on members of an entire race a lesser start in life, and then to expect from them a degree of resolution that has never been demanded from your own race?[9]

---

[8] Although violence in nonurban areas is increasing, children in poor, unstable neighborhoods are more likely to be assaulted than their counterparts in affluent or stable suburbs. The ultimate violence is murder. Homicide has been the leading cause of death among African Americans age 15 to 34 since 1978. The lifetime risk of violent death for young black males is 1 in 27, and for black females, 1 in 17. By contrast, 1 in 205 young white males and 1 in 496 white females are murdered. See "Is Youth Violence Just Another Fact of Life?" (www.apa.org, June, 2000). According to the Federal Bureau of Investigation, between 1985 and 1995, for black and white older adolescents, firearm murders were the most rapidly increasing cause of death. "In some areas of the country, it is now more likely for a black male of 15 to 25 years old to die from homicide than it was for a U.S. soldier to be killed on a tour of duty in Vietnam." (New York Times, December 7, 1990).

[9] Hacker, 218-219.

What the Church Must Do

In different ways, I have been dealing with this question from the first page of this book. I have been dealing with why white Americans, white church leaders, have felt that it was their right to treat black people in a way they would never treat themselves.

Earlier I quoted Hacker, who completed his book in 1992, as saying that after centuries of slavery and subordination of African Americans by white Americans, "a huge racial chasm remains, and there are few signs that the coming century will see it closed." As I write this, we are starting the new century, and my mission is to do everything I can to help close that racial chasm. Obviously, this is something that all of us, white, black, red, yellow and brown must do together.

I am writing about white prejudice against black people because that is my mission from God, and it is my mission because I am a black American and because white racism against Blacks has been the central race problem in America. I have experienced it, and so did my parents, their parents and their parents before them, all the way back to my first ancestors who were brought here from Africa. I welcome people of other colors to expose and root out racism against them. We know that in John 8:32, Jesus says, **"And you shall know the truth, and the truth shall make you free."** When we all know the truth about racism, we will all be free of it. The only way that the chasm of racism will close is for everyone to understand that we are all one, as God made us.

I might have focused this book on the role of big business in promulgating racism, or the role of education or politics or government; unfortunately, each segment of society has played and continues to play its part in racism. I'm writing about the Church because that is also my mission, because the Lord Jesus Christ is at the center of my life, and because, as the previous chapters show, the Church has played an important part in perpetuating racism. Some prominent leaders of the Church have supported or appeared to support racism. Many others have remained silent, when the only true Christian response is to speak out and act to end it. The Church's role is doubly sinful, because not only does it go against God's Word about the different nations of people, it also goes against what Jesus says about the Church.

In Matthew 5:13, Jesus tells us:

"You are the salt of the earth...."

In Matthew 5:14, Jesus tells us:

"You are the light of the world...."

What a responsibility and a privilege to be **the salt of the earth** and **the light of the world!** How miserably the Church has failed until now!

When Africans were brought to America as slaves, instead of some churches coming out for the abolition of slavery, the Church as a whole should have thrown God's light on the evil institution to make sure that it ended as quickly as it began. But the majority of churches supported slavery or turned away and remained silent.[10] After almost two and a half centuries slavery was finally abolished,

---

[10] While not all churches supported racism, even some that initially opposed it changed their stand when it seemed to go against the desires of their members. The Quakers, who initiated the abolition movement, stayed true to their beliefs, but the Baptist and Methodist churches, which were opposed to slavery in the years following the Revolutionary War, did not. With the rise of the cotton industry and the increased demand for slaves, these evangelicals exchanged their stand against slavery for the ideology of the regeneration of society through the regeneration of the individual.

The Episcopalian Church did not address the issue of slavery. Its leaders were even unwilling to allow their one Negro church, St. Thomas Episcopal Church in Philadelphia, to fully participate in the Protestant Episcopal Convention. See Joseph R. Washington, Jr., *Black Religion: The Negro and Christianity in the United States* (Boston: Beacon Press, 1964), 186-187, 190-191.

but black people were still terrorized by racist acts, denied their rights as citizens, and kept subordinate to white society.[11] We have already shown what some church leaders wrote in their commentaries on

---

It's interesting to look briefly at some of the events in the Methodist Church's changing point of view towards slavery, because they show how directly the members' needs affected the Church's position. All three founding fathers of the Methodist faith were opposed to slavery and, at their 1780 Church Convention, it was agreed that any traveling preacher owning slaves would be required to free them. But this proved easier said than done, so the issue of slavery had to be readdressed at both the 1783 and 1784 conventions before a definitive stance was finally taken. Any church member owning slaves was then mandated to sign emancipation papers or withdraw his church membership. The buying and selling of slaves for any reason other than to free them was banned. But, again, this proved difficult to enforce, as Thomas Coke, one of the founders, was personally soon to discover. After speaking against slavery in 1785, Coke was threatened by a mob and served with indictments in two Virginia counties. One woman even offered 50 pounds — which was then a large amount of money — to anyone who would give him 100 lashes. It was not long before the Methodist Church repealed its ruling against slavery, claiming that given the great opposition and the infantile stage of the Church, it would not be prudent to push things to extremity. See Albert J. Raboteau, *Slave Religion: The "Invisible Institution" in the Antebellum South*, 143-144.

[11] Unfortunately, the killing and terrorizing of black Americans by whites is not a thing of the past. At the time of this writing, the Southern Poverty Law Center, a nonprofit organization established to track and fight hate crimes in the United States, published its "Decade in Review." It declared that in the 1990s, "hate crimes and terrorist attacks grabbed headlines like never before.... Although the extreme right had left a trail of bloodshed across the nation in the 1980s, in the 1990s the pace and severity of radical activity ... overshadowed the events of the previous decade." Some of the gruesome hate crimes perpetrated against African Americans during the previous decade include the Florida parking lot murder of Harold Mansfield, an African-American sailor who had just come home from the Gulf War, by a "reverend" in

the Bible. Did they use the Scriptures to stand up for black people? No, these so-called Christian leaders falsified the Bible in order to speak against black people with prejudice. They did this even though

---

the neo-Nazi Church of the Creator; a rash of cross-burnings in black neighborhoods in Shreveport, Louisiana, on the day that Wayne Pierce, state Klan leader, began a four-month sentence for firearms violations; the murder of a homeless black man by neo-Nazi skinheads in Birmingham, Alabama, shortly after one of the skinheads attended a rally where former Klansman Bill Riccio spoke; and the brutal murder in Jasper, Texas, of African-American James Byrd, Jr. by three white supremacists who chained Byrd's ankles to the back of a truck and dragged him for miles until his head was severed from his body. "The Intelligence Report," Winter 2000, Issue 97 (Montgomery, Alabama: Southern Poverty Law Center), 9-27.

In the last three months of 1999, at least 27 hate crimes against black citizens were reported, ranging from murder to physical and verbal attacks to burning crosses on the lawns of black and interracial couples to racist graffiti. The number of active hate groups nationwide includes 138 Ku Klux Klan, 130 neo-Nazi and 40 racist skinhead groups. There are also 21 black separatist groups. "The Intelligence Report," 30, 58-60.

Burnings seem to have long been a favored manner of demonstrating hate toward Blacks and they continue to be so to this day. Among the many church burnings in the 1990s was the destruction of two churches near Manning, South Carolina. On June 20th and 21st, 1995, Ku Klux Klan members, Timothy Welch and another young man, Christopher Cox, burned Macedonia Baptist and Mt. Zion AME Churches. They and two older accomplices, Arthur Haley and Hubert Rowell, were found guilty of these acts of arson and sentenced to 15 to 21 years in prison (later reduced to 12 years for Cox and Welch for testifying in the civil suit against the Klan). Both churches have since been rebuilt. See PBS online, *www.itvs.rg/forgottenfires/story* for more details, and the documentary based on this incident.

It is important to note that the hate crimes listed above do not include the everyday practice in American life of racial profiling, which result in the humiliation of and lethal violence toward innocent black

their actions were in direct opposition to the Word — even though they should have known from the Bible that not taking a stand on behalf of those who were treated as the least of society was the same as not taking a stand for the Lord Jesus Christ Himself. For Jesus tells us in Matthew 25:45:

> **"Assuredly, I say to you, inasmuch as you did not do it to one of the least of these, you did not do it to Me."**

Every time the Church did not protect a black man from a lynch mob or make sure that a black child was not barred entry to a white school, every time the Church did not support black Americans in being equal members of society, the Church didn't just fail its responsibility to black people, it failed its responsibility to itself and the Lord Jesus Christ.

1 Peter 4:17 says:

> **For the time has come for judgment to begin at the house of God; and if it begins with us first, what will be the end of those who do not obey the gospel of God?**

The Bible has been telling us this for almost 2,000 years, but apparently many within the Church have misunderstood it. They have not realized how they will be judged for making judgments about

---

Americans. Incidents of racial profiling include the intrusive, traumatic strip-searching of nearly twice as many African-American women as white men and women by U.S. Customs service inspectors, despite statistical evidence that African-American women returning from abroad were no more likely to carry contraband than white women. In 1998, black women who were U.S. citizens were also nine times more likely than white women who were U.S. citizens to be X-rayed following frisking or being patted down, even though they were "less than half as likely to be found carrying contraband as white women." Black men who were U.S. citizens were also nearly nine times as likely as white men and women to be X-rayed. See *Los Angeles Times*, A-16, April 10, 2000.

black people; they have not realized that their judgments directly disobey the Gospel of God. Why? Because they have never really understood the Gospel of God, or they have understood it only in a segregated way, as if it applied to white people in one sense and to black people in another sense, the sense of black people being inferior. They have not understood that the concept of inferiority based on skin color or anything else is in opposition to the Gospel.

John 3:16 tells us:

> **"For God so loved the world that He gave His only begotten Son, that whoever believes in Him should not perish but have everlasting life."**

The Christian leaders and their followers who have believed in racial division and the inferiority of black people have also believed that they believed in Jesus Christ, but we know by their words that they have not lived what Jesus taught. Indeed, as we've seen, despite what some Bible commentators have written, Jesus *forbids* division within the Church.

Romans 16:17 says:

> **Now I urge you, brethren, note those who cause divisions and offenses, contrary to the doctrine which you learned, and avoid them.**

What is the doctrine that Christians are supposed to learn about how we are to treat our fellow human beings? At the core of Christian doctrine is God's admonition that we are not supposed to show partiality to anyone.

In Acts 10:34-35, Peter says:

> **"In truth I perceive that God shows no partiality.**
>
> **"But in every nation whoever fears Him and works righteousness is accepted by Him."**

In this verse, Peter illustrates what he means by **"God shows no partiality"**; he explains that **"whoever fears Him and works righteousness is accepted by Him."** Peter is clearly telling us that God accepts *everyone* who works righteousness; God makes no gradations in his acceptance among black, white, red, yellow, or brown. How could He, since **"God shows no partiality"**?

This lesson about partiality is taught in Scripture after Scripture. 1 Peter 1:17 says:

And if you call on the Father, who without partiality judges according to each one's work …

It couldn't be stated any more plainly than this: God judges **… without partiality … according to each one's work.…**

First Timothy 5:21 tells us:

I charge you before God and the Lord Jesus Christ and the elect angels that you observe these things without … partiality.

Romans 2:10-11 states:

but glory, honor, and peace to everyone who works what is good, to the Jew first and also the Greek

For there is no partiality with God.

There is no partiality with God, so there should be no partiality with human beings. This is what the Bible is telling us. It's why Galatians 3:28 says:

There is neither Jew nor Greek, there is neither slave nor free, there is neither male nor female; for you are all one in Christ Jesus.

Why we should ignore outward appearances is also stated in Galatians 2:6, when Paul tells us:

> **But from those who seemed to be something — whatever they were, it makes no difference to me; God shows personal favoritism to no man — for those who seemed to be something added nothing to me.**

This verse is the key to why focusing on externals, why being a racist, flies in the face of everything God teaches us. Paul says, **from those who *seemed* to be something**. I italicized the word *seemed* to emphasize that whatever someone seems to be is only external. It is not essence. I've said before that the color of my skin says nothing about my character or my integrity, nor does a red person's, yellow person's, brown person's or white person's skin color say anything about his or her character or integrity. Yet we've seen white Bible commentators assuming that the color of my skin says *everything* about me and puts me in a different, and lower, position than theirs.

It's remarkable to me that these people could have missed the fact that from the beginning God has told us that we are *not* our material bodies.

In Genesis 1:26, as He is about to create Adam, God says:

> **"Let Us make man in Our image, according to Our likeness...."**

We know from John 4:24, KJV, from Jesus's own words, that **God is a Spirit: and they that worship him must worship him in spirit and in truth.** Thus, the image and likeness of God — which He describes as **"Our"** because along with Him He is also including Jesus and the Holy Spirit — is not a physical image and likeness; it is the spirit within the physical body of man that is the image and likeness of God.[12]

What is man's physical body? Genesis 2:7 tells us:

---

[12] For a complete discussion of this issue, see *Race, Religion & Racism,* Vol. 1, 101-111.

And the Lord God formed man of the dust of the ground, and breathed into his nostrils the breath of life; and man became a living being.

Thus, our physical bodies are literally **the dust of the ground**. This is repeated in Genesis 3:19, which says:

"In the sweat of your face you shall eat bread
Till you return to the ground,
For out of it you were taken; for dust you are,
And to dust you shall return."

No wonder the Bible constantly tells us God shows no partiality. No wonder James 2:9 warns us:

but if you show partiality, you commit sin, and are convicted by the law as transgressors...

The wonder is that so many Church leaders have not recognized that showing partiality to white people over black people is a sin. It has been in the Bible in black and white all this time.

To make it crystal clear that all of the people God created are one, Acts 17:26 says:

"And He has made from one blood every nation of men to dwell on all the face of the earth...."

One blood — not one blood for every so-called race as some of the Church leaders whose commentary we have looked at have said.

1 Corinthians 15:39 tells us:

All flesh is not the same flesh, but there is one kind of flesh of men....

Humanity is "one blood" and "one kind of flesh." This is what the Scriptures tell us. It couldn't be said any more simply.

229

And to all these flesh bodies that God has given us, God gives life. As Acts 17:24-25 explains:

"God, who made the world and everything in it, since He is Lord of heaven and earth, does not dwell in temples made with hands.

"Nor is He worshiped with men's hands, as though He needed anything, since He gives to all life, breath, and all things."

Second Corinthians 5:14-15, 17 states:

For the love of Christ compels us, because we judge thus: that if One died for all, then all died;

and He died for all, that those who live should live no longer for themselves, but for Him who died for them and rose again....

Therefore, if anyone is in Christ, he is a new creation; old things have passed away; behold, all things have become new.

Some Christian leaders have ignored the fact that all of us of every color are part of the same race, the human race, and that as Christians we are all one in Jesus. But this Scripture tells us that in Christ, old things pass away and all things become new. This means that anyone who up to now may not have known God's teaching against racism can in Christ renounce racist thoughts and ways and become new.

Earlier we looked at 1 Peter 4:17, which says:

For the time has come for judgment to begin at the house of God; and if it begins with us first, what will be the end of those who do not obey the gospel of God?

Let this warning also be an inspiration. If the Church finally becomes the house of God that it was meant to be and leads the way against racism as it was always meant to do, it will light the way for everyone else. If the Church takes on its role as **the salt of the earth** and **the light of the world** so that all Christians cease to hold racist thoughts in their minds and practice racism in their lives, if all Christians everywhere condemn racism as the sin it is, the "huge racial chasm" will finally close.

The Old Testament tells us in Leviticus 19:34: **"The stranger who dwells among you shall be to you as one born among you, and you shall love him as yourself; for you were strangers in the land of Egypt."** In the New Testament, Jesus reminds us of what God said in His commandments: **"Love your neighbor as yourself"** (Romans 13:9).

Jesus offers us hope, and He also tells us that we will be judged by our actions.

As Revelation 22:12-14, 16 says:

> **"And behold, I am coming quickly, and My reward is with Me, to give to everyone according to his work.**
>
> **"I am the Alpha and the Omega, the Beginning and the End, the First and the Last."**
>
> **Blessed are those who do His commandments, that they may have the right to the tree of life, and may enter through the gates into the city....**
>
> **"I, Jesus, have sent My angel to testify to you these things in the churches. I am the Root and the Offspring of David, the Bright and Morning Star."**

Appendix

With the exception of the verses from 2 Samuel 11:6-17 immediately below, which are taken from the *New King James Version* of the Bible, all other biblical quotes are from the *King James Version*.

Chapter 2

2 Samuel 11: 6-17, from Page 27

11: 6   Then David sent to Joab, *saying*, "Send me Uriah the Hittite." And Joab sent Uriah to David.

7   When Uriah had come to him, David asked how Joab was doing, and how the people were doing, and how the war prospered.

8   And David said to Uriah, "Go down to your house, and wash your feet." So Uriah departed from the king's house, and a gift *of food* from the king followed him.

9   But Uriah slept at the door of the king's house with all the servants of his lord, and did not go down to his house.

10   So when they told David, saying, "Uriah did not go down to his house," David said to Uriah, "Did you not come from a journey? Why did you not go down to your house?"

11   And Uriah said to David, "The ark and Israel and Judah are dwelling in tents, and my lord Joab and the servants of my lord are encamped in the open fields. Shall I then go to my house to eat and drink, and to lie with my wife? *As* you live, and *as* your soul lives, I will not do this thing."

12   Then David said to Uriah, "Wait here today also, and tomorrow I will let you depart." So Uriah remained in Jerusalem that day and the next.

13   Now when David had called him, he ate and drank before him; and he made him drunk. And at evening he went out to lie on his bed with the servants of his lord, but did not go down to his house.

14 In the morning it happened that David wrote a letter to Joab and sent *it* by the hand of Uriah.

15 And he wrote in the letter, saying, "Set Uriah in the forefront of the hottest battle, and retreat from him, that he may be struck down and die."

16 So it was, while Joab besieged the city, that he assigned Uriah to a place where he knew there *were* valiant men.

17 Then the men of the city came out and fought with Joab. And *some* of the people of the servants of David fell; and Uriah the Hittite died also.

Chapter 4

Exodus 3:7-10, from Page 36

3: 7 And the LORD said, I have surely seen the affliction of my people which are in Egypt, and have heard their cry by reason of their taskmasters; for I know their sorrows;

8 And I am come down to deliver them out of the hand of the Egyptians, and to bring them up out of that land unto a good land and a large, unto a land flowing with milk and honey; unto the place of the Canaanites, and the Hittites, and the Amorites, and the Perizzites, and the Hivites, and the Jebusites.

9 Now therefore, behold, the cry of the children of Israel is come unto me: and I have also seen the oppression wherewith the Egyptians oppress them.

10 Come now therefore, and I will send thee unto Pharaoh, that thou mayest bring forth my people the children of Israel out of Egypt.

Nehemiah, chapters 9-13, from Page 39

9: 1 Now in the twenty and fourth day of this month the children of Israel were assembled with fasting, and with sackclothes, and earth upon them.

2 And the seed of Israel separated themselves from all strangers, and stood and confessed their sins, and the iniquities of their fathers.

3 And they stood up in their place, and read in the book of the law of the LORD their God one fourth part of the day; and another fourth part they confessed, and worshipped the LORD their God.

4 Then stood up upon the stairs, of the Levites, Jeshua, and Bani, Kadmiel, Shebaniah, Bunni, Sherebiah, Bani, and Chenani, and cried with a loud voice unto the LORD their God.

5   Then the Levites, Jeshua, and Kadmiel, Bani, Hashabniah, Sherebiah, Hodijah, Shebaniah, and Pethahiah, said, Stand up and bless the LORD your God for ever and ever: and blessed be thy glorious name, which is exalted above all blessing and praise.

6   Thou, even thou, art LORD alone; thou hast made heaven, the heaven of heavens, with all their host, the earth, and all things that are therein, the seas, and all that is therein, and thou preservest them all; and the host of heaven worshippeth thee.

7   Thou art the LORD the God, who didst choose Abram, and broughtest him forth out of Ur of the Chaldees, and gavest him the name of Abraham;

8   And foundest his heart faithful before thee, and madest a covenant with him to give the land of the Canaanites, the Hittites, the Amorites, and the Perizzites, and the Jebusites, and the Girgashites, to give it, I say, to his seed, and hast performed thy words; for thou art righteous:

9   And didst see the affliction of our fathers in Egypt, and heardest their cry by the Red sea;

10 And showedst signs and wonders upon Pharaoh, and on all his servants, and on all the people of his land: for thou knewest that they dealt proudly against them. So didst thou get thee a name, as it is this day.

11 And thou didst divide the sea before them, so that they went through the midst of the sea on the dry land; and their persecutors thou threwest into the deeps, as a stone into the mighty waters.

12 Moreover thou leddest them in the day by a cloudy pillar; and in the night by a pillar of fire, to give them light in the way wherein they should go.

13 Thou camest down also upon mount Sinai, and spakest with them from heaven, and gavest them right judgments, and true laws, good statutes and commandments:

14 And madest known unto them thy holy sabbath, and commandedst them precepts, statutes, and laws, by the hand of Moses thy servant:

15 And gavest them bread from heaven for their hunger, and broughtest forth water for them out of the rock for their thirst, and promisedst them that they should go in to possess the land which thou hadst sworn to give them.

16 But they and our fathers dealt proudly, and hardened their necks, and hearkened not to thy commandments,

17 And refused to obey, neither were mindful of thy wonders that thou didst among them; but hardened their necks, and in their rebellion appointed a captain to return to their bondage: but thou art a God ready to pardon, gracious and merciful, slow to anger, and of great kindness, and forsookest them not.

18 Yea, when they had made them a molten calf, and said, This is thy God that brought thee up out of Egypt, and had wrought great provocations;

19 Yet thou in thy manifold mercies forsookest them not in the wilderness: the pillar of the cloud departed not from them by day, to lead them in the way; neither the pillar of fire by night, to show them light, and the way wherein they should go.

20 Thou gavest also thy good spirit to instruct them, and withheldest not thy manna from their mouth, and gavest them water for their thirst.

21 Yea, forty years didst thou sustain them in the wilderness, so that they lacked nothing; their clothes waxed not old, and their feet swelled not.

22 Moreover thou gavest them kingdoms and nations, and didst divide them into corners: so they possessed the land of Sihon, and the land of the king of Heshbon, and the land of Og king of Bashan.

23 Their children also multipliedst thou as the stars of heaven, and broughtest them into the land, concerning which thou hadst promised to their fathers, that they should go in to possess it.

24 So the children went in and possessed the land, and thou subduedst before them the inhabitants of the land, the Canaanites, and gavest them into their hands, with their kings, and the people of the land, that they might do with them as they would.

25 And they took strong cities, and a fat land, and possessed houses full of all goods, wells digged, vineyards, and oliveyards, and fruit trees in abundance: so they did eat, and were filled, and became fat, and delighted themselves in thy great goodness.

26 Nevertheless they were disobedient, and rebelled against thee, and cast thy law behind their backs, and slew thy prophets which testified against them to turn them to thee, and they wrought great provocations.

27 Therefore thou deliveredst them into the hand of their enemies, who vexed them: and in the time of their trouble, when they cried unto thee, thou heardest them from heaven; and according to thy manifold mercies thou gavest them saviours, who saved them out of the hand of their enemies.

28 But after they had rest, they did evil again before thee: therefore leftest thou them in the hand of their enemies, so that they had the dominion over them: yet when they returned, and cried unto thee, thou heardest them from heaven; and many times didst thou deliver them according to thy mercies;

29 And testifiedst against them, that thou mightest bring them again unto thy law: yet they dealt proudly, and hearkened not unto thy commandments,

Appendix

but sinned against thy judgments, (which if a man do, he shall live in them;) and withdrew the shoulder, and hardened their neck, and would not hear.

30 Yet many years didst thou forbear them, and testifiedst against them by thy spirit in thy prophets: yet would they not give ear: therefore gavest thou them into the hand of the people of the lands.

31 Nevertheless for thy great mercies' sake thou didst not utterly consume them, nor forsake them; for thou art a gracious and merciful God.

32 Now therefore, our God, the great, the mighty, and the terrible God, who keepest covenant and mercy, let not all the trouble seem little before thee, that hath come upon us, on our kings, on our princes, and on our priests, and on our prophets, and on our fathers, and on all thy people, since the time of the kings of Assyria unto this day.

33 Howbeit thou art just in all that is brought upon us; for thou hast done right, but we have done wickedly:

34 Neither have our kings, our princes, our priests, nor our fathers, kept thy law, nor hearkened unto thy commandments and thy testimonies, wherewith thou didst testify against them.

35 For they have not served thee in their kingdom, and in thy great goodness that thou gavest them, and in the large and fat land which thou gavest before them, neither turned they from their wicked works.

36 Behold, we are servants this day, and for the land that thou gavest unto our fathers to eat the fruit thereof and the good thereof, behold, we are servants in it:

37 And it yieldeth much increase unto the kings whom thou hast set over us because of our sins: also they have dominion over our bodies, and over our cattle, at their pleasure, and we are in great distress.

38 And because of all this we make a sure covenant, and write it; and our princes, Levites, and priests, seal unto it.

10: 1 Now those that sealed were, Nehemiah, the Tirshatha, the son of Hachaliah, and Zidkijah,

2 Seraiah, Azariah, Jeremiah,

3 Pashur, Amariah, Malchijah,

4 Hattush, Shebaniah, Malluch,

5 Harim, Meremoth, Obadiah,

6 Daniel, Ginnethon, Baruch,

7 Meshullam, Abijah, Mijamin,

8   Maaziah, Bilgai, Shemaiah: these were the priests.

9   And the Levites: both Jeshua the son of Azaniah, Binnui of the sons of Henadad, Kadmiel;

10 And their brethren, Shebaniah, Hodijah, Kelita, Pelaiah, Hanan,

11 Micha, Rehob, Hashabiah,

12 Zaccur, Sherebiah, Shebaniah,

13 Hodijah, Bani, Beninu.

14 The chief of the people; Parosh, Pahathmoab, Elam, Zatthu, Bani,

15 Bunni, Azgad, Bebai,

16 Adonijah, Bigvai, Adin,

17 Ater, Hizkijah, Azzur,

18 Hodijah, Hashum, Bezai,

19 Hariph, Anathoth, Nebai,

20 Magpiash, Meshullam, Hezir,

21 Meshezabeel, Zadok, Jaddua,

22 Pelatiah, Hanan, Anaiah,

23 Hoshea, Hananiah, Hashub,

24 Hallohesh, Pileha, Shobek,

25 Rehum, Hashabnah, Maaseiah,

26 And Ahijah, Hanan, Anan,

27 Malluch, Harim, Baanah.

28 And the rest of the people, the priests, the Levites, the porters, the singers, the Nethinims, and all they that had separated themselves from the people of the lands unto the law of God, their wives, their sons, and their daughters, every one having knowledge, and having understanding;

29 They clave to their brethren, their nobles, and entered into a curse, and into an oath, to walk in God's law, which was given by Moses the servant of God, and to observe and do all the commandments of the LORD our Lord, and his judgments and his statutes;

30 And that we would not give our daughters unto the people of the land, nor take their daughters for our sons:

31 And if the people of the land bring ware or any victuals on the sabbath day to sell, that we would not buy it of them on the sabbath, or on the holy day: and that we would leave the seventh year, and the exaction of every debt.

32 Also we made ordinances for us, to charge ourselves yearly with the third part of a shekel for the service of the house of our God;

33 For the showbread, and for the continual meat offering, and for the continual burnt offering, of the sabbaths, of the new moons, for the set feasts, and for the holy things, and for the sin offerings to make an atonement for Israel, and for all the work of the house of our God.

34 And we cast the lots among the priests, the Levites, and the people, for the wood offering, to bring it into the house of our God, after the houses of our fathers, at times appointed year by year, to burn upon the altar of the LORD our God, as it is written in the law:

35 And to bring the firstfruits of our ground, and the firstfruits of all fruit of all trees, year by year, unto the house of the LORD:

36 Also the firstborn of our sons, and of our cattle, as it is written in the law, and the firstlings of our herds and of our flocks, to bring to the house of our God, unto the priests that minister in the house of our God:

37 And that we should bring the firstfruits of our dough, and our offerings, and the fruit of all manner of trees, of wine and of oil, unto the priests, to the chambers of the house of our God; and the tithes of our ground unto the Levites, that the same Levites might have the tithes in all the cities of our tillage.

38 And the priest the son of Aaron shall be with the Levites, when the Levites take tithes: and the Levites shall bring up the tithe of the tithes unto the house of our God, to the chambers, into the treasure house.

39 For the children of Israel and the children of Levi shall bring the offering of the corn, of the new wine, and the oil, unto the chambers, where are the vessels of the sanctuary, and the priests that minister, and the porters, and the singers: and we will not forsake the house of our God.

11: 1 And the rulers of the people dwelt at Jerusalem: the rest of the people also cast lots, to bring one of ten to dwell in Jerusalem the holy city, and nine parts to dwell in other cities.

2 And the people blessed all the men, that willingly offered themselves to dwell at Jerusalem.

3 Now these are the chief of the province that dwelt in Jerusalem: but in the cities of Judah dwelt every one in his possession in their cities, to wit, Israel, the priests, and the Levites, and the Nethinims, and the children of Solomon's servants.

4 And at Jerusalem dwelt certain of the children of Judah, and of the children of Benjamin. Of the children of Judah; Athaiah the son of Uzziah, the son

of Zechariah, the son of Amariah, the son of Shephatiah, the son of Mahalaleel, of the children of Perez;

5 And Maaseiah the son of Baruch, the son of Colhozeh, the son of Hazaiah, the son of Adaiah, the son of Joiarib, the son of Zechariah, the son of Shiloni.

6 All the sons of Perez that dwelt at Jerusalem were four hundred threescore and eight valiant men.

7 And these are the sons of Benjamin; Sallu the son of Meshullam, the son of Joed, the son of Pedaiah, the son of Kolaiah, the son of Maaseiah, the son of Ithiel, the son of Jesaiah.

8 And after him Gabbai, Sallai, nine hundred twenty and eight.

9 And Joel the son of Zichri was their overseer: and Judah the son of Senuah was second over the city.

10 Of the priests: Jedaiah the son of Joiarib, Jachin.

11 Seraiah the son of Hilkiah, the son of Meshullam, the son of Zadok, the son of Meraioth, the son of Ahitub, was the ruler of the house of God.

12 And their brethren that did the work of the house were eight hundred twenty and two: and Adaiah the son of Jeroham, the son of Pelaliah, the son of Amzi, the son of Zechariah, the son of Pashur, the son of Malchiah,

13 And his brethren, chief of the fathers, two hundred forty and two: and Amashai the son of Azareel, the son of Ahasai, the son of Meshillemoth, the son of Immer,

14 And their brethren, mighty men of valour, an hundred twenty and eight: and their overseer was Zabdiel, the son of one of the great men.

15 Also of the Levites: Shemaiah the son of Hashub, the son of Azrikam, the son of Hashabiah, the son of Bunni;

16 And Shabbethai and Jozabad, of the chief of the Levites, had the oversight of the outward business of the house of God.

17 And Mattaniah the son of Micha, the son of Zabdi, the son of Asaph, was the principal to begin the thanksgiving in prayer: and Bakbukiah the second among his brethren, and Abda the son of Shammua, the son of Galal, the son of Jeduthun.

18 All the Levites in the holy city were two hundred fourscore and four.

19 Moreover the porters, Akkub, Talmon, and their brethren that kept the gates, were an hundred seventy and two.

20 And the residue of Israel, of the priests, and the Levites, were in all the cities of Judah, every one in his inheritance.

21 But the Nethinims dwelt in Ophel: and Ziha and Gispa were over the Nethinims.

22 The overseer also of the Levites at Jerusalem was Uzzi the son of Bani, the son of Hashabiah, the son of Mattaniah, the son of Micha. Of the sons of Asaph, the singers were over the business of the house of God.

23 For it was the king's commandment concerning them, that a certain portion should be for the singers, due for every day.

24 And Pethahiah the son of Meshezabeel, of the children of Zerah the son of Judah, was at the king's hand in all matters concerning the people.

25 And for the villages, with their fields, some of the children of Judah dwelt at Kirjatharba, and in the villages thereof, and at Dibon, and in the villages thereof, and at Jekabzeel, and in the villages thereof,

26 And at Jeshua, and at Moladah, and at Bethphelet,

27 And at Hazarshual, and at Beersheba, and in the villages thereof,

28 And at Ziklag, and at Mekonah, and in the villages thereof,

29 And at Enrimmon, and at Zareah, and at Jarmuth,

30 Zanoah, Adullam, and in their villages, at Lachish, and the fields thereof, at Azekah, and in the villages thereof. And they dwelt from Beersheba unto the valley of Hinnom.

31 The children also of Benjamin from Geba dwelt at Michmash, and Aija, and Bethel, and in their villages,

32 And at Anathoth, Nob, Ananiah,

33 Hazor, Ramah, Gittaim,

34 Hadid, Zeboim, Neballat,

35 Lod, and Ono, the valley of craftsmen.

36 And of the Levites were divisions in Judah, and in Benjamin.

12: 1 Now these are the priests and the Levites that went up with Zerubbabel the son of Shealtiel, and Jeshua: Seraiah, Jeremiah, Ezra,

2 Amariah, Malluch, Hattush,

3 Shechaniah, Rehum, Meremoth,

4 Iddo, Ginnetho, Abijah,

5 Miamin, Maadiah, Bilgah,

6 Shemaiah, and Joiarib, Jedaiah,

7 Sallu, Amok, Hilkiah, Jedaiah. These were the chief of the priests and of their brethren in the days of Jeshua.

8 Moreover the Levites: Jeshua, Binnui, Kadmiel, Sherebiah, Judah, and Mattaniah, which was over the thanksgiving, he and his brethren.

9 Also Bakbukiah and Unni, their brethren, were over against them in the watches.

10 And Jeshua begat Joiakim, Joiakim also begat Eliashib, and Eliashib begat Joiada,

11 And Joiada begat Jonathan, and Jonathan begat Jaddua.

12 And in the days of Joiakim were priests, the chief of the fathers: of Seraiah, Meraiah; of Jeremiah, Hananiah;

13 Of Ezra, Meshullam; of Amariah, Jehohanan;

14 Of Melicu, Jonathan; of Shebaniah, Joseph;

15 Of Harim, Adna; of Meraioth, Helkai;

16 Of Iddo, Zechariah; of Ginnethon, Meshullam;

17 Of Abijah, Zichri; of Miniamin, of Moadiah, Piltai;

18 Of Bilgah, Shammua; of Shemaiah, Jehonathan;

19 And of Joiarib, Mattenai; of Jedaiah, Uzzi;

20 Of Sallai, Kallai; of Amok, Eber;

21 Of Hilkiah, Hashabiah; of Jedaiah, Nethaneel.

22 The Levites in the days of Eliashib, Joiada, and Johanan, and Jaddua, were recorded chief of the fathers: also the priests, to the reign of Darius the Persian.

23 The sons of Levi, the chief of the fathers, were written in the book of the chronicles, even until the days of Johanan the son of Eliashib.

24 And the chief of the Levites: Hashabiah, Sherebiah, and Jeshua the son of Kadmiel, with their brethren over against them, to praise and to give thanks, according to the commandment of David the man of God, ward over against ward.

25 Mattaniah, and Bakbukiah, Obadiah, Meshullam, Talmon, Akkub, were porters keeping the ward at the thresholds of the gates.

26 These were in the days of Joiakim the son of Jeshua, the son of Jozadak, and in the days of Nehemiah the governor, and of Ezra the priest, the scribe.

27 And at the dedication of the wall of Jerusalem they sought the Levites out of all their places, to bring them to Jerusalem, to keep the dedication with gladness, both with thanksgivings, and with singing, with cymbals, psalteries, and with harps.

Appendix

28 And the sons of the singers gathered themselves together, both out of the plain country round about Jerusalem, and from the villages of Netophathi;

29 Also from the house of Gilgal, and out of the fields of Geba and Azmaveth: for the singers had builded them villages round about Jerusalem.

30 And the priests and the Levites purified themselves, and purified the people, and the gates, and the wall.

31 Then I brought up the princes of Judah upon the wall, and appointed two great companies of them that gave thanks, whereof one went on the right hand upon the wall toward the dung gate:

32 And after them went Hoshaiah, and half of the princes of Judah,

33 And Azariah, Ezra, and Meshullam,

34 Judah, and Benjamin, and Shemaiah, and Jeremiah,

35 And certain of the priests' sons with trumpets; namely, Zechariah the son of Jonathan, the son of Shemaiah, the son of Mattaniah, the son of Michaiah, the son of Zaccur, the son of Asaph:

36 And his brethren, Shemaiah, and Azarael, Milalai, Gilalai, Maai, Nethaneel, and Judah, Hanani, with the musical instruments of David the man of God, and Ezra the scribe before them.

37 And at the fountain gate, which was over against them, they went up by the stairs of the city of David, at the going up of the wall, above the house of David, even unto the water gate eastward.

38 And the other company of them that gave thanks went over against them, and I after them, and the half of the people upon the wall, from beyond the tower of the furnaces even unto the broad wall;

39 And from above the gate of Ephraim, and above the old gate, and above the fish gate, and the tower of Hananeel, and the tower of Meah, even unto the sheep gate: and they stood still in the prison gate.

40 So stood the two companies of them that gave thanks in the house of God, and I, and the half of the rulers with me:

41 And the priests; Eliakim, Maaseiah, Miniamin, Michaiah, Elioenai, Zechariah, and Hananiah, with trumpets;

42 And Maaseiah, and Shemaiah, and Eleazar, and Uzzi, and Jehohanan, and Malchijah, and Elam, and Ezer. And the singers sang loud, with Jezrahiah their overseer.

43 Also that day they offered great sacrifices, and rejoiced: for God had made them rejoice with great joy: the wives also and the children rejoiced: so that the joy of Jerusalem was heard even afar off.

44 And at that time were some appointed over the chambers for the treasures, for the offerings, for the firstfruits, and for the tithes, to gather into them out of the fields of the cities the portions of the law for the priests and Levites: for Judah rejoiced for the priests and for the Levites that waited.

45 And both the singers and the porters kept the ward of their God, and the ward of the purification, according to the commandment of David, and of Solomon his son.

46 For in the days of David and Asaph of old there were chief of the singers, and songs of praise and thanksgiving unto God.

47 And all Israel in the days of Zerubbabel, and in the days of Nehemiah, gave the portions of the singers and the porters, every day his portion: and they sanctified holy things unto the Levites; and the Levites sanctified them unto the children of Aaron.

13: 1 On that day they read in the book of Moses in the audience of the people; and therein was found written, that the Ammonite and the Moabite should not come into the congregation of God for ever;

2 Because they met not the children of Israel with bread and with water, but hired Balaam against them, that he should curse them: howbeit our God turned the curse into a blessing.

3 Now it came to pass, when they had heard the law, that they separated from Israel all the mixed multitude.

4 And before this, Eliashib the priest, having the oversight of the chamber of the house of our God, was allied unto Tobiah:

5 And he had prepared for him a great chamber, where aforetime they laid the meat offerings, the frankincense, and the vessels, and the tithes of the corn, the new wine, and the oil, which was commanded to be given to the Levites, and the singers, and the porters; and the offerings of the priests.

6 But in all this time was not I at Jerusalem: for in the two and thirtieth year of Artaxerxes king of Babylon came I unto the king, and after certain days obtained I leave of the king:

7 And I came to Jerusalem, and understood of the evil that Eliashib did for Tobiah, in preparing him a chamber in the courts of the house of God.

8 And it grieved me sore: therefore I cast forth all the household stuff of Tobiah out of the chamber.

9 Then I commanded, and they cleansed the chambers: and thither brought I again the vessels of the house of God, with the meat offering and the frankincense.

10 And I perceived that the portions of the Levites had not been given them: for the Levites and the singers, that did the work, were fled every one to his field.

11 Then contended I with the rulers, and said, Why is the house of God forsaken? And I gathered them together, and set them in their place.

12 Then brought all Judah the tithe of the corn and the new wine and the oil unto the treasuries.

13 And I made treasurers over the treasuries, Shelemiah the priest, and Zadok the scribe, and of the Levites, Pedaiah: and next to them was Hanan the son of Zaccur, the son of Mattaniah: for they were counted faithful, and their office was to distribute unto their brethren.

14 Remember me, O my God, concerning this, and wipe not out my good deeds that I have done for the house of my God, and for the offices thereof.

15 In those days saw I in Judah some treading wine presses on the sabbath, and bringing in sheaves, and lading asses; as also wine, grapes, and figs, and all manner of burdens, which they brought into Jerusalem on the sabbath day: and I testified against them in the day wherein they sold victuals.

16 There dwelt men of Tyre also therein, which brought fish, and all manner of ware, and sold on the sabbath unto the children of Judah, and in Jerusalem.

17 Then I contended with the nobles of Judah, and said unto them, What evil thing is this that ye do, and profane the sabbath day?

18 Did not your fathers thus, and did not our God bring all this evil upon us, and upon this city? yet ye bring more wrath upon Israel by profaning the sabbath.

19 And it came to pass, that when the gates of Jerusalem began to be dark before the sabbath, I commanded that the gates should be shut, and charged that they should not be opened till after the sabbath: and some of my servants set I at the gates, that there should no burden be brought in on the sabbath day.

20 So the merchants and sellers of all kind of ware lodged without Jerusalem once or twice.

21 Then I testified against them, and said unto them, Why lodge ye about the wall? if ye do so again, I will lay hands on you. From that time forth came they no more on the sabbath.

22 And I commanded the Levites that they should cleanse themselves, and that they should come and keep the gates, to sanctify the sabbath day. Remember me, O my God, concerning this also, and spare me according to the greatness of thy mercy.

23 In those days also saw I Jews that had married wives of Ashdod, of Ammon, and of Moab:

24 And their children spake half in the speech of Ashdod, and could not speak in the Jews' language, but according to the language of each people.

25 And I contended with them, and cursed them, and smote certain of them, and plucked off their hair, and made them swear by God, saying, Ye shall not give your daughters unto their sons, nor take their daughters unto your sons, or for yourselves.

26 Did not Solomon king of Israel sin by these things? yet among many nations was there no king like him, who was beloved of his God, and God made him king over all Israel: nevertheless even him did outlandish women cause to sin.

27 Shall we then hearken unto you to do all this great evil, to transgress against our God in marrying strange wives?

28 And one of the sons of Joiada, the son of Eliashib the high priest, was son in law to Sanballat the Horonite: therefore I chased him from me.

29 Remember them, O my God, because they have defiled the priesthood, and the covenant of the priesthood, and of the Levites.

30 Thus cleansed I them from all strangers, and appointed the wards of the priests and the Levites, every one in his business;

31 And for the wood offering, at times appointed, and for the firstfruits. Remember me, O my God, for good.

Jeremiah 50, from Page 40

50: 1 The word that the LORD spake against Babylon and against the land of the Chaldeans by Jeremiah the prophet.

2 Declare ye among the nations, and publish, and set up a standard; publish, and conceal not: say, Babylon is taken, Bel is confounded, Merodach is broken in pieces; her idols are confounded, her images are broken in pieces.

3 For out of the north there cometh up a nation against her, which shall make her land desolate, and none shall dwell therein: they shall remove, they shall depart, both man and beast.

4 In those days, and in that time, saith the LORD, the children of Israel shall come, they and the children of Judah together, going and weeping: they shall go, and seek the LORD their God.

5 They shall ask the way to Zion with their faces thitherward, saying, Come, and let us join ourselves to the LORD in a perpetual covenant that shall not be forgotten.

6   My people hath been lost sheep: their shepherds have caused them to go astray, they have turned them away on the mountains: they have gone from mountain to hill, they have forgotten their restingplace.

7   All that found them have devoured them: and their adversaries said, We offend not, because they have sinned against the LORD, the habitation of justice, even the LORD, the hope of their fathers.

8   Remove out of the midst of Babylon, and go forth out of the land of the Chaldeans, and be as the he goats before the flocks.

9   For, lo, I will raise and cause to come up against Babylon an assembly of great nations from the north country: and they shall set themselves in array against her; from thence she shall be taken: their arrows shall be as of a mighty expert man; none shall return in vain.

10 And Chaldea shall be a spoil: all that spoil her shall be satisfied, saith the LORD.

11 Because ye were glad, because ye rejoiced, O ye destroyers of mine heritage, because ye are grown fat as the heifer at grass, and bellow as bulls;

12 Your mother shall be sore confounded; she that bare you shall be ashamed: behold, the hindermost of the nations shall be a wilderness, a dry land, and a desert.

13 Because of the wrath of the LORD it shall not be inhabited, but it shall be wholly desolate: every one that goeth by Babylon shall be astonished, and hiss at all her plagues.

14 Put yourselves in array against Babylon round about: all ye that bend the bow, shoot at her, spare no arrows: for she hath sinned against the LORD.

15 Shout against her round about: she hath given her hand: her foundations are fallen, her walls are thrown down: for it is the vengeance of the LORD: take vengeance upon her; as she hath done, do unto her.

16 Cut off the sower from Babylon, and him that handleth the sickle in the time of harvest: for fear of the oppressing sword they shall turn every one to his people, and they shall flee every one to his own land.

17 Israel is a scattered sheep; the lions have driven him away: first the king of Assyria hath devoured him; and last this Nebuchadrezzar king of Babylon hath broken his bones.

18 Therefore thus saith the LORD of hosts, the God of Israel; Behold, I will punish the king of Babylon and his land, as I have punished the king of Assyria.

19 And I will bring Israel again to his habitation, and he shall feed on Carmel and Bashan, and his soul shall be satisfied upon mount Ephraim and Gilead.

20 In those days, and in that time, saith the LORD, the iniquity of Israel shall be sought for, and there shall be none; and the sins of Judah, and they shall not be found: for I will pardon them whom I reserve.

21 Go up against the land of Merathaim, even against it, and against the inhabitants of Pekod: waste and utterly destroy after them, saith the LORD, and do according to all that I have commanded thee.

22 A sound of battle is in the land, and of great destruction.

23 How is the hammer of the whole earth cut asunder and broken! how is Babylon become a desolation among the nations!

24 I have laid a snare for thee, and thou art also taken, O Babylon, and thou wast not aware: thou art found, and also caught, because thou hast striven against the LORD.

25 The LORD hath opened his armoury, and hath brought forth the weapons of his indignation: for this is the work of the Lord GOD of hosts in the land of the Chaldeans.

26 Come against her from the utmost border, open her storehouses: cast her up as heaps, and destroy her utterly: let nothing of her be left.

27 Slay all her bullocks; let them go down to the slaughter: woe unto them! for their day is come, the time of their visitation.

28 The voice of them that flee and escape out of the land of Babylon, to declare in Zion the vengeance of the LORD our God, the vengeance of his temple.

29 Call together the archers against Babylon: all ye that bend the bow, camp against it round about; let none thereof escape: recompense her according to her work; according to all that she hath done, do unto her: for she hath been proud against the LORD, against the Holy One of Israel.

30 Therefore shall her young men fall in the streets, and all her men of war shall be cut off in that day, saith the LORD.

31 Behold, I am against thee, O thou most proud, saith the Lord GOD of hosts: for thy day is come, the time that I will visit thee.

32 And the most proud shall stumble and fall, and none shall raise him up: and I will kindle a fire in his cities, and it shall devour all round about him.

33 Thus saith the LORD of hosts; The children of Israel and the children of Judah were oppressed together: and all that took them captives held them fast; they refused to let them go.

34 Their Redeemer is strong; the LORD of hosts is his name: he shall thoroughly plead their cause, that he may give rest to the land, and disquiet the inhabitants of Babylon.

35 A sword is upon the Chaldeans, saith the LORD, and upon the inhabitants of Babylon, and upon her princes, and upon her wise men.

36 A sword is upon the liars; and they shall dote: a sword is upon her mighty men; and they shall be dismayed.

37 A sword is upon their horses, and upon their chariots, and upon all the mingled people that are in the midst of her; and they shall become as women: a sword is upon her treasures; and they shall be robbed.

38 A drought is upon her waters; and they shall be dried up: for it is the land of graven images, and they are mad upon their idols.

39 Therefore the wild beasts of the desert with the wild beasts of the islands shall dwell there, and the owls shall dwell therein: and it shall be no more inhabited for ever; neither shall it be dwelt in from generation to generation.

40 As God overthrew Sodom and Gomorrah and the neighbour cities thereof, saith the LORD; so shall no man abide there, neither shall any son of man dwell therein.

41 Behold, a people shall come from the north, and a great nation, and many kings shall be raised up from the coasts of the earth.

42 They shall hold the bow and the lance: they are cruel, and will not show mercy: their voice shall roar like the sea, and they shall ride upon horses, every one put in array, like a man to the battle, against thee, O daughter of Babylon.

43 The king of Babylon hath heard the report of them, and his hands waxed feeble: anguish took hold of him, and pangs as of a woman in travail.

44 Behold, he shall come up like a lion from the swelling of Jordan unto the habitation of the strong: but I will make them suddenly run away from her: and who is a chosen man, that I may appoint over her? for who is like me? and who will appoint me the time? and who is that shepherd that will stand before me?

45 Therefore hear ye the counsel of the LORD, that he hath taken against Babylon; and his purposes, that he hath purposed against the land of the Chaldeans: Surely the least of the flock shall draw them out: surely he shall make their habitation desolate with them.

46 At the noise of the taking of Babylon the earth is moved, and the cry is heard among the nations.

Ezekiel 30, from Page 40

30: 1 The word of the LORD came again unto me, saying,

2   Son of man, prophesy and say, Thus saith the Lord GOD; Howl ye, Woe worth the day!

3   For the day is near, even the day of the LORD is near, a cloudy day; it shall be the time of the heathen.

4   And the sword shall come upon Egypt, and great pain shall be in Ethiopia, when the slain shall fall in Egypt, and they shall take away her multitude, and her foundations shall be broken down.

5   Ethiopia, and Libya, and Lydia, and all the mingled people, and Chub, and the men of the land that is in league, shall fall with them by the sword.

6   Thus saith the LORD; They also that uphold Egypt shall fall; and the pride of her power shall come down: from the tower of Syene shall they fall in it by the sword, saith the Lord GOD.

7   And they shall be desolate in the midst of the countries that are desolate, and her cities shall be in the midst of the cities that are wasted.

8   And they shall know that I am the LORD, when I have set a fire in Egypt, and when all her helpers shall be destroyed.

9   In that day shall messengers go forth from me in ships to make the careless Ethiopians afraid, and great pain shall come upon them, as in the day of Egypt: for, lo, it cometh.

10 Thus saith the Lord GOD; I will also make the multitude of Egypt to cease by the hand of Nebuchadrezzar king of Babylon.

11 He and his people with him, the terrible of the nations, shall be brought to destroy the land: and they shall draw their swords against Egypt, and fill the land with the slain.

12 And I will make the rivers dry, and sell the land into the hand of the wicked: and I will make the land waste, and all that is therein, by the hand of strangers: I the LORD have spoken it.

13 Thus saith the Lord GOD; I will also destroy the idols, and I will cause their images to cease out of Noph; and there shall be no more a prince of the land of Egypt: and I will put a fear in the land of Egypt.

14 And I will make Pathros desolate, and will set fire in Zoan, and will execute judgments in No.

15 And I will pour my fury upon Sin, the strength of Egypt; and I will cut off the multitude of No.

16 And I will set fire in Egypt: Sin shall have great pain, and No shall be rent asunder, and Noph shall have distresses daily.

17 The young men of Aven and of Pibeseth shall fall by the sword: and these cities shall go into captivity.

18 At Tehaphnehes also the day shall be darkened, when I shall break there the yokes of Egypt: and the pomp of her strength shall cease in her: as for her, a cloud shall cover her, and her daughters shall go into captivity.

19 Thus will I execute judgments in Egypt: and they shall know that I am the LORD.

20 And it came to pass in the eleventh year, in the first month, in the seventh day of the month, that the word of the LORD came unto me, saying,

21 Son of man, I have broken the arm of Pharaoh king of Egypt; and, lo, it shall not be bound up to be healed, to put a roller to bind it, to make it strong to hold the sword.

22 Therefore thus saith the Lord GOD; Behold, I am against Pharaoh king of Egypt, and will break his arms, the strong, and that which was broken; and I will cause the sword to fall out of his hand.

23 And I will scatter the Egyptians among the nations, and will disperse them through the countries.

24 And I will strengthen the arms of the king of Babylon, and put my sword in his hand: but I will break Pharaoh's arms, and he shall groan before him with the groanings of a deadly wounded man.

25 But I will strengthen the arms of the king of Babylon, and the arms of Pharaoh shall fall down; and they shall know that I am the LORD, when I shall put my sword into the hand of the king of Babylon, and he shall stretch it out upon the land of Egypt.26   And I will scatter the Egyptians among the nations, and disperse them among the countries; and they shall know that I am the LORD.

Genesis 24:12-67, from Page 44

24: 12 And he said, O LORD God of my master Abraham, I pray thee, send me good speed this day, and show kindness unto my master Abraham.

13 Behold, I stand here by the well of water; and the daughters of the men of the city come out to draw water:

14 And let it come to pass, that the damsel to whom I shall say, Let down thy pitcher, I pray thee, that I may drink; and she shall say, Drink, and I will give thy camels drink also: let the same be she that thou hast appointed for thy servant Isaac; and thereby shall I know that thou hast showed kindness unto my master.

15 And it came to pass, before he had done speaking, that, behold, Rebekah came out, who was born to Bethuel, son of Milcah, the wife of Nahor, Abraham's brother, with her pitcher upon her shoulder.

16 And the damsel was very fair to look upon, a virgin, neither had any man known her: and she went down to the well, and filled her pitcher, and came up.

17 And the servant ran to meet her, and said, Let me, I pray thee, drink a little water of thy pitcher.

18 And she said, Drink, my lord: and she hasted, and let down her pitcher upon her hand, and gave him drink.

19 And when she had done giving him drink, she said, I will draw water for thy camels also, until they have done drinking.

20 And she hasted, and emptied her pitcher into the trough, and ran again unto the well to draw water, and drew for all his camels.

21 And the man wondering at her held his peace, to wit whether the LORD had made his journey prosperous or not.

22 And it came to pass, as the camels had done drinking, that the man took a golden earring of half a shekel weight, and two bracelets for her hands of ten shekels weight of gold;

23 And said, Whose daughter art thou? tell me, I pray thee: is there room in thy father's house for us to lodge in?

24 And she said unto him, I am the daughter of Bethuel the son of Milcah, which she bare unto Nahor.

25 She said moreover unto him, We have both straw and provender enough, and room to lodge in.

26 And the man bowed down his head, and worshipped the LORD.

27 And he said, Blessed be the LORD God of my master Abraham, who hath not left destitute my master of his mercy and his truth: I being in the way, the LORD led me to the house of my master's brethren.

28 And the damsel ran, and told them of her mother's house these things.

29 And Rebekah had a brother, and his name was Laban: and Laban ran out unto the man, unto the well.

Appendix

30 And it came to pass, when he saw the earring and bracelets upon his sister's hands, and when he heard the words of Rebekah his sister, saying, Thus spake the man unto me; that he came unto the man; and, behold, he stood by the camels at the well.

31 And he said, Come in, thou blessed of the LORD; wherefore standest thou without? for I have prepared the house, and room for the camels.

32 And the man came into the house: and he ungirded his camels, and gave straw and provender for the camels, and water to wash his feet, and the men's feet that were with him.

33 And there was set meat before him to eat: but he said, I will not eat, until I have told mine errand. And he said, Speak on.

34 And he said, I am Abraham's servant.

35 And the LORD hath blessed my master greatly; and he is become great: and he hath given him flocks, and herds, and silver, and gold, and menservants, and maidservants, and camels, and asses.

36 And Sarah my master's wife bare a son to my master when she was old: and unto him hath he given all that he hath.

37 And my master made me swear, saying, Thou shalt not take a wife to my son of the daughters of the Canaanites, in whose land I dwell:

38 But thou shalt go unto my father's house, and to my kindred, and take a wife unto my son.

39 And I said unto my master, Peradventure the woman will not follow me.

40 And he said unto me, The LORD, before whom I walk, will send his angel with thee, and prosper thy way; and thou shalt take a wife for my son of my kindred, and of my father's house:

41 Then shalt thou be clear from this my oath, when thou comest to my kindred; and if they give not thee one, thou shalt be clear from my oath.

42 And I came this day unto the well, and said, O LORD God of my master Abraham, if now thou do prosper my way which I go:

43 Behold, I stand by the well of water; and it shall come to pass, that when the virgin cometh forth to draw water, and I say to her, Give me, I pray thee, a little water of thy pitcher to drink;

44 And she say to me, Both drink thou, and I will also draw for thy camels: let the same be the woman whom the LORD hath appointed out for my master's son.

45 And before I had done speaking in mine heart, behold, Rebekah came forth with her pitcher on her shoulder; and she went down unto the well, and drew water: and I said unto her, Let me drink, I pray thee.

253

46 And she made haste, and let down her pitcher from her shoulder, and said, Drink, and I will give thy camels drink also: so I drank, and she made the camels drink also.

47 And I asked her, and said, Whose daughter art thou? And she said, The daughter of Bethuel, Nahor's son, whom Milcah bare unto him: and I put the earring upon her face, and the bracelets upon her hands.

48 And I bowed down my head, and worshipped the LORD, and blessed the LORD God of my master Abraham, which had led me in the right way to take my master's brother's daughter unto his son.

49 And now if ye will deal kindly and truly with my master, tell me: and if not, tell me; that I may turn to the right hand, or to the left.

50 Then Laban and Bethuel answered and said, The thing proceedeth from the LORD: we cannot speak unto thee bad or good.

51 Behold, Rebekah is before thee, take her, and go, and let her be thy master's son's wife, as the LORD hath spoken.

52 And it came to pass, that, when Abraham's servant heard their words, he worshipped the LORD, bowing himself to the earth.

53 And the servant brought forth jewels of silver, and jewels of gold, and raiment, and gave them to Rebekah: he gave also to her brother and to her mother precious things.

54 And they did eat and drink, he and the men that were with him, and tarried all night; and they rose up in the morning, and he said, Send me away unto my master.

55 And her brother and her mother said, Let the damsel abide with us a few days, at the least ten; after that she shall go.

56 And he said unto them, Hinder me not, seeing the LORD hath prospered my way; send me away that I may go to my master.

57 And they said, We will call the damsel, and inquire at her mouth.

58 And they called Rebekah, and said unto her, Wilt thou go with this man? And she said, I will go.

59 And they sent away Rebekah their sister, and her nurse, and Abraham's servant, and his men.

60 And they blessed Rebekah, and said unto her, Thou art our sister, be thou the mother of thousands of millions, and let thy seed possess the gate of those which hate them.

61 And Rebekah arose, and her damsels, and they rode upon the camels, and followed the man: and the servant took Rebekah, and went his way.

62 And Isaac came from the way of the well Lahairoi; for he dwelt in the south country.

63 And Isaac went out to meditate in the field at the eventide: and he lifted up his eyes, and saw, and, behold, the camels were coming.

64 And Rebekah lifted up her eyes, and when she saw Isaac, she lighted off the camel.

65 For she *had* said unto the servant, What man is this that walketh in the field to meet us? And the servant *had* said, It is my master: therefore she took a vail, and covered herself.

66 And the servant told Isaac all things that he had done

67 And Isaac brought her into his mother Sarah's tent, and took Rebekah, and she became his wife; and he loved her: and Isaac was comforted after his mother's *death*.

Chapter 5

Genesis 36, from Page 51

36: 1 Now these are the generations of Esau, who is Edom.

2 Esau took his wives of the daughters of Canaan; Adah the daughter of Elon the Hittite, and Aholibamah the daughter of Anah the daughter of Zibeon the Hivite;

3 And Bashemath Ishmael's daughter, sister of Nebajoth.

4 And Adah bare to Esau Eliphaz; and Bashemath bare Reuel;

5 And Aholibamah bare Jeush, and Jaalam, and Korah: these are the sons of Esau, which were born unto him in the land of Canaan.

6 And Esau took his wives, and his sons, and his daughters, and all the persons of his house, and his cattle, and all his beasts, and all his substance, which he had got in the land of Canaan; and went into the country from the face of his brother Jacob.

7 For their riches were more than that they might dwell together; and the land wherein they were strangers could not bear them because of their cattle.

8 Thus dwelt Esau in mount Seir: Esau is Edom.

9 And these are the generations of Esau the father of the Edomites in mount Seir:

10 These are the names of Esau's sons; Eliphaz the son of Adah the wife of Esau, Reuel the son of Bashemath the wife of Esau.

11 And the sons of Eliphaz were Teman, Omar, Zepho, and Gatam, and Kenaz.

12 And Timna was concubine to Eliphaz Esau's son; and she bare to Eliphaz Amalek: these were the sons of Adah Esau's wife.

13 And these are the sons of Reuel; Nahath, and Zerah, Shammah, and Mizzah: these were the sons of Bashemath Esau's wife.

14 And these were the sons of Aholibamah, the daughter of Anah the daughter of Zibeon, Esau's wife: and she bare to Esau Jeush, and Jaalam, and Korah.

15 These were dukes of the sons of Esau: the sons of Eliphaz the firstborn son of Esau; duke Teman, duke Omar, duke Zepho, duke Kenaz,

16 Duke Korah, duke Gatam, and duke Amalek: these are the dukes that came of Eliphaz in the land of Edom; these were the sons of Adah.

17 And these are the sons of Reuel Esau's son; duke Nahath, duke Zerah, duke Shammah, duke Mizzah: these are the dukes that came of Reuel in the land of Edom; these are the sons of Bashemath Esau's wife.

18 And these are the sons of Aholibamah Esau's wife; duke Jeush, duke Jaalam, duke Korah: these were the dukes that came of Aholibamah the daughter of Anah, Esau's wife.

19 These are the sons of Esau, who is Edom, and these are their dukes.

20 These are the sons of Seir the Horite, who inhabited the land; Lotan, and Shobal, and Zibeon, and Anah,

21 And Dishon, and Ezer, and Dishan: these are the dukes of the Horites, the children of Seir in the land of Edom.

22 And the children of Lotan were Hori and Hemam; and Lotan's sister was Timna.

23 And the children of Shobal were these; Alvan, and Manahath, and Ebal, Shepho, and Onam.

24 And these are the children of Zibeon; both Ajah, and Anah: this was that Anah that found the mules in the wilderness, as he fed the asses of Zibeon his father.

25 And the children of Anah were these; Dishon, and Aholibamah the daughter of Anah.

26 And these are the children of Dishon; Hemdan, and Eshban, and Ithran, and Cheran.

27 The children of Ezer are these; Bilhan, and Zaavan, and Akan.

28 The children of Dishan are these; Uz, and Aran.

29 These are the dukes that came of the Horites; duke Lotan, duke Shobal, duke Zibeon, duke Anah,

30 Duke Dishon, duke Ezer, duke Dishan: these are the dukes that came of Hori, among their dukes in the land of Seir.

31 And these are the kings that reigned in the land of Edom, before there reigned any king over the children of Israel.

32 And Bela the son of Beor reigned in Edom: and the name of his city was Dinhabah.

33 And Bela died, and Jobab the son of Zerah of Bozrah reigned in his stead.

34 And Jobab died, and Husham of the land of Temani reigned in his stead.

35 And Husham died, and Hadad the son of Bedad, who smote Midian in the field of Moab, reigned in his stead: and the name of his city was Avith.

36 And Hadad died, and Samlah of Masrekah reigned in his stead.

37 And Samlah died, and Saul of Rehoboth by the river reigned in his stead.

38 And Saul died, and Baalhanan the son of Achbor reigned in his stead.

39 And Baalhanan the son of Achbor died, and Hadar reigned in his stead: and the name of his city was Pau; and his wife's name was Mehetabel, the daughter of Matred, the daughter of Mezahab.

40 And these are the names of the dukes that came of Esau, according to their families, after their places, by their names; duke Timnah, duke Alvah, duke Jetheth,

41 Duke Aholibamah, duke Elah, duke Pinon,

42 Duke Kenaz, duke Teman, duke Mibzar,

43 Duke Magdiel, duke Iram: these be the dukes of Edom, according to their habitations in the land of their possession: he is Esau the father of the Edomites.

Chapter 7

I Kings 11, Page 75

11: 1 But king Solomon loved many strange women, together with the daughter of Pharaoh, women of the Moabites, Ammonites, Edomites, Zidonians, and Hittites;

2   Of the nations concerning which the LORD said unto the children of Israel, Ye shall not go in to them, neither shall they come in unto you: for surely they will turn away your heart after their gods: Solomon clave unto these in love.

3   And he had seven hundred wives, princesses, and three hundred concubines: and his wives turned away his heart.

4   For it came to pass, when Solomon was old, that his wives turned away his heart after other gods: and his heart was not perfect with the LORD his God, as was the heart of David his father.

5   For Solomon went after Ashtoreth the goddess of the Zidonians, and after Milcom the abomination of the Ammonites.

6   And Solomon did evil in the sight of the LORD, and went not fully after the LORD, as did David his father.

7   Then did Solomon build an high place for Chemosh, the abomination of Moab, in the hill that is before Jerusalem, and for Molech, the abomination of the children of Ammon.

8   And likewise did he for all his strange wives, which burnt incense and sacrificed unto their gods.

9   And the LORD was angry with Solomon, because his heart was turned from the LORD God of Israel, which had appeared unto him twice,

10 And had commanded him concerning this thing, that he should not go after other gods: but he kept not that which the LORD commanded.

11 Wherefore the LORD said unto Solomon, Forasmuch as this is done of thee, and thou hast not kept my covenant and my statutes, which I have commanded thee, I will surely rend the kingdom from thee, and will give it to thy servant.

12 Notwithstanding in thy days I will not do it for David thy father's sake: but I will rend it out of the hand of thy son.

13 Howbeit I will not rend away all the kingdom; but will give one tribe to thy son for David my servant's sake, and for Jerusalem's sake which I have chosen.

14 And the LORD stirred up an adversary unto Solomon, Hadad the Edomite: he was of the king's seed in Edom.

15 For it came to pass, when David was in Edom, and Joab the captain of the host was gone up to bury the slain, after he had smitten every male in Edom;

16 (For six months did Joab remain there with all Israel, until he had cut off every male in Edom:)

Appendix

17 That Hadad fled, he and certain Edomites of his father's servants with him, to go into Egypt; Hadad being yet a little child.

18 And they arose out of Midian, and came to Paran: and they took men with them out of Paran, and they came to Egypt, unto Pharaoh king of Egypt; which gave him an house, and appointed him victuals, and gave him land.

19 And Hadad found great favour in the sight of Pharaoh, so that he gave him to wife the sister of his own wife, the sister of Tahpenes the queen.

20 And the sister of Tahpenes bare him Genubath his son, whom Tahpenes weaned in Pharaoh's house: and Genubath was in Pharaoh's household among the sons of Pharaoh.

21 And when Hadad heard in Egypt that David slept with his fathers, and that Joab the captain of the host was dead, Hadad said to Pharaoh, Let me depart, that I may go to mine own country.

22 Then Pharaoh said unto him, But what hast thou lacked with me, that, behold, thou seekest to go to thine own country? And he answered, Nothing: howbeit let me go in any wise.

23 And God stirred him up another adversary, Rezon the son of Eliadah, which fled from his lord Hadadezer king of Zobah:

24 And he gathered men unto him, and became captain over a band, when David slew them of Zobah: and they went to Damascus, and dwelt therein, and reigned in Damascus.

25 And he was an adversary to Israel all the days of Solomon, beside the mischief that Hadad did: and he abhorred Israel, and reigned over Syria.

26 And Jeroboam the son of Nebat, an Ephrathite of Zereda, Solomon's servant, whose mother's name was Zeruah, a widow woman, even he lifted up his hand against the king.

27 And this was the cause that he lifted up his hand against the king: Solomon built Millo, and repaired the breaches of the city of David his father.

28 And the man Jeroboam was a mighty man of valour: and Solomon seeing the young man that he was industrious, he made him ruler over all the charge of the house of Joseph.

29 And it came to pass at that time when Jeroboam went out of Jerusalem, that the prophet Ahijah the Shilonite found him in the way; and he had clad himself with a new garment; and they two were alone in the field:

30 And Ahijah caught the new garment that was on him, and rent it in twelve pieces:

31 And he said to Jeroboam, Take thee ten pieces: for thus saith the LORD, the God of Israel, Behold, I will rend the kingdom out of the hand of Solomon, and will give ten tribes to thee:

32 (But he shall have one tribe for my servant David's sake, and for Jerusalem's sake, the city which I have chosen out of all the tribes of Israel:)

33 Because that they have forsaken me, and have worshipped Ashtoreth the goddess of the Zidonians, Chemosh the god of the Moabites, and Milcom the god of the children of Ammon, and have not walked in my ways, to do that which is right in mine eyes, and to keep my statutes and my judgments, as did David his father.

34 Howbeit I will not take the whole kingdom out of his hand: but I will make him prince all the days of his life for David my servant's sake, whom I chose, because he kept my commandments and my statutes:

35 But I will take the kingdom out of his son's hand, and will give it unto thee, even ten tribes.

36 And unto his son will I give one tribe, that David my servant may have a light alway before me in Jerusalem, the city which I have chosen me to put my name there.

37 And I will take thee, and thou shalt reign according to all that thy soul desireth, and shalt be king over Israel.

38 And it shall be, if thou wilt hearken unto all that I command thee, and wilt walk in my ways, and do that is right in my sight, to keep my statutes and my commandments, as David my servant did; that I will be with thee, and build thee a sure house, as I built for David, and will give Israel unto thee.

39 And I will for this afflict the seed of David, but not for ever.

40 Solomon sought therefore to kill Jeroboam. And Jeroboam arose, and fled into Egypt, unto Shishak king of Egypt, and was in Egypt until the death of Solomon.

41 And the rest of the acts of Solomon, and all that he did, and his wisdom, are they not written in the book of the acts of Solomon?

42 And the time that Solomon reigned in Jerusalem over all Israel was forty years.

43 And Solomon slept with his fathers, and was buried in the city of David his father: and Rehoboam his son reigned in his stead.

Chapter 8

Isaiah 2:2-4, from Page 86

2: 2 And it shall come to pass in the last days, that the mountain of the Lord's house shall be established in the top of the mountains, and shall be exalted above the hills, and all nations shall flow unto it.

3 And many people shall go and say, Come ye, and let us go up to the mountain of the LORD, to the house of the God of Jacob; and he will teach us of his ways, and we will walk in his paths: for out of Zion shall go forth the law, and the word of the LORD from Jerusalem.

4 And he shall judge among the nations, and shall rebuke many people: and they shall beat their swords into plowshares, and their spears into pruninghooks: nation shall not lift up sword against nation, neither shall they learn war any more.

Ezekiel 37, from Page 86

37: 1 The hand of the LORD was upon me, and carried me out in the spirit of the LORD, and set me down in the midst of the valley which was full of bones,

2 And caused me to pass by them round about: and, behold, there were very many in the open valley; and, lo, they were very dry.

3 And he said unto me, Son of man, can these bones live? And I answered, O Lord GOD, thou knowest.

4 Again he said unto me, Prophesy upon these bones, and say unto them, O ye dry bones, hear the word of the LORD.

5 Thus saith the Lord GOD unto these bones; Behold, I will cause breath to enter into you, and ye shall live:

6 And I will lay sinews upon you, and will bring up flesh upon you, and cover you with skin, and put breath in you, and ye shall live; and ye shall know that I am the LORD.

7 So I prophesied as I was commanded: and as I prophesied, there was a noise, and behold a shaking, and the bones came together, bone to his bone.

8 And when I beheld, lo, the sinews and the flesh came up upon them, and the skin covered them above: but there was no breath in them.

261

9   Then said he unto me, Prophesy unto the wind, prophesy, son of man, and say to the wind, Thus saith the Lord GOD; Come from the four winds, O breath, and breathe upon these slain, that they may live.

10 So I prophesied as he commanded me, and the breath came into them, and they lived, and stood up upon their feet, an exceeding great army.

11 Then he said unto me, Son of man, these bones are the whole house of Israel: behold, they say, Our bones are dried, and our hope is lost: we are cut off for our parts.

12 Therefore prophesy and say unto them, Thus saith the Lord GOD; Behold, O my people, I will open your graves, and cause you to come up out of your graves, and bring you into the land of Israel.

13 And ye shall know that I am the LORD, when I have opened your graves, O my people, and brought you up out of your graves,

14 And shall put my spirit in you, and ye shall live, and I shall place you in your own land: then shall ye know that I the LORD have spoken it, and performed it, saith the LORD.

15 The word of the LORD came again unto me, saying,

16 Moreover, thou son of man, take thee one stick, and write upon it, For Judah, and for the children of Israel his companions: then take another stick, and write upon it, For Joseph, the stick of Ephraim, and for all the house of Israel his companions:

17 And join them one to another into one stick; and they shall become one in thine hand.

18 And when the children of thy people shall speak unto thee, saying, Wilt thou not show us what thou meanest by these?

19 Say unto them, Thus saith the Lord GOD; Behold, I will take the stick of Joseph, which is in the hand of Ephraim, and the tribes of Israel his fellows, and will put them with him, even with the stick of Judah, and make them one stick, and they shall be one in mine hand.

20 And the sticks whereon thou writest shall be in thine hand before their eyes.

21 And say unto them, Thus saith the Lord GOD; Behold, I will take the children of Israel from among the heathen, whither they be gone, and will gather them on every side, and bring them into their own land:

22 And I will make them one nation in the land upon the mountains of Israel; and one king shall be king to them all: and they shall be no more two nations, neither shall they be divided into two kingdoms any more at all:

23 Neither shall they defile themselves any more with their idols, nor with their detestable things, nor with any of their transgressions: but I will save them out of all their dwellingplaces, wherein they have sinned, and will cleanse them: so shall they be my people, and I will be their God.

24 And David my servant shall be king over them; and they all shall have one shepherd: they shall also walk in my judgments, and observe my statutes, and do them.

25 And they shall dwell in the land that I have given unto Jacob my servant, wherein your fathers have dwelt; and they shall dwell therein, even they, and their children, and their children's children for ever: and my servant David shall be their prince for ever.

26 Moreover I will make a covenant of peace with them; it shall be an everlasting covenant with them: and I will place them, and multiply them, and will set my sanctuary in the midst of them for evermore.

27 My tabernacle also shall be with them: yea, I will be their God, and they shall be my people.

28 And the heathen shall know that I the LORD do sanctify Israel, when my sanctuary shall be in the midst of them for evermore.

Ezekiel 47:13-23, from Page 86

47: 13 Thus saith the Lord GOD; This shall be the border, whereby ye shall inherit the land according to the twelve tribes of Israel: Joseph shall have two portions.

14 And ye shall inherit it, one as well as another: concerning the which I lifted up mine hand to give it unto your fathers: and this land shall fall unto you for inheritance.

15 And this shall be the border of the land toward the north side, from the great sea, the way of Hethlon, as men go to Zedad;

16 Hamath, Berothah, Sibraim, which is between the border of Damascus and the border of Hamath; Hazarhatticon, which is by the coast of Hauran.

17 And the border from the sea shall be Hazarenan, the border of Damascus, and the north northward, and the border of Hamath. And this is the north side.

18 And the east side ye shall measure from Hauran, and from Damascus, and from Gilead, and from the land of Israel by Jordan, from the border unto the east sea. And this is the east side.

19 And the south side southward, from Tamar even to the waters of strife in Kadesh, the river to the great sea. And this is the south side southward.

20 The west side also shall be the great sea from the border, till a man come over against Hamath. This is the west side.

21 So shall ye divide this land unto you according to the tribes of Israel.

22 And it shall come to pass, that ye shall divide it by lot for an inheritance unto you, and to the strangers that sojourn among you, which shall beget children among you: and they shall be unto you as born in the country among the children of Israel; they shall have inheritance with you among the tribes of Israel.

23 And it shall come to pass, that in what tribe the stranger sojourneth, there shall ye give him his inheritance, saith the Lord GOD.

Ezekiel 48:1-35, from Page 86

48: 1 Now these are the names of the tribes. From the north end to the coast of the way of Hethlon, as one goeth to Hamath, Hazarenan, the border of Damascus northward, to the coast of Hamath; for these are his sides east and west; a portion for Dan.

2 And by the border of Dan, from the east side unto the west side, a portion for Asher.

3 And by the border of Asher, from the east side even unto the west side, a portion for Naphtali.

4 And by the border of Naphtali, from the east side unto the west side, a portion for Manasseh.

5 And by the border of Manasseh, from the east side unto the west side, a portion for Ephraim.

6 And by the border of Ephraim, from the east side even unto the west side, a portion for Reuben.

7 And by the border of Reuben, from the east side unto the west side, a portion for Judah.

8 And by the border of Judah, from the east side unto the west side, shall be the offering which ye shall offer of five and twenty thousand reeds in breadth, and in length as one of the other parts, from the east side unto the west side: and the sanctuary shall be in the midst of it.

9 The oblation that ye shall offer unto the LORD shall be of five and twenty thousand in length, and of ten thousand in breadth.

10 And for them, even for the priests, shall be this holy oblation; toward the north five and twenty thousand in length, and toward the west ten thousand in breadth, and toward the east ten thousand in breadth, and toward the

south five and twenty thousand in length: and the sanctuary of the LORD shall be in the midst thereof.

11 It shall be for the priests that are sanctified of the sons of Zadok; which have kept my charge, which went not astray when the children of Israel went astray, as the Levites went astray.

12 And this oblation of the land that is offered shall be unto them a thing most holy by the border of the Levites.

13 And over against the border of the priests the Levites shall have five and twenty thousand in length, and ten thousand in breadth: all the length shall be five and twenty thousand, and the breadth ten thousand.

14 And they shall not sell of it, neither exchange, nor alienate the firstfruits of the land: for it is holy unto the LORD.

15 And the five thousand, that are left in the breadth over against the five and twenty thousand, shall be a profane place for the city, for dwelling, and for suburbs: and the city shall be in the midst thereof.

16 And these shall be the measures thereof; the north side four thousand and five hundred, and the south side four thousand and five hundred, and on the east side four thousand and five hundred, and the west side four thousand and five hundred.

17 And the suburbs of the city shall be toward the north two hundred and fifty, and toward the south two hundred and fifty, and toward the east two hundred and fifty, and toward the west two hundred and fifty.

18 And the residue in length over against the oblation of the holy portion shall be ten thousand eastward, and ten thousand westward: and it shall be over against the oblation of the holy portion; and the increase thereof shall be for food unto them that serve the city.

19 And they that serve the city shall serve it out of all the tribes of Israel.

20 All the oblation shall be five and twenty thousand by five and twenty thousand: ye shall offer the holy oblation foursquare, with the possession of the city.

21 And the residue shall be for the prince, on the one side and on the other of the holy oblation, and of the possession of the city, over against the five and twenty thousand of the oblation toward the east border, and westward over against the five and twenty thousand toward the west border, over against the portions for the prince: and it shall be the holy oblation; and the sanctuary of the house shall be in the midst thereof.

22 Moreover from the possession of the Levites, and from the possession of the city, being in the midst of that which is the prince's, between the border of Judah and the border of Benjamin, shall be for the prince.

23 As for the rest of the tribes, from the east side unto the west side, Benjamin shall have a portion.

24 And by the border of Benjamin, from the east side unto the west side, Simeon shall have a portion.

25 And by the border of Simeon, from the east side unto the west side, Issachar a portion.

26 And by the border of Issachar, from the east side unto the west side, Zebulun a portion.

27 And by the border of Zebulun, from the east side unto the west side, Gad a portion.

28 And by the border of Gad, at the south side southward, the border shall be even from Tamar unto the waters of strife in Kadesh, and to the river toward the great sea.

29 This is the land which ye shall divide by lot unto the tribes of Israel for inheritance, and these are their portions, saith the Lord GOD.

30 And these are the goings out of the city on the north side, four thousand and five hundred measures.

31 And the gates of the city shall be after the names of the tribes of Israel: three gates northward; one gate of Reuben, one gate of Judah, one gate of Levi.

32 And at the east side four thousand and five hundred: and three gates; and one gate of Joseph, one gate of Benjamin, one gate of Dan.

33 And at the south side four thousand and five hundred measures: and three gates; one gate of Simeon, one gate of Issachar, one gate of Zebulun.

34 At the west side four thousand and five hundred, with their three gates; one gate of Gad, one gate of Asher, one gate of Naphtali.

35 It was round about eighteen thousand measures: and the name of the city from that day shall be, The LORD is there.

Zechariah 14:16-21, from Page 86

14: 16 And it shall come to pass, that every one that is left of all the nations which came against Jerusalem shall even go up from year to year to worship the King, the LORD of hosts, and to keep the feast of tabernacles.

17 And it shall be, that whoso will not come up of all the families of the earth unto Jerusalem to worship the King, the LORD of hosts, even upon them shall be no rain.

Appendix

18 And if the family of Egypt go not up, and come not, that have no rain; there shall be the plague, wherewith the LORD will smite the heathen that come not up to keep the feast of tabernacles.

19 This shall be the punishment of Egypt, and the punishment of all nations that come not up to keep the feast of tabernacles.

20 In that day shall there be upon the bells of the horses, HOLINESS UNTO THE LORD; and the pots in the LORD'S house shall be like the bowls before the altar.

21 Yea, every pot in Jerusalem and in Judah shall be holiness unto the LORD of hosts: and all they that sacrifice shall come and take of them, and seethe therein: and in that day there shall be no more the Canaanite in the house of the LORD of hosts.

Luke 1:32-33, from Page 86

1: 32 He shall be great, and shall be called the Son of the Highest: and the Lord God shall give unto him the throne of his father David:

33 And he shall reign over the house of Jacob for ever; and of his kingdom there shall be no end.

Revelation 7:1-8, from Page 86

7: 1 And after these things I saw four angels standing on the four corners of the earth, holding the four winds of the earth, that the wind should not blow on the earth, nor on the sea, nor on any tree.

2 And I saw another angel ascending from the east, having the seal of the living God: and he cried with a loud voice to the four angels, to whom it was given to hurt the earth and the sea,

3 Saying, Hurt not the earth, neither the sea, nor the trees, till we have sealed the servants of our God in their foreheads.

4 And I heard the number of them which were sealed: and there were sealed an hundred and forty and four thousand of all the tribes of the children of Israel.

5 Of the tribe of Juda were sealed twelve thousand. Of the tribe of Reuben were sealed twelve thousand. Of the tribe of Gad were sealed twelve thousand.

6 Of the tribe of Aser were sealed twelve thousand. Of the tribe of Nephthalim were sealed twelve thousand. Of the tribe of Manasses were sealed twelve thousand.

7   Of the tribe of Simeon were sealed twelve thousand. Of the tribe of Levi were sealed twelve thousand. Of the tribe of Issachar were sealed twelve thousand.

8   Of the tribe of Zabulon were sealed twelve thousand. Of the tribe of Joseph were sealed twelve thousand. Of the tribe of Benjamin were sealed twelve thousand.

Revelation 14:1-5, from Page 86

14: 1   And I looked, and, lo, a Lamb stood on the mount Sion, and with him an hundred forty and four thousand, having his Father's name written in their foreheads.

2   And I heard a voice from heaven, as the voice of many waters, and as the voice of a great thunder: and I heard the voice of harpers harping with their harps:

3   And they sung as it were a new song before the throne, and before the four beasts, and the elders: and no man could learn that song but the hundred and forty and four thousand, which were redeemed from the earth.

4   These are they which were not defiled with women; for they are virgins. These are they which follow the Lamb whithersoever he goeth. These were redeemed from among men, being the firstfruits unto God and to the Lamb.

5   And in their mouth was found no guile: for they are without fault before the throne of God.

Acts 17:26, from Page 87

17: 26 And hath made of one blood all nations of men for to dwell on all the face of the earth, and hath determined the times before appointed, and the bounds of their habitation;

Genesis 10: 5, 32, from Page 87

10: 5   By these were the isles of the Gentiles divided in their lands; every one after his tongue, after their families, in their nations.

32   These are the families of the sons of Noah, after their generations, in their nations: and by these were the nations divided in the earth after the flood.

Genesis 11:8-9, from Page 87

11: 8   So the LORD scattered them abroad from thence upon the face of all the earth: and they left off to build the city.

Appendix

9 Therefore is the name of it called Babel; because the LORD did there confound the language of all the earth: and from thence did the LORD scatter them abroad upon the face of all the earth.

Deuteronomy 32:8, from Page 87

32: 8 When the Most High divided to the nations their inheritance, when he separated the sons of Adam, he set the bounds of the people according to the number of the children of Israel.

Daniel 7:13-14, from Page 87

7: 13 I saw in the night visions, and, behold, one like the Son of man came with the clouds of heaven, and came to the Ancient of days, and they brought him near before him.

14 And there was given him dominion, and glory, and a kingdom, that all people, nations, and languages, should serve him: his dominion is an everlasting dominion, which shall not pass away, and his kingdom that which shall not be destroyed.

Zechariah 14, from Page 87

14:1 Behold, the day of the LORD cometh, and thy spoil shall be divided in the midst of thee.

2 For I will gather all nations against Jerusalem to battle; and the city shall be taken, and the houses rifled, and the women ravished; and half of the city shall go forth into captivity, and the residue of the people shall not be cut off from the city.

3 Then shall the LORD go forth, and fight against those nations, as when he fought in the day of battle.

4 And his feet shall stand in that day upon the mount of Olives, which is before Jerusalem on the east, and the mount of Olives shall cleave in the midst thereof toward the east and toward the west, and there shall be a very great valley; and half of the mountain shall remove toward the north, and half of it toward the south.

5 And ye shall flee to the valley of the mountains; for the valley of the mountains shall reach unto Azal: yea, ye shall flee, like as ye fled from before the earthquake in the days of Uzziah king of Judah: and the LORD my God shall come, and all the saints with thee.

6 And it shall come to pass in that day, that the light shall not be clear, nor dark:

7   But it shall be one day which shall be known to the LORD, not day, nor night: but it shall come to pass, that at evening time it shall be light.

8   And it shall be in that day, that living waters shall go out from Jerusalem; half of them toward the former sea, and half of them toward the hinder sea: in summer and in winter shall it be.

9   And the LORD shall be king over all the earth: in that day shall there be one LORD, and his name one.

10 All the land shall be turned as a plain from Geba to Rimmon south of Jerusalem: and it shall be lifted up, and inhabited in her place, from Benjamin's gate unto the place of the first gate, unto the corner gate, and from the tower of Hananeel unto the king's winepresses.

11 And men shall dwell in it, and there shall be no more utter destruction; but Jerusalem shall be safely inhabited.

12 And this shall be the plague wherewith the LORD will smite all the people that have fought against Jerusalem; Their flesh shall consume away while they stand upon their feet, and their eyes shall consume away in their holes, and their tongue shall consume away in their mouth.

13 And it shall come to pass in that day, that a great tumult from the LORD shall be among them; and they shall lay hold every one on the hand of his neighbour, and his hand shall rise up against the hand of his neighbour.

14 And Judah also shall fight at Jerusalem; and the wealth of all the heathen round about shall be gathered together, gold, and silver, and apparel, in great abundance.

15 And so shall be the plague of the horse, of the mule, of the camel, and of the ass, and of all the beasts that shall be in these tents, as this plague.

16 And it shall come to pass, that every one that is left of all the nations which came against Jerusalem shall even go up from year to year to worship the King, the LORD of hosts, and to keep the feast of tabernacles.

17 And it shall be, that whoso will not come up of all the families of the earth unto Jerusalem to worship the King, the LORD of hosts, even upon them shall be no rain.

18 And if the family of Egypt go not up, and come not, that have no rain; there shall be the plague, wherewith the LORD will smite the heathen that come not up to keep the feast of tabernacles.

19 This shall be the punishment of Egypt, and the punishment of all nations that come not up to keep the feast of tabernacles.

20 In that day shall there be upon the bells of the horses, HOLINESS UNTO THE LORD; and the pots in the LORD'S house shall be like the bowls before the altar.

21 Yea, every pot in Jerusalem and in Judah shall be holiness unto the LORD of hosts: and all they that sacrifice shall come and take of them, and seethe therein: and in that day there shall be no more the Canaanite in the house of the LORD of hosts.

Revelation 21:24, from Page 87

21:24 And the nations of them which are saved shall walk in the light of it: and the kings of the earth do bring their glory and honour into it.

Deuteronomy 23:1-3, from Page 88

23:1 He that is wounded in the stones, or hath his privy member cut off, shall not enter into the congregation of the LORD.

2 A bastard shall not enter into the congregation of the LORD; even to his tenth generation shall he not enter into the congregation of the LORD.

3 An Ammonite or Moabite shall not enter into the congregation of the LORD; even to their tenth generation shall they not enter into the congregation of the LORD for ever:

Ezra 10:8, from Page 88

10:8 And that whosoever would not come within three days, according to the counsel of the princes and the elders, all his substance should be forfeited, and himself separated from the congregation of those that had been carried away.

Nehemiah 9:2, from Page 88

9:2 And the seed of Israel separated themselves from all strangers, and stood and confessed their sins, and the iniquities of their fathers.

Nehemiah 10:28, from Page 88

10:28 And the rest of the people, the priests, the Levites, the porters, the singers, the Nethinims, and all they that had separated themselves from the people of the lands unto the law of God, their wives, their sons, and their daughters, every one having knowledge, and having understanding;

Revelation 7:7-17, from Page 89

7:7 Of the tribe of Simeon were sealed twelve thousand. Of the tribe of Levi were sealed twelve thousand. Of the tribe of Issachar were sealed twelve thousand.

8   Of the tribe of Zabulon were sealed twelve thousand. Of the tribe of Joseph were sealed twelve thousand. Of the tribe of Benjamin were sealed twelve thousand.

9   After this I beheld, and, lo, a great multitude, which no man could number, of all nations, and kindreds, and people, and tongues, stood before the throne, and before the Lamb, clothed with white robes, and palms in their hands;

10   And cried with a loud voice, saying, Salvation to our God which sitteth upon the throne, and unto the Lamb.

11   And all the angels stood round about the throne, and about the elders and the four beasts, and fell before the throne on their faces, and worshipped God,

12   Saying, Amen: Blessing, and glory, and wisdom, and thanksgiving, and honour, and power, and might, be unto our God for ever and ever. Amen.

13   And one of the elders answered, saying unto me, What are these which are arrayed in white robes? and whence came they?

14   And I said unto him, Sir, thou knowest. And he said to me, These are they which came out of great tribulation, and have washed their robes, and made them white in the blood of the Lamb.

15   Therefore are they before the throne of God, and serve him day and night in his temple: and he that sitteth on the throne shall dwell among them.

16   They shall hunger no more, neither thirst any more; neither shall the sun light on them, nor any heat.

17   For the Lamb which is in the midst of the throne shall feed them, and shall lead them unto living fountains of waters: and God shall wipe away all tears from their eyes.

Revelation 14:1-5, from Page 89

14: 1   And I looked, and, lo, a Lamb stood on the mount Sion, and with him an hundred forty and four thousand, having his Father's name written in their foreheads.

2   And I heard a voice from heaven, as the voice of many waters, and as the voice of a great thunder: and I heard the voice of harpers harping with their harps:

3   And they sung as it were a new song before the throne, and before the four beasts, and the elders: and no man could learn that song but the hundred and forty and four thousand, which were redeemed from the earth.

4   These are they which were not defiled with women; for they are virgins. These are they which follow the Lamb whithersoever he goeth. These were redeemed from among men, being the firstfruits unto God and to the Lamb.

5   And in their mouth was found no guile: for they are without fault before the throne of God.

Numbers 12:11-16, from Page 93

12: 11   And Aaron said unto Moses, Alas, my lord, I beseech thee, lay not the sin upon us, wherein we have done foolishly, and wherein we have sinned.

12   Let her not be as one dead, of whom the flesh is half consumed when he cometh out of his mother's womb.

13   And Moses cried unto the LORD, saying, Heal her now, O God, I beseech thee.

14   And the LORD said unto Moses, If her father had but spit in her face, should she not be ashamed seven days? let her be shut out from the camp seven days, and after that let her be received in again.

15   And Miriam was shut out from the camp seven days: and the people journeyed not till Miriam was brought in again.

16   And afterward the people removed from Hazeroth, and pitched in the wilderness of Paran.

Matthew 18:15-17, from Page 95

18: 15   Moreover if thy brother shall trespass against thee, go and tell him his fault between thee and him alone: if he shall hear thee, thou hast gained thy brother.

16   But if he will not hear thee, then take with thee one or two more, that in the mouth of two or three witnesses every word may be established.

17   And if he shall neglect to hear them, tell it unto the church: but if he neglect to hear the church, let him be unto thee as a heathen man and a publican.

1 Corinthians 5: 9-13, from Page 95

5: 9   I wrote unto you in an epistle not to company with fornicators:

10   Yet not altogether with the fornicators of this world, or with the covetous, or extortioners, or with idolaters; for then must ye needs go out of the world.

11 But now I have written unto you not to keep company, if any man that is called a brother be a fornicator, or covetous, or an idolater, or a railer, or a drunkard, or an extortioner; with such an one no not to eat.

12 For what have I to do to judge them also that are without? do not ye judge them that are within?

13 But them that are without God judgeth. Therefore put away from among yourselves that wicked person.

1 Corinthians 6:15, from Page 95

6: 15 Know ye not that your bodies are the members of Christ? shall I then take the members of Christ, and make them the members of an harlot? God forbid.

2 Corinthians 6:14-18, from Page 95

6: 14 Be ye not unequally yoked together with unbelievers: for what fellowship hath righteousness with unrighteousness? and what communion hath light with darkness?

15 And what concord hath Christ with Belial? or what part hath he that believeth with an infidel?

16 And what agreement hath the temple of God with idols? for ye are the temple of the living God; as God hath said, I will dwell in them, and walk in them; and I will be their God, and they shall be my people.

17 Wherefore come out from among them, and be ye separate, saith the Lord, and touch not the unclean thing; and I will receive you,

18 And will be a Father unto you, and ye shall be my sons and daughters, saith the Lord Almighty.

2 Thessalonians 3:6-16, from Page 95

3: 6 Now we command you, brethren, in the name of our Lord Jesus Christ, that ye withdraw yourselves from every brother that walketh disorderly, and not after the tradition which he received of us.

7 For yourselves know how ye ought to follow us: for we behaved not ourselves disorderly among you;

8 Neither did we eat any man's bread for nought; but wrought with labour and travail night and day, that we might not be chargeable to any of you:

9   Not because we have not power, but to make ourselves an ensample unto you to follow us.

10 For even when we were with you, this we commanded you, that if any would not work, neither should he eat.

11 For we hear that there are some which walk among you disorderly, working not at all, but are busybodies.

12 Now them that are such we command and exhort by our Lord Jesus Christ, that with quietness they work, and eat their own bread.

13 But ye, brethren, be not weary in well doing.

14 And if any man obey not our word by this epistle, note that man, and have no company with him, that he may be ashamed.

15 Yet count him not as an enemy, but admonish him as a brother.

16 Now the Lord of peace himself give you peace always by all means. The Lord be with you all.

1 Timothy 6:5, from Page 95

6: 5   Perverse disputings of men of corrupt minds, and destitute of the truth, supposing that gain is godliness: from such withdraw thyself.

2 Timothy 3:5, from Page 95

3: 5   Having a form of godliness, but denying the power thereof: from such turn away.

x

Bibliography

This bibliography is not a complete record of all the works and sources consulted in the researching and writing of this book. It only indicates the substance and range of reading upon which the ideas and text were formed and is intended to serve as a convenience for those who wish to pursue the study of this subject further.

"Aetna Reviewing Archived Insurance Policies on Slaves," *Los Angeles Times* [from *The Washington Post*], March 8, 2000, A-15.

Albu, Emily, William J. Frost, Howard Clark Kee, Carter Lindberg and Dana L. Robert, *Christianity: A Social and Cultural History* (New York: Prentice Hall, Inc., 1998).

American Church Clergy and Parish Directory for 1905, (Uniontown, Pennsylvania: Frederic E.J. Lloyd, 1905).

Anderson, Claud, *Black Labor, White Wealth: The Search for Power and Economic Justice* (Bethesda, Maryland: PowerNomics Corporation of America, Inc., 1994).

Atkinson, Edward, "The Negro A Beast," *North American Review*, (August, 1905).

Berardi, Gayle K. and Thomas W. Segady, "The Development of African-American Newspapers in the American West: A Sociohistorical Perspective," *Journal of Negro History*, v. 75, no. 3/4, (Summer/Autumn, 1990): 96-111.

"Bombs, Bullets, Bodies: The Decade in Review," *Intelligence Report*, no. 97 (Winter 2000): 9-29.

Bond, Horace Mann, "The Influence of Personalities on the Public Education of Negroes in Alabama, I," *Journal of Negro Education*, v. 6, no.1 (January 1937): 17-29.

Bowden, Henry Warner, "Scofield, Cyrus Ingerson," *Dictionary of American Religious Biography,* 2nd ed. (Westport, Connecticut: Greenwood Press, 1993): 477-478.

Briggs, Charles A., Francis Brown and S.R. Driver, *The New Brown-Driver-Briggs-Gesenius Hebrew-English Lexicon* (Oxford, England: J.P. Greene Sr., 1979).

Briggs, Charles A., Francis Brown and S.R. Driver, *A Hebrew-English Lexicon of the Old Testament* (Oxford, England: Clarendon Press, 1951).

Broadman Bible Commentary, 12 vols., rev. (Broadman Press: 1969).

Brown, William Montgomery, *The Crucial Race Question, or Where and How Shall the Color Line Be Drawn?* (Arkansas Churchman's Publishing Company, 1907).

Brundage, W. Fitzhugh, *Lynching in the New South: Georgia and Virginia, 1880-1930* (Chicago: University of Illinois Press, 1993).

Burgess, Stanley M. and Gary B. McGee, *The Dictionary of Pentecostal and Charismatic Movements* (Grand Rapids, Michigan: Regency, Zondervan Publishing House, 1988).

Carroll, Charles, *The Tempter of Eve* (St. Louis, Missouri: Adamic Publishing Co., 1902).

Clary, Johnny Lee, *Boys in the Hoods: One Man's Journey From Hatred to Love* (Bakersfield, California: Pneuma Life Publishing, 1995).

Dake, Finis Jennings, ed., *Dake's Annotated Reference Bible* (Lawrenceville, Georgia.: Dake Bible Sales, Inc., 1963, 1971).

Davis, Abraham L. and Barbara Luck Graham, *The Supreme Court, Race, and Civil Rights* (Thousand Oaks: Sage Publications, Inc., 1995).

Dennis, R. Ethel, *The Black People of America: Illustrated History* (New Haven, Readers Press 1970).

Bibliography

Donovan, Frank, *Mr. Jefferson's Declaration: The Story Behind the Declaration of Independence* (New York: Dodd, Mead & Company, 1968).

Dormon, James H., "Shaping the Popular Image of Post-Reconstruction American Blacks: The 'Coon Song' Phenomenon of the Gilded Age," *American Quarterly*, v. 40, no. 4 (December 1988): 450-451.

Ehrlich, Walter, "The Origins of the Dred Scott Case," *Journal of Negro History*, v. 59, no. 2 (April, 1974): 133-142.

Eliade, Mircea, ed., *The Encyclopedia of Religion, 16* vols. (New York: MacMillan Publishing, 1987).

Encyclopedia Judaica, (Jerusalem: Keter Publishing House Limited, 1971).

Fehrenbacher, Don E., "The Origins and Purpose of Lincoln's 'House Divided' Speech," *Mississippi Valley Historical Review*, v. 46, no. 4 (March, 1960): 615-643.

Flanders, Stephen A., *Atlas of American Migration* (New York: Facts on File, Inc., 1998).

Fulop, Timothy E. and Albert J. Raboteau, eds., *African-American Religion: Interpretive Essays in History and Culture* (New York: Routledge, 1997).

Ginzberg, Louis, *The Legends of the Jews, Volume 1* (Philadelphia: Jewish Publication Society of America, 1909-1938).

Ginzburg, Ralph, *100 Years of Lynching* (New York: Lancer Books, 1962).

Goux, Lynette, "Women of the Bible," *Jimmy Swaggart Ministries Bible,* Marvin Solum, ed. (Dallas: Heritage Publishers Incorporated, 1983): xix-xx.

Greenberg, Joseph H., Christy G. Turner II and Stephen L. Zegura, "The Settlement of the Americas: A Comparison of the Linguistic, Dental, and

Genetic Evidence," *Current Anthropology*, v. 27, no. 5 (December 1986): 477-497.

Hacker, Andrew, *Two Nations, Black and White, Separate, Hostile, Unequal* (New York: Charles Scribner Sons, 1992).

Hansen, Klaus J., *Mormonism and the American Experience* (Chicago: University of Chicago Press, 1981).

Harlan, Louis R., "Booker T. Washington and the Voice of the Negro, 1904-1907," *Journal of Southern History*, v. 45, no. 1 (February 1979): 56

Harris, R. Laird, Gleason L. Archer, Jr. and Bruce K. Waltke, *Theological Wordbook of the Old Testament* (Chicago: Moody Bible Institute, 1980).

Haycock, Kati and Susana M. Navarro, "A Report From the Achievement Council," *Unfinished Business: Fulfilling Our Children's Promise* (Oakland, California: Inkworks Press, 1990): 3, 4.

"Higher Ratio of Black Women Strip-Searched at Airports," *Los Angeles Times*, April 10, 2000, A16.

Hodder, F.H., "Some Phases of the Dred Scott Case," *Mississippi Valley Historical Review,* v. 16, no. 1 (June 1929): 3-22

Hood, Robert E., *Begrimed and Black: Christian Traditions on Blacks and Blackness* (Minneapolis: Fortress Press, 1994).

Hrdlicka, Alec, "Transpacific Migrations," in *Man*, Royal Anthropological Institute, v. 17, (February 1917): 29-30.

Irvin, Maurice I, "Grace and Race," *Alliance Life*, v. 130, no. 24 (August 9, 1995): 6, 12.

"Is Youth Violence Just Another Fact of Life?" www.apa.org/ppo/violence/html (June 2000).

Bibliography

Leach, Edmund, "Noah's Second Son: A Lady Day Sermon at King's College Cambridge," *Anthropology Today*, v. 4, no. 4 (August, 1988): 2-5.

Lloyd's Clerical Directory: A Treasury of Information for the Clergy and Laity of the Protestant Episcopal Church in the United States, and the Church of England in Canada and Newfoundland (Chicago: American Church Publishing Company, 1910).

Logan, Rayford W., "The Progress of the Negro After a Century of Emancipation," *Journal of Negro Education*, v. 32, no. 4 (Autumn, 1963): 323.

Love, Spencie, *One Blood: The Death and Resurrection of Charles R. Drew* (Chapel Hill: University of North Carolina Press, 1996).

Matthew Henry's Commentary (Grand Rapids, Michigan: Regency Reference Library, Zondervan Publishing House, 1960).

McKenzie, Stephen L., *All God's Children: A Biblical Critique of Racism* (Louisville, Kentucky: Westminster John Knox Press, 1997).

Melton, J. Gordon, "William Montgomery Brown," *Religious Leaders of America: A Biographical Guide to Founders and Leaders of Religious Bodies, Churches, and Spiritual Groups in America* (Detroit: Gale Research, Inc., 1991).

Miller, John Chester, *The Wolf by the Ears: Thomas Jefferson and Slavery* (Charlottesville, Virginia: The Free Press, 1977).

Montgomery, Rich, "Photo Exhibit Resurrects Grim History of Missouri," (Knight-Ridder/Tribune News Service, March 1, 2000).

Muhammad, Elijah, *Message to the Black Man in America* (Chicago: Muhammad Mosque of Islam No.2, 1965).

Oakes, James and James Gilreath, ed., "Why Slaves Can't Read: The Political Significance of Jefferson's Racism," in *Thomas Jefferson and the Education of a Citizen* (Washington D.C.: Library of Congress, 1999): 177-192.

Otabil, Mensa, *Beyond the Rivers of Ethiopia: A Biblical Revelation on God's Purpose for the Black Race* (Bakersfield, California: Pneuma Life Publishing, 1993).

Price, Frederick K.C., *Race, Religion & Racism: A Bold Encounter With Division in the Church,* v.1 (Los Angeles, California: Faith One Publishing, 1999).

Raboteau, Albert J., *Slave Religion: The "Invisible Institution" in the Antebellum South* (New York: Oxford University Press, 1978).

Rampersad, Arnold, "W.E.B. Du Bois as a Man of Literature," *American Literature,* v. 51, no. 1 (March 1979): 50-68.

Reiss, Oscar, *Blacks in Colonial America* (North Carolina: McFarland & Company, Inc., 1997).

Rhodes, James Ford, *History of the United States From the Compromise of 1850* (Chicago: University of Chicago Press, 1966).

Rice, Chris, "Changing Habits of the Heart," *Alliance Life,* v. 130, no. 24 (August 9, 1995): 9.

Rogers, J.A., *Sex and Race: Negro-Caucasian Mixing in All Ages and All Lands,* v. I, 9th ed. (St. Petersburg, Florida: Helga M. Rogers, 1967).

Rogers, J.A., *Sex and Race: Why White and Black Mix in Spite of Opposition,* v. III, 5th ed. (St. Petersburg, Florida: Helga M. Rogers, 1944; reprint, 1972).

Scofield, Cyrus Ingerson, ed., *The Scofield Reference Bible* (New York: Oxford University Press, rev., 1917).

Singal, Daniel Joseph, "Ulrich B. Phillips: The Old South as the New," *Journal of American History,* v. 63, no. 4 (March 1977): 871-891.

Smock, Raymond W., ed. "Scott v. Sanford (The Dred Scott Decision)," in *Landmark Documents on the U.S. Congress* (Washington, D.C: Congressional Quarterly, 1999): 185-192.

Bibliography

Strong, James, *The New Strong's Exhaustive Concordance of the Bible*, Nelson's Comfort Print ed. (Nashville: Thomas Nelson Publishers, 1995).

"Texaco Chairman on Alleged Racial Slurs by Executives," *Historic Documents of 1996* (Washington, D.C.: Congressional Quarterly Inc., 1997): 764-769.

Tocqueville, Alexis de, *Democracy in America*, 2 vols. (New York: Altred A. Knopf, 1989).

"Topical Index to the Bible: From Genesis to Revelation," in *The Holy Bible* [New King James Version] (Nashville: Thomas Nelson, Inc., 1982): 3-296.

Vine, W.E., *Vine's Expository Dictionary of Old and New Testament Words* (Nashville: Thomas Nelson, Publishers, 1984, 1996).

Washington , Joseph R. Jr., *Black Religion: The Negro and Christianity in the United States* (Boston: Beacon Press, 1964).

Weathers, Diane, "Corporate Race Wars," *Essence*, v. 28, no. 6 (October 1997): 80-88.

Wells, Amy Stuart and Robert L. Crain, *Stepping Over the Color Line: African-American Students in White Suburban Schools* (New Haven, Connecticut: Yale University Press, 1997).

Wilson, William, *New Wilson's Old Testament Word Studies* (Grand Rapids, Michigan: Kregel Publications, 1987, rev. from 1978).

Woodward, C. Vann, *The Strange Career of Jim Crow*, 3rd rev. ed. (New York: Oxford University Press, 1974).

Young, Robert, *Young's Analytical Concordance to the Bible* (Peabody, Maine: Hendrickson Publishers).

Youngs, J. William T., *The Congregationalists*, Denominations in America, no. 4 (Westport, Connecticut.: Greenwood Press, 1990).

Index

The italicized *n* following page numbers refers to information to be found in footnotes; *nn* refers to more than one footnote on a page.

Frost, William, 21n
Fulop, Timothy E., 145n

genealogies
    children of Israel, 52-54
    of Isaac (son of Abraham), 55
    of Ishmael (son of Abraham),
        54-55
    of Jesus Christ, 24-27
genetic inheritance, and racial
    disparities, 217
Ginzberg, Louis, 197-198, 198n,
    200
Ginzburg, Ralph, 132n
Good Samaritan parable, 135
Gordon-Reed, Annette, 157n
grace of God, 139n
Graham, Barbara Luck, 162n
Graham, Billy, 133
Graves, John Temple, 164n,
    164-166

Hacker, Andrew, 216-221
Haley, Arthur, 224n
Ham, Debra Newman, 148n
Ham (son of Noah)
    curse of Ham myth, 10n, 111-
        114, 112n, 131, 189-205
    descendants of an inferior
        race, 111-114, 198
    meaning of word Ham, 17n
Hansen, Klaus J., 206-213
Harlan, Louis R., 164n
Harris, R. Laird, 32-33
hate crimes, 223-224n
Haycock, Kati, 141-142n
Haygood, Atticus G., 131
Hemings, Sally, relationship with
    Thomas Jefferson, 156-
    157n
Henry, Matthew, 43
Historic Documents of 1996,
    184n
*History of the United States From
    the Compromise of 1850*
    (Rhodes), 151-153

Hitler, Adolf, 8
Hodder, F.H., 154n, 160n
homicide, among African
    Americans, 220n, 220
Hood, Robert E., 190n

idol worship, 38-39, 64-66, 71-
    73, 79-80
image of God, 66
impartiality of God, 71, 82, 226-
    227
inferiority in the races
    assumption of white
        superiority, 2
    inferior vs. superior race, 178
    See also black inferiority
interracial marriage
    Abraham and Hagar as
        example of, 15-17
    amalgamation as a crime, 7-8
    amalgamation of the races,
        175
    Dake's views on miscegenation
        as against God's will, 36-
        41, 70-80
    fear of, 2, 8
    letter of disapproval, 116-117
    Moses and Ethiopian wife, 18-
        21, 28, 92-93, 176
    with pagans, 71
    practical considerations
        against, 21
    Price's position on, 20-22
    prohibitions against, 11
    restrictions for Believers, 20,
        28-29, 38, 42-43, 47, 62-
        64, 120-121
    Salmon and Rahab as example
        of, 23-26
    sinfulness of, 176
    unlawful in God's plan, 118-
        119
    See also miscegenation
Irvin, Maurice I., 133-135, 134n

Index

Index

Tamar, 25, 26
The Tempter of Eve (Carroll), 2-8, 112, 173
Terry, Wallace, 149n
Texaco scandal, prejudicial remarks, 184n, 184
The Theological Wordbook of the Old Testament (Harris, Archer, and Waltke), 32-33
Thomas Jefferson: An Intimate History (Brodie), 157n
Thomas Jefferson and Sally Hemings (Gordon-Reed), 157n
Thomas Jefferson and the Education of a Citizen, 155n
Tocqueville, Alexis de, 217-219, 218n
truthfulness, 7, 81-96, 120, 213n, 221
Turner, Nat, 159n
Tuskegee Study, syphilis experiment, 143-144nn
Two Nations, Black and White, Separate, Hostile, Unequal (Hacker), 216-221

unity (and division) of the Church, 166-176
Uriah (husband of Bathsheba), 26-27

Vesey, Denmark, 159n, 160n
Vine, W.E., 139n
Vine's Expository Dictionary of Old and New Testament Words, 139n
violence
   death of African Americans, 220n
   hate crimes, 223-224n
   white violence against black communities, 150n, 223-224n

violence *(continued)*
   See also lynchings
Vonderlehr, Raymond, 144n

Waltke, Bruce K., 32-33
Washington, Joseph R., Jr., 146n, 222n
Weathers, Diane, 184n
Welch, Timothy, 224n
Wells, Amy Stuart, 141n, 149-150n
White Anglo-Saxon Protestant (WASP), 167
white superiority
   Aryan White man's country, 181
   Church membership restrictions, 167-168, 179-181
   intelligence, 199
   See also inferiority in the races
white supremacist's recorded message, 129-130
Wilson, William, 32n
witnesses, of the Word, 16
The Wolf by the Ears: Thomas Jefferson and Slavery (Miller), 155-156, 156-157nn, 189
Woodward, C. Vann, 6n, 148n

Young, Brigham, 206-209
Young's Analytical Concordance to the Bible (Young), 32
Youngs, J. William T., 111n

Zipporah (wife of Moses), 18-19

Scriptural Index

All biblical quotes are taken from the New King James Version unless otherwise noted.

Books by
Frederick K.C. Price, D.D.

INTEGRITY
The Guarantee for Success

HIGHER FINANCE
How to Live Debt-Free

RACE, RELIGION & RACISM, VOLUME 1
A Bold Encounter With Division in the Church

THE TRUTH ABOUT ...THE BIBLE

THE TRUTH ABOUT ...DEATH

THE TRUTH ABOUT ...DISASTERS

THE TRUTH ABOUT ...FATE

THE TRUTH ABOUT ...FEAR

THE TRUTH ABOUT ...HOMOSEXUALITY

THE TRUTH ABOUT ...RACE

THE TRUTH ABOUT ...WORRY

LIVING IN HOSTILE TERRITORY
A Survival Guide for the Overcoming Christian

DR. PRICE'S GOLDEN NUGGETS
A Treasury of Wisdom for Both Ministers and Laypeople

BUILDING ON A FIRM FOUNDATION

FIVE LITTLE FOXES OF FAITH

THE HOLY SPIRIT:
The Helper We All Need

THE CHRISTIAN FAMILY:
Practical Insight for Family Living
(formerly *MARRIAGE AND THE FAMILY)*

IDENTIFIED WITH CHRIST:
A Complete Cycle From Defeat to Victory

THE CHASTENING OF THE LORD

TESTING THE SPIRITS

BEWARE! THE LIES OF SATAN

THE WAY, THE WALK,
AND THE WARFARE OF THE BELIEVER
(A Verse-by-Verse Study on the Book of Ephesians)

THREE KEYS TO POSITIVE CONFESSION

THE PROMISED LAND
(A New Era for the Body of Christ)

A NEW LAW FOR A NEW PEOPLE

THE VICTORIOUS, OVERCOMING LIFE
(A Verse-by-Verse Study on the Book of Colossians)

NAME IT AND CLAIM IT!
The Power of Positive Confession

PRACTICAL SUGGESTIONS FOR SUCCESSFUL MINISTRY

WALKING IN GOD'S WORD
Through His Promises

HOMOSEXUALITY:
State of Birth or State of Mind?

CONCERNING THOSE WHO HAVE FALLEN ASLEEP

THE ORIGIN OF SATAN

LIVING IN THE REALM OF THE SPIRIT

HOW TO BELIEVE GOD FOR A MATE

THANK GOD FOR EVERYTHING?

FAITH, FOOLISHNESS, OR PRESUMPTION?

THE HOLY SPIRIT —
The Missing Ingredient

NOW FAITH IS
Substance Evidence — Hebrews 11:1

HOW TO OBTAIN STRONG FAITH
Six Principles

IS HEALING FOR ALL?

HOW FAITH WORKS

About the Author

Dr. Frederick K.C. Price is a world-renowned teacher of the biblical principles of faith, healing, prosperity and the Holy Spirit. During his more than 45 years in Ministry, countless lives have been changed by his dynamic and insightful teaching that truly tells it like it is.

His television program, *Ever Increasing Faith*, has been broadcast throughout the world for more than 20 years and airs in 15 of the 20 largest markets in America, reaching an audience of more than 15 million households each week. His radio program is heard on stations across the world, including the continent of Europe via short wave radio.

Author of more than 40 popular books teaching practical application of biblical principles, Dr. Price is also the founder and pastor of one of America's largest church congregations, with a membership of more than 18,000. The church sanctuary, the FaithDome, is among the most notable and largest in the nation, with a seating capacity of more than 10,000.

In 1990, Dr. Price founded the Fellowship of Inner City Word of Faith Ministries (FICWFM) that comprises more than 300 ministries throughout the world.

Dr. Price holds an honorary Doctorate of Divinity degree from Oral Roberts University and an honorary diploma from Rhema Bible Training Center.

Dr. Frederick K.C. Price is a 1998 recipient of the Horatio Alger Award. Each year, this prestigious honor is bestowed upon ten "outstanding Americans who exemplify inspirational success, triumph over adversity, and an uncommon commitment to helping others...." Dr. Price also received the 1998 Southern Christian Leadership Conference's Kelly Miller Smith Interfaith Award. This award is given to clergy who have made the most significant contribution through religious expression affecting the nation and the world.